POSTCARD HISTORY SERIES

Westwood

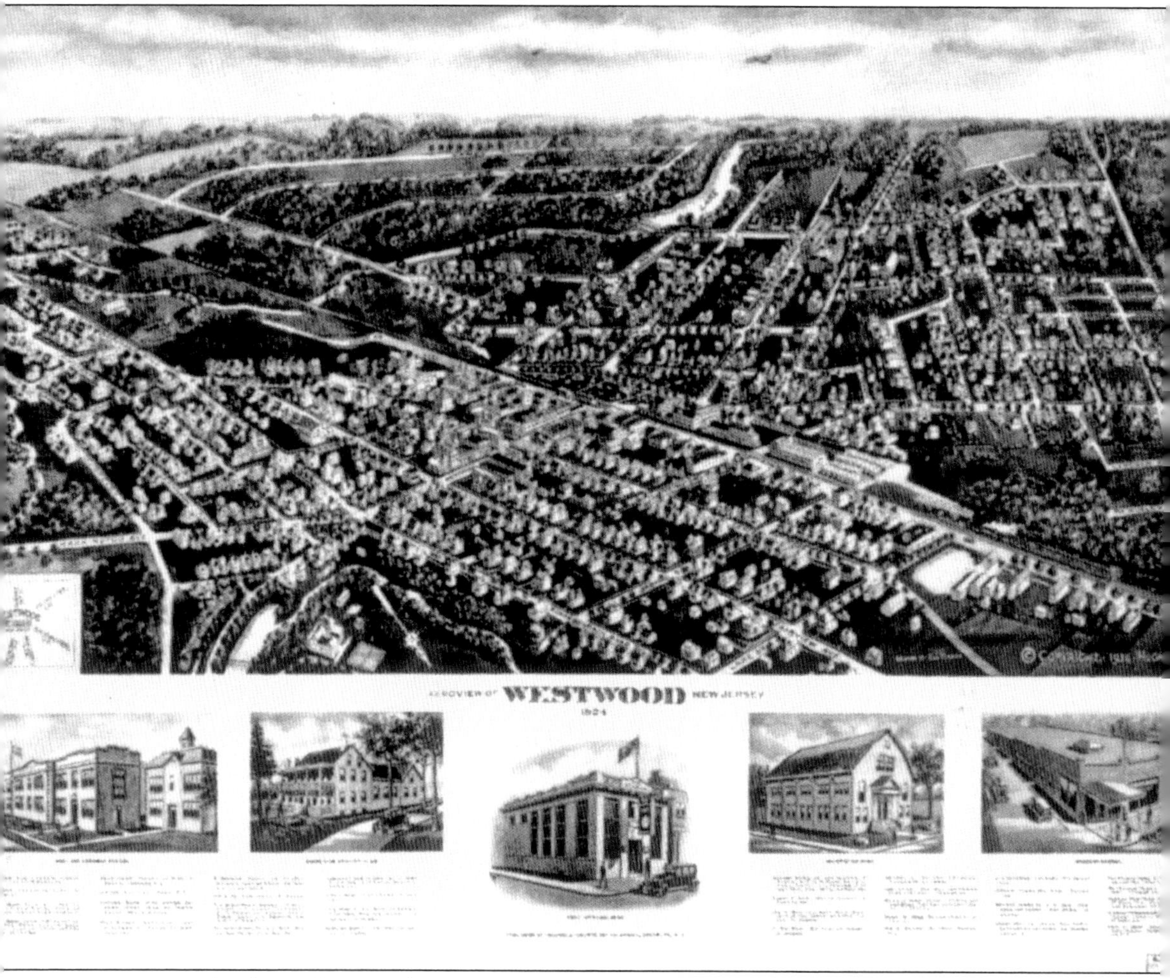

Westwood is located in northern Bergen County, in the center of Pascack Valley. The town of Westwood has always offered, and continues to offer a rare combination of natural beauty, historic picturesque homes, varied recreational attractions, and a thriving downtown area.

POSTCARD HISTORY SERIES

Westwood

Michael Pellegrino

ARCADIA
PUBLISHING

ISBN 978-0-7385-3659-0

Published by Arcadia Publishing
Charleston, South Carolina

Printed in the United States of America

Library of Congress Catalog Card Number: 2004107292

For all general information contact Arcadia Publishing at:
Telephone 843-853-2070
Fax 843-853-0044
E-mail sales@arcadiapublishing.com
For customer service and orders:
Toll-Free 1-888-313-2665

Visit us on the Internet at www.arcadiapublishing.com

All royalties are to be donated to the Westwood Heritage Society.

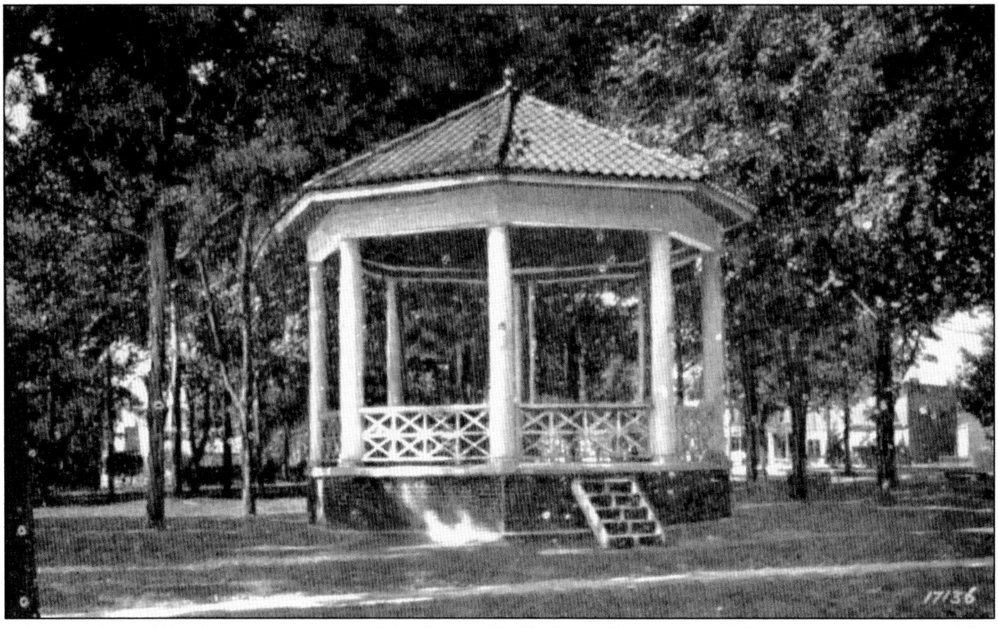

The bandstand in Veterans Memorial Park was built by volunteers and has been maintained by volunteers ever since. It is symbolic of Westwood's volunteerism, natural beauty, and recreational opportunities. Dedicated on August 2, 1922, its cost was just $1,500. The bandstand was rehabilitated and rededicated on May 29, 1989, in honor of Westwood's veterans.

Contents

Acknowledgments

Great appreciation is owed to everyone who has contributed to this book. It would be impractical to name everyone who has provided historical background for each of the postcards. Most of the images can still be recognized today, but many of the scenes could not be identified without the assistance of lifelong residents and local historians. Lee Tremble, Richard Muzio, Florine Ponton, Joseph Oettinger Jr., Susan Mueller, Leigh Hopper, Robert Todd, Jim Sealy, Helen Whalen, and Katherine Randall are just a few friends who helped to flesh out the stories behind each postcard. I owe great appreciation to the Westwood Heritage Society and the late Cheryl Todd, who preserved an enormous amount of historical artifacts for the public's use. Computer scanning equipment and storage space were generously provided by Nancy and Michael Ruane of Revelation Software in Westwood. I also thank my wife, Jennifer, and our children, Jessica and Nicholas, for patiently allowing me the time to collect these postcards and write this book.

These fine resources were heavily relied upon:

~ *The Westwood Centennial Journal,* published in 1994 by the Westwood Heritage Society.
~ *The 75th Anniversary Journal,* published in 1969 by the Borough of Westwood.
~ *Pascack Valley Tales,* published in 1993 by the Pascack Historical Society.
~ *Bogert's Mill, Westwood – The Earliest Pascack Mill Site,* published in 1990 by the Pascack Historical Society.
~ *History of Westwood, Bergen County & New Jersey,* published in 1942 by the Westwood High School Faculty.
~ *Westwood Tercentenary Journal,* published in 1964 by the Borough of Westwood.

The postcards reprinted in this book are from the author's collection and other collections generously contributed by the Westwood Heritage Society, the Pascack Historical Society, and individual postcard collectors Susan Mueller, Helen Whalen, Ellen Marcoux (nee Archibald), and Gloria Van Overloop (nee Henninger). These contributions are greatly appreciated.

Introduction

Most people are surprised by the number of postcards depicting scenes of Westwood. In present times, Westwood is certainly not considered to be a vacation spot. Throughout the first half of the 1900s, however, there seems to have been a large demand for Westwood postcards. There are over 180 postcards reprinted in this book, and there certainly are more to be found. Postcards of Westwood scenes date back as far as 1906, and they provide a fair depiction of Westwood's culture and history. Postcards were used like phone calls are used today. People would send a card to confirm an arrival time, check on a family member, or share some family news. The period from 1905 through 1915 has been referred to as the "golden age of postcards," with up to one billion postcards mailed each year in the United States.

The settlement that later became Westwood has truly been "the hub of the Pascack Valley" since the mid-1700s, when the region's first grain mill drew visitors from all of the neighboring settlements. The town has always attracted visitors to its businesses, places of worship, and social events. Westwood was also known for its early establishment of a volunteer fire department, a post office, a bank, schools, and the Pascack Valley Hospital. For a period of time, Westwood's streams, ponds, and undeveloped natural settings made it a country getaway destination for city dwellers.

Residents and visitors used postcards depicting these attractions, and these postcards now provide an interesting window into the history of Westwood.

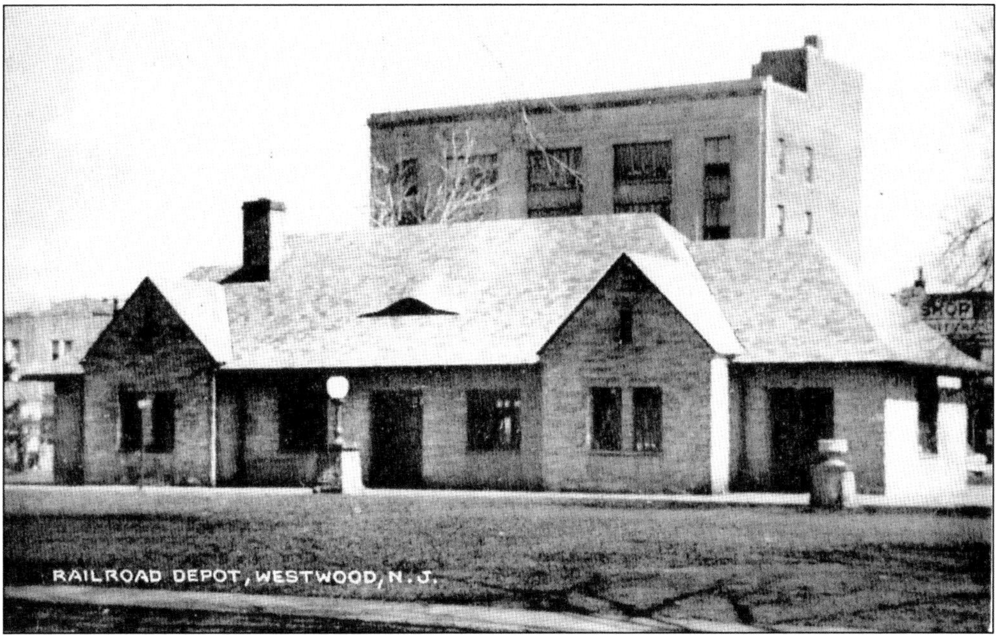

This image shows the Westwood train station, current home of the Westwood Heritage Society Museum.

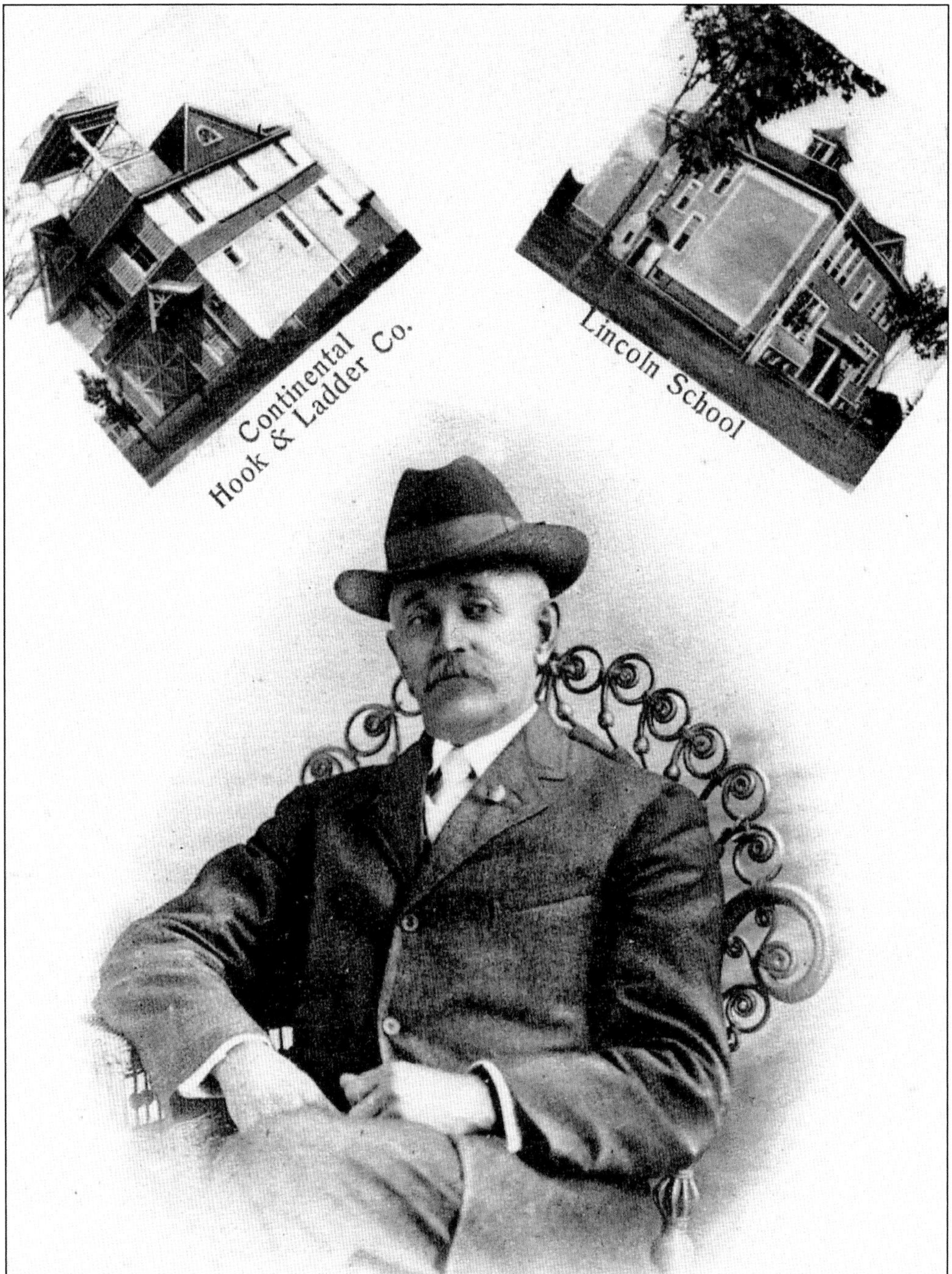

Thomas E. Brickell was one of Westwood's early mayors.

One

A Historical Overview

A brief historical overview is helpful in order to put the stories behind each postcard in context. Before adopting the name Westwood on March 10, 1870, the community was known as Pleasantville. The name Westwood was selected by a Mr. Scott who lived in Eastwood (now River Vale). Scott was permitted to choose the name because he donated the slate roofing materials for the train station that was being built at the time. Westwood remained part of Washington Township until May 8, 1894, when it formally incorporated into a borough form of government. The original train station, pictured *c.* 1900, stood on the east side of the tracks and accommodated horse buggies.

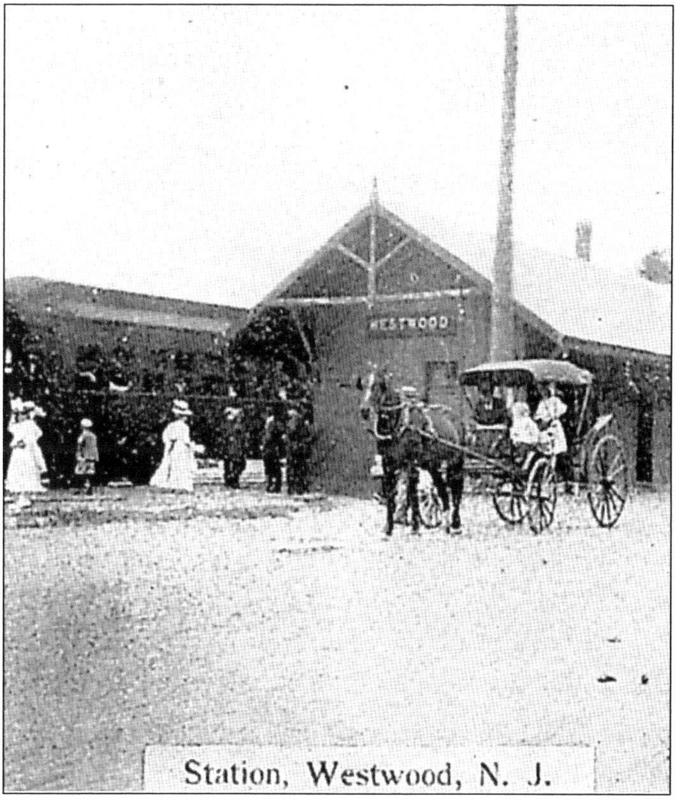

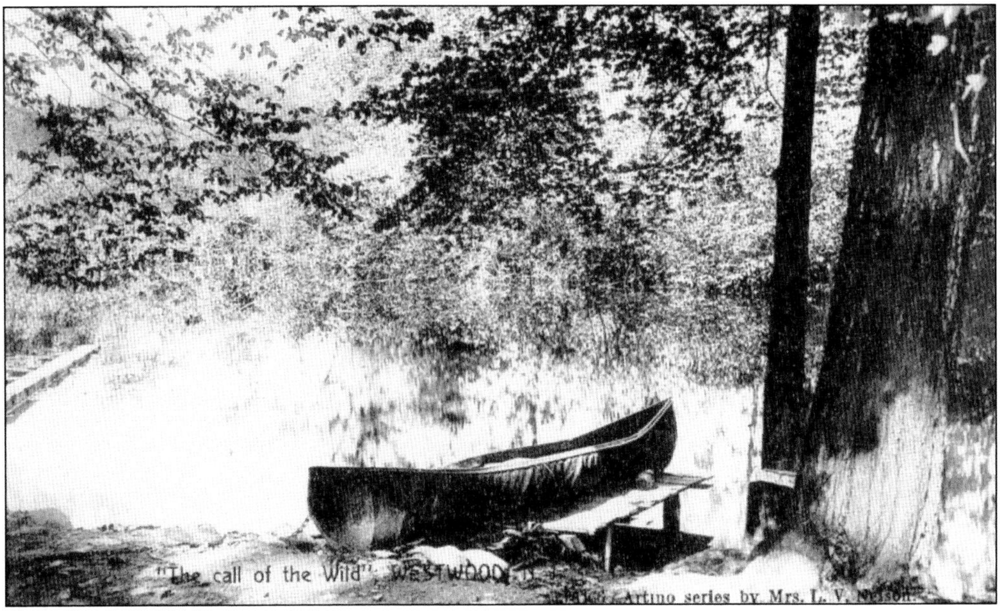

The Lenni Lenape Indians inhabited this part of the state and shared it with transient trappers until permanent settlers began to enter in the mid-1700s. The earliest settlers appear to have been Dutch. They settled here to farm and mill grain.

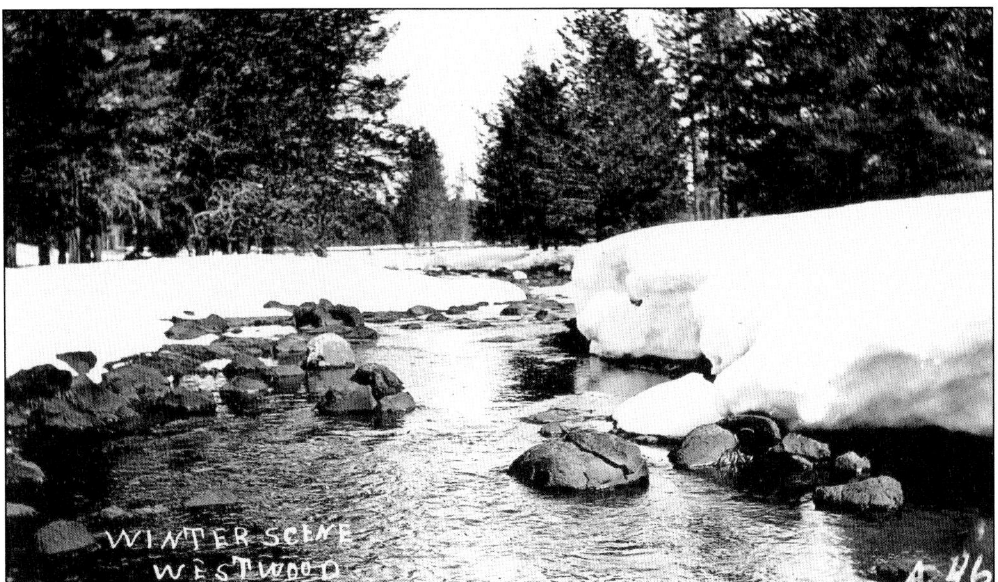

Influence of the early Dutch and American Indian inhabitants is evident in the names of some streams and streets such as Pascack, Musquapsink (the brook that feeds Bogert's Pond), and Kinderkamack, which is said to be a Lenni Lenape term for "place where the rooster crows." It is also said to be a Dutch term for "place where the children play."

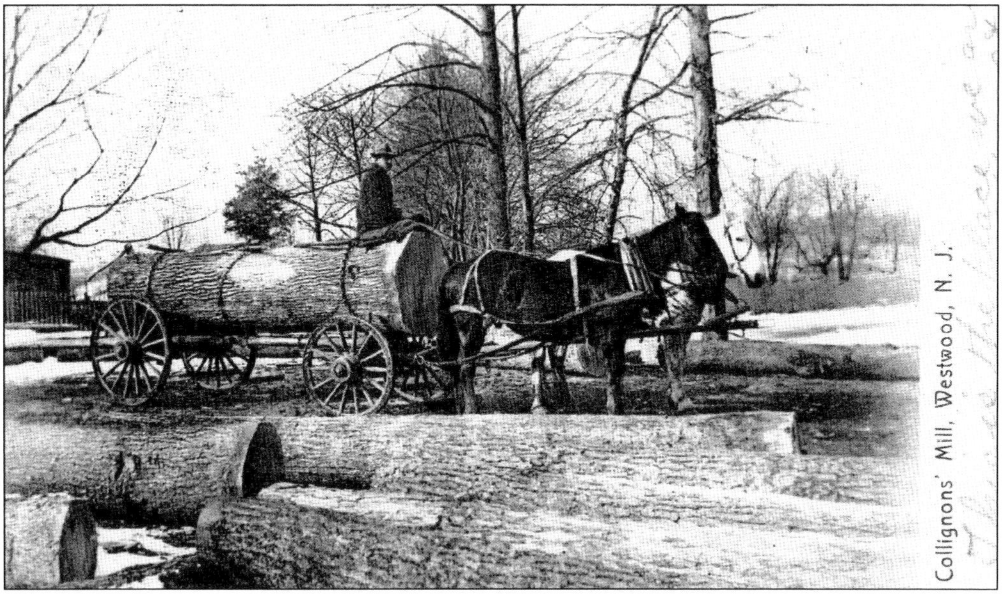

The two biggest factors leading to the settlement and growth of Westwood were the mills and the train station. They attracted commerce and visitors and set the stage for Westwood's development. Collignon's Mill was one of the earliest businesses in the Westwood area.

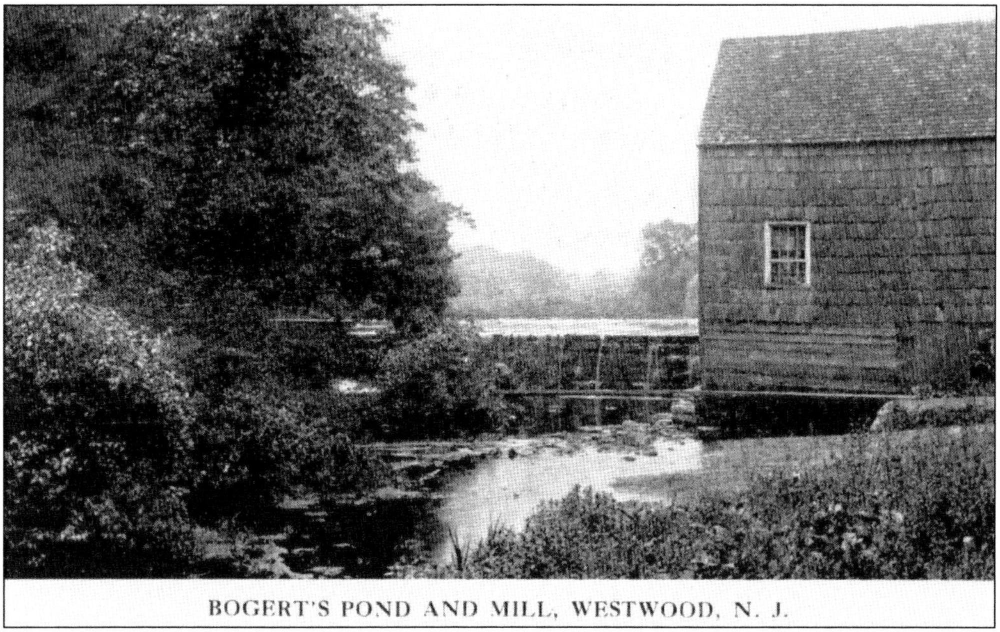

Much of this town was originally granted to Gilliam Bogert, who then parceled off lots to each of his children as they were married. In this way, the family names Bogert, Brickell, Hopper, and Demarest became well known in Westwood. Through the years, these family members invested in the growth of Westwood by serving as postmasters, business owners, and political leaders.

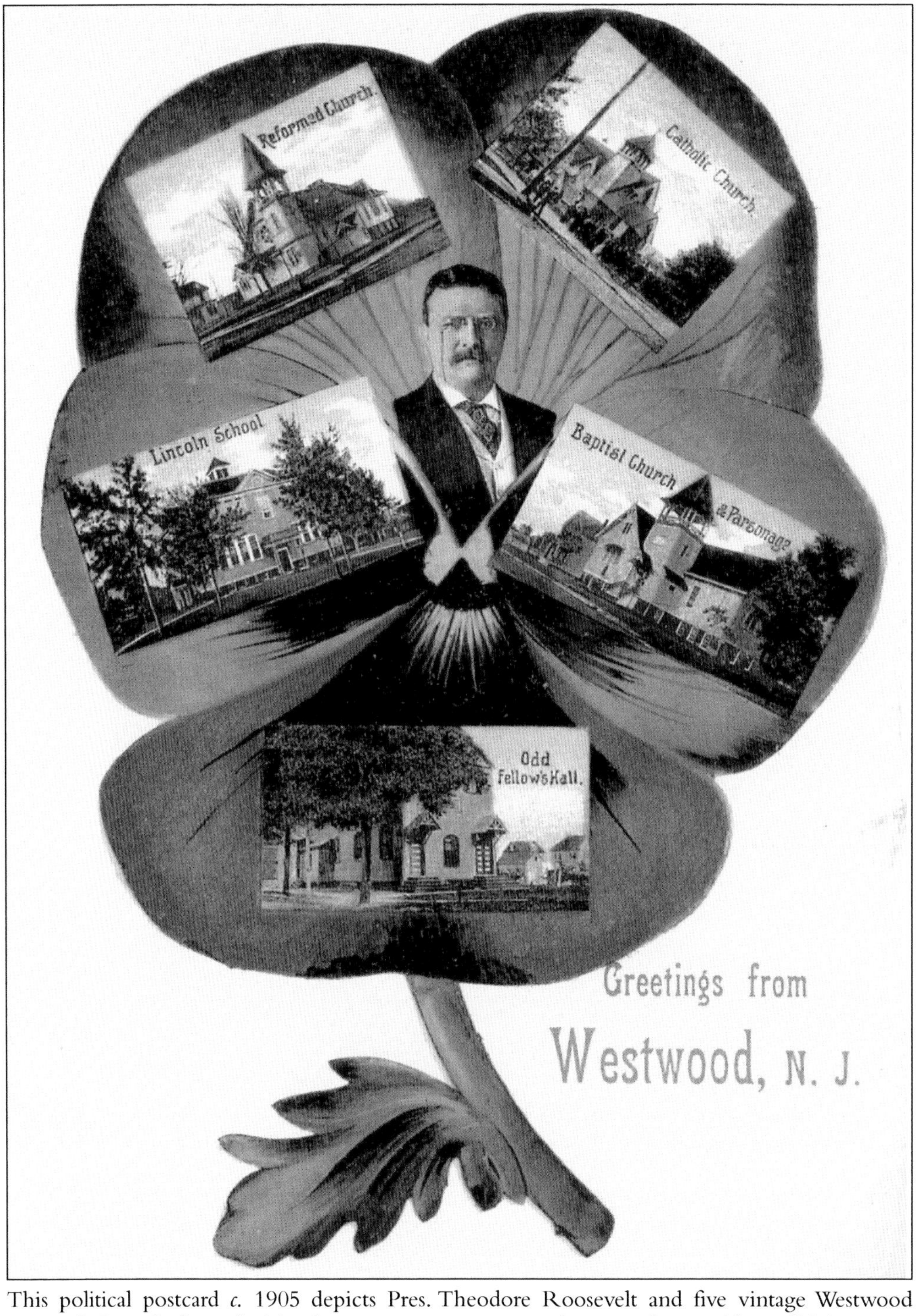

This political postcard *c.* 1905 depicts Pres. Theodore Roosevelt and five vintage Westwood postcards. Long before television became common, postcards were often used by politicians as an inexpensive way to identify themselves with a local region. By including himself among images of Westwood's schools, churches, and the Odd Fellows Hall social center, the president promoted an image of being a part of the local community.

Two

The Community

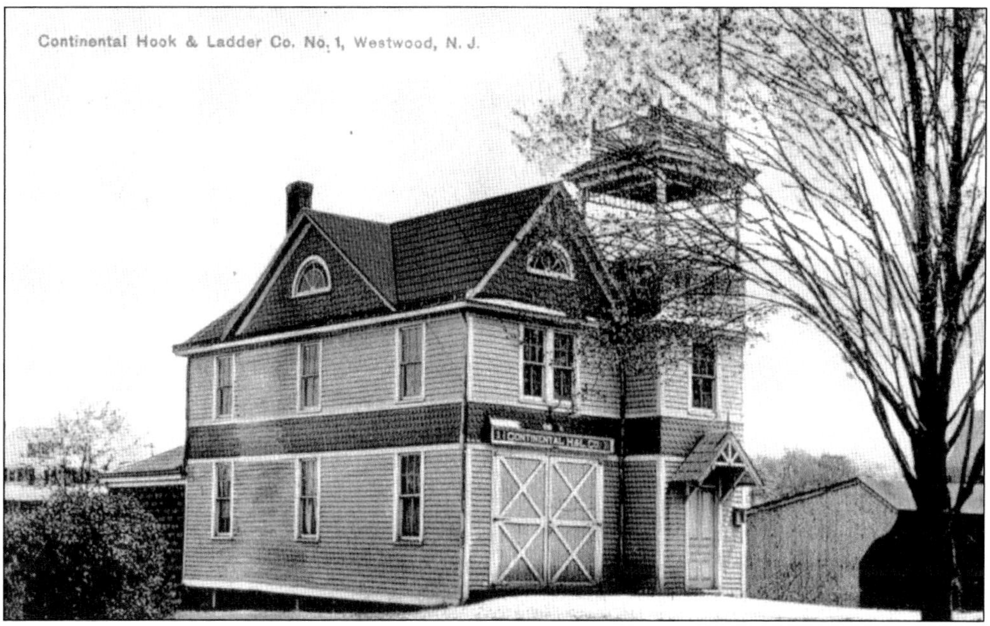

Westwood's first firefighting unit, the Continental Hook and Ladder Company No. 1, was formed by a group of concerned residents on February 17, 1894. Officers were elected and a fund-raiser was held at Odd Fellows Hall (discussed on pages 24–25) to collect money for new equipment. The group raised $350 and purchased a hand-drawn hook and ladder wagon. George T. Brickell, who owned the local general store, donated a lot on Center Avenue by a deed dated April 27, 1894, containing a perpetual condition that the land must be used for a firehouse. This land continues to be the location of the new Westwood Firehouse. Construction of the first firehouse was completed in September 1894. The firehouse was also used for borough council meetings, and in the spring of 1898, the municipal court began hearing cases there. On April 27, 1900, the fire department transferred the title to the borough of Westwood.

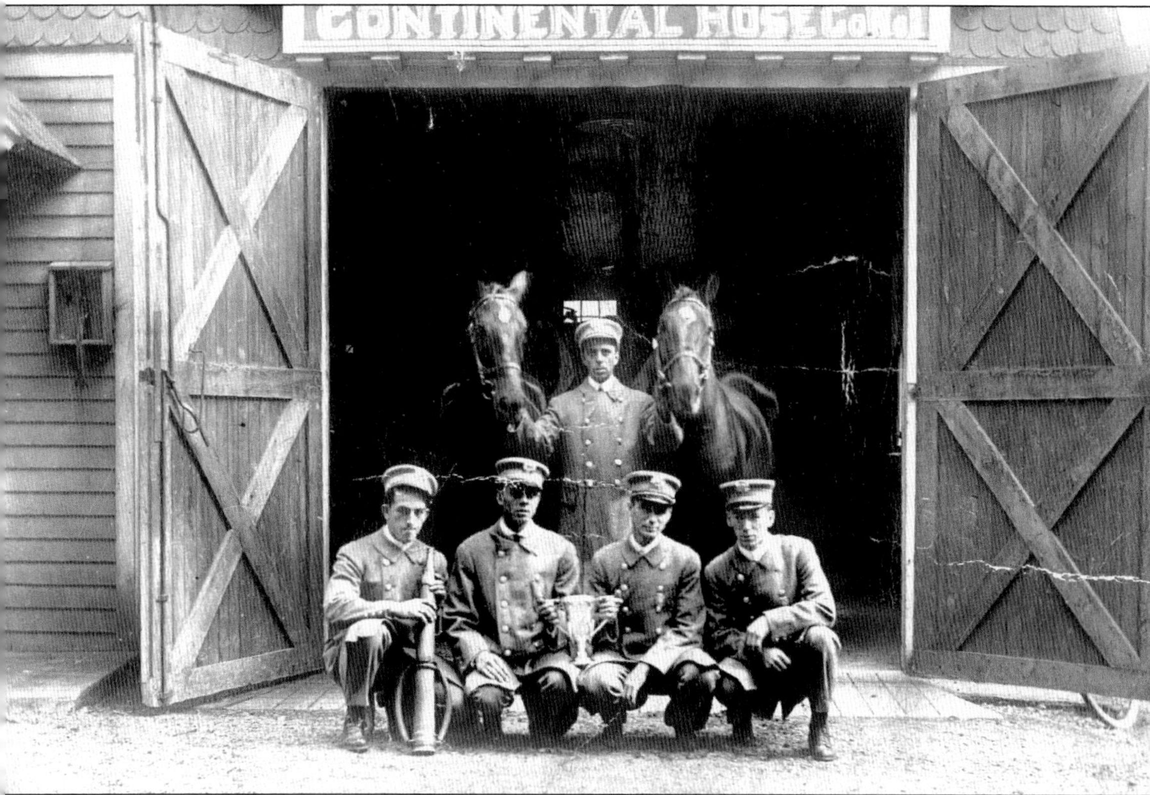

The original firehouse (pictured on the previous page) was expanded *c.* 1910 to add a second bay for the Continental Hose Company No. 1. Westwood's first fire hydrant was installed in 1894 at the corner of Broadway and Westwood Avenue, shortly after C. S. DeBaun built the town's first pressurized water system.

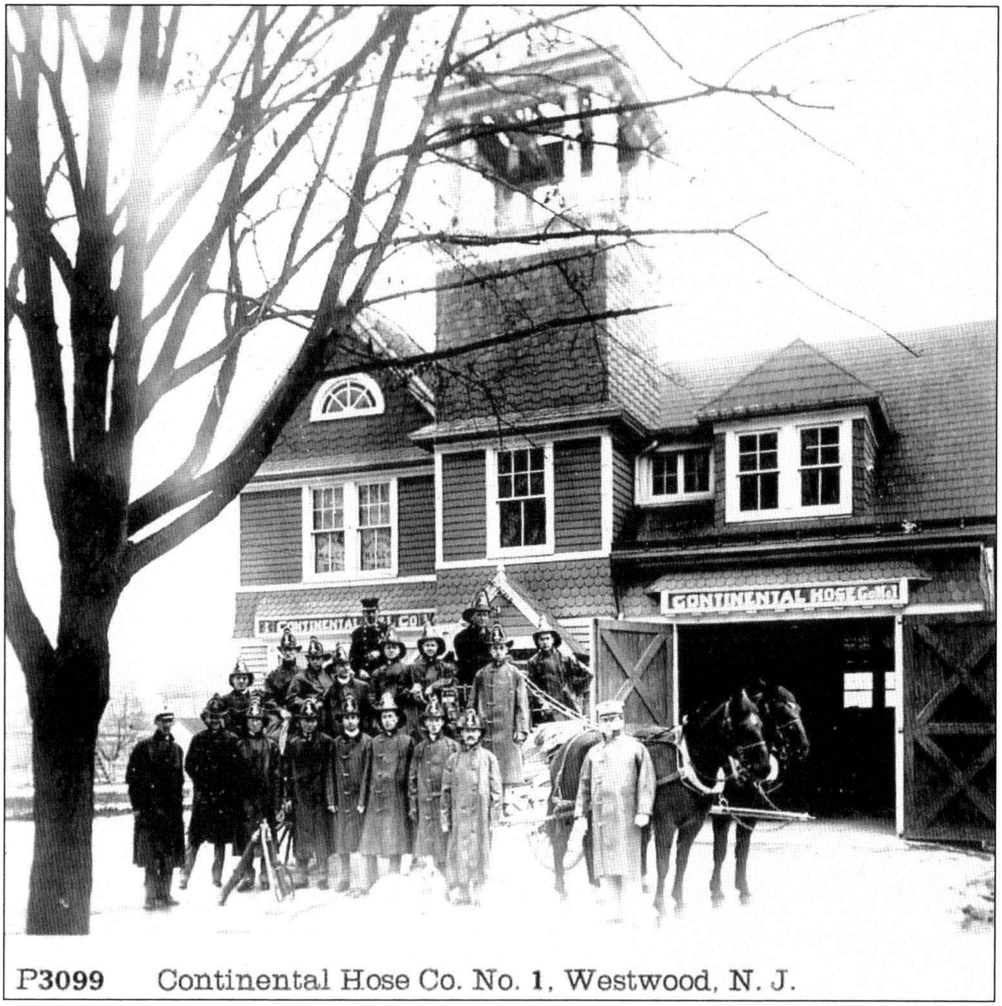

Prince and Belle were the names of these two black fire horses, which were purchased in June 1911. The horse-drawn fire wagons had been replaced by motorized fire trucks by 1918.

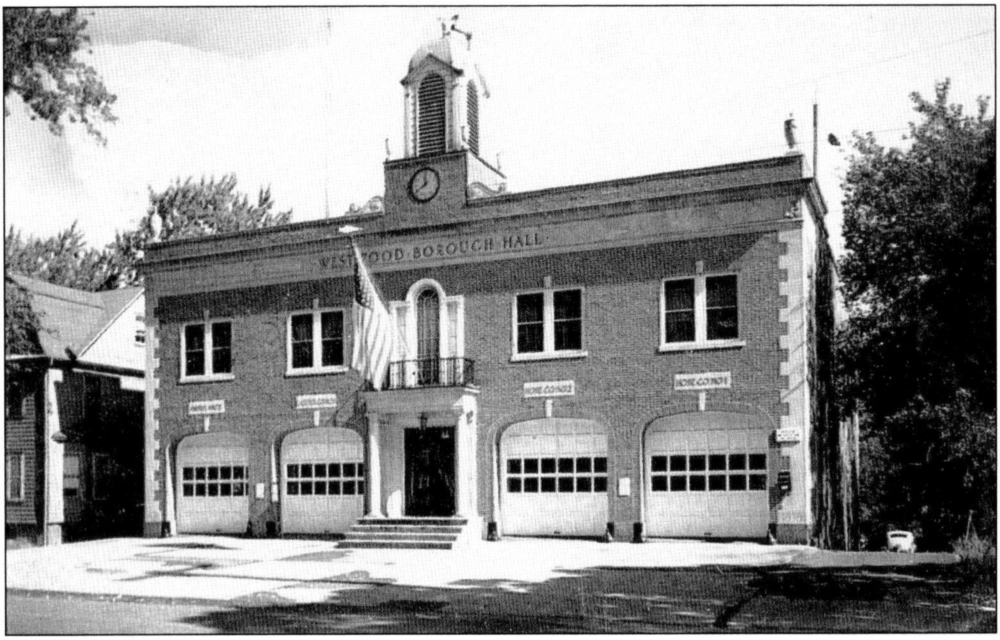

In 1928, the original firehouse was demolished, and the borough constructed a multipurpose municipal building that housed the fire department on the ground level, with second-floor accommodations for the police department, municipal court, and the mayor and council.

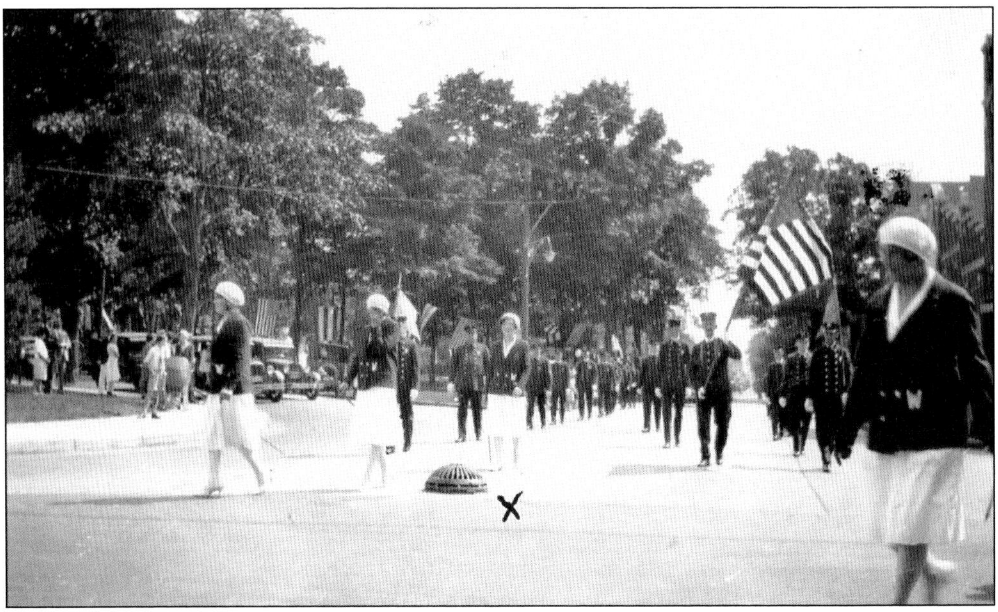

The Ladies Auxiliary of the Westwood Volunteer Fire Department been raising money and assisting the department since 1928. This 1930 postcard shows members of the auxiliary marching in a parade at the corner of Washington and Third Avenues.

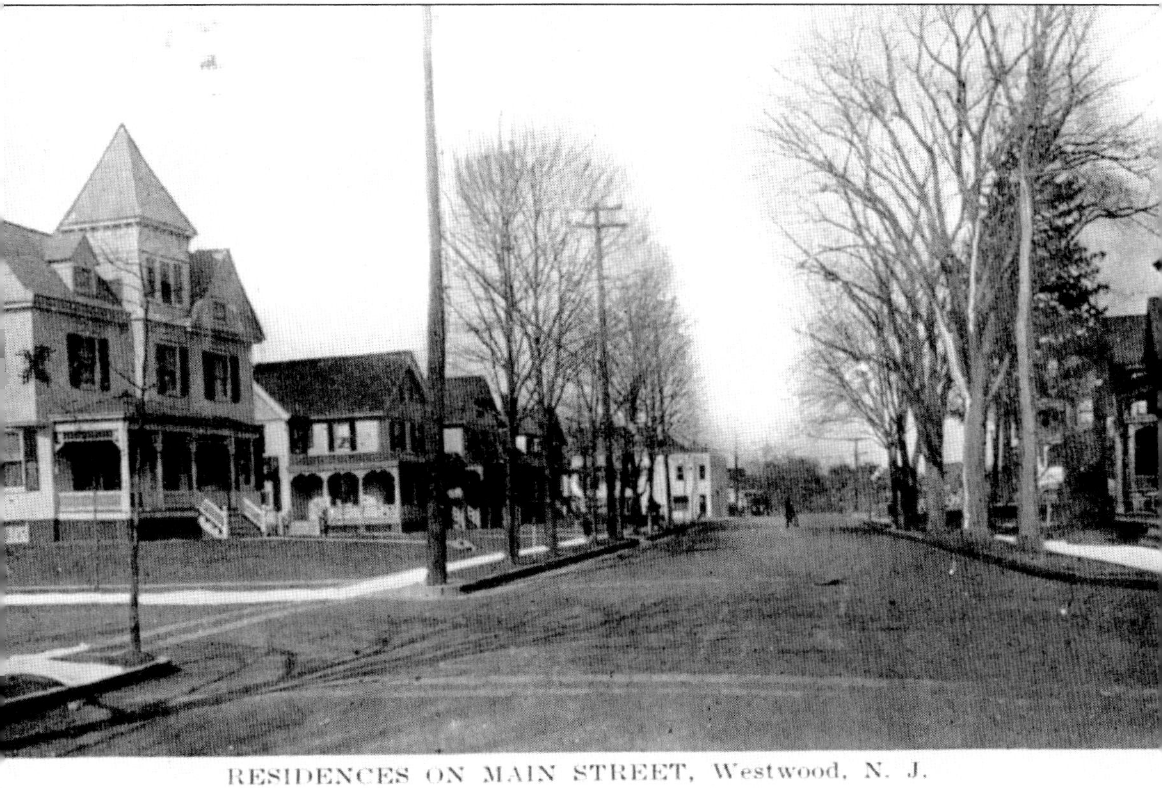

Prior to the official federal appointment of a postmaster in 1862, George T. Brickell distributed mail from his home, pictured on the left, which, coincidently, was located where the present post office stands today, at the corner of Westwood and Fairview Avenues. At that time, Westwood Avenue was known as Main Street and it was predominantly a residential street.

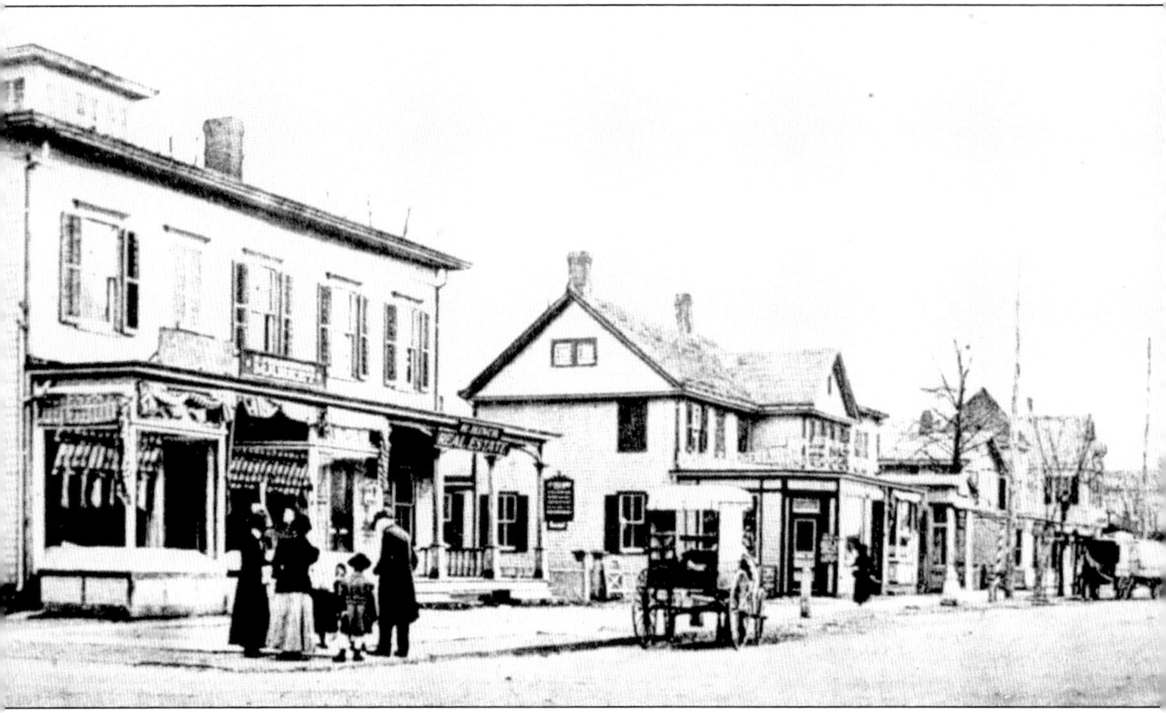

The post office later moved to the Van Emburgh & Bogert General Store, built in 1869, and Isaac D. Bogert served as Westwood's postmaster for the next 20 years. Bogert also served as mayor for three terms, from 1894 to 1895, 1899 to 1903, and 1908 to 1910. The store was located at the corner of Main Street and Railroad Avenue (now Westwood Avenue and Broadway). General stores were the center of the local economy, so it was common for the post office to be housed in them. The card shows the view looking south from the corner of Railroad Avenue and Main Street.

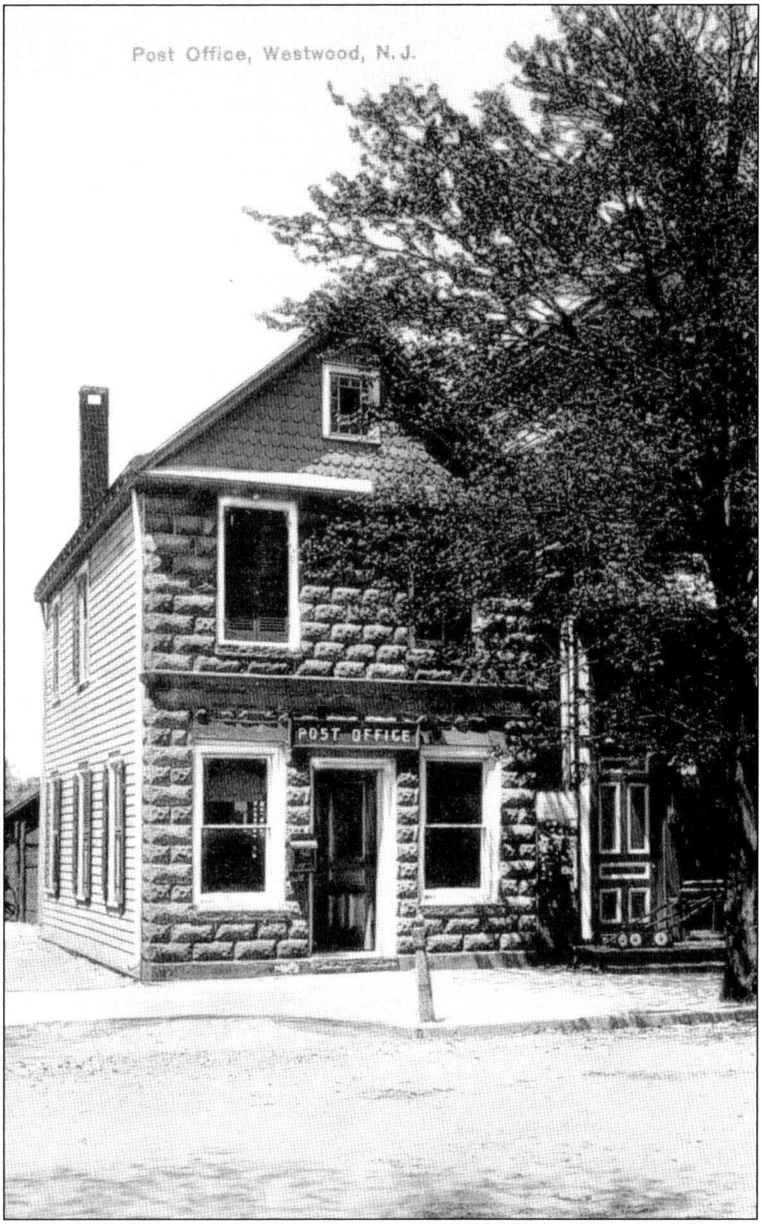

Mail was delivered from a distribution hub in Hackensack to the general store by stagecoach on a weekly basis, and residents would gather at the store on mail day to await incoming correspondence. At that time, there were only about 25 households in Westwood. Thus, everyone knew each other, and mail day offered a chance to socialize and catch up on local gossip and events. By 1870, mail could be delivered on a daily basis because the railroad was extended from Hackensack, through Westwood, to Hillsdale. This railroad extension changed the lives of Westwood residents in countless ways, but the daily delivery of mail must have made an enormous impact on businesses and residents. Westwood became officially incorporated in 1894, and Thomas E. Brickell served as postmaster and, later, as mayor. On March 27, 1895, Brickell moved the post office to its own building, pictured here, at 89 Westwood Avenue. The first mailman was Gene Perry, who delivered the mail by horse and buggy.

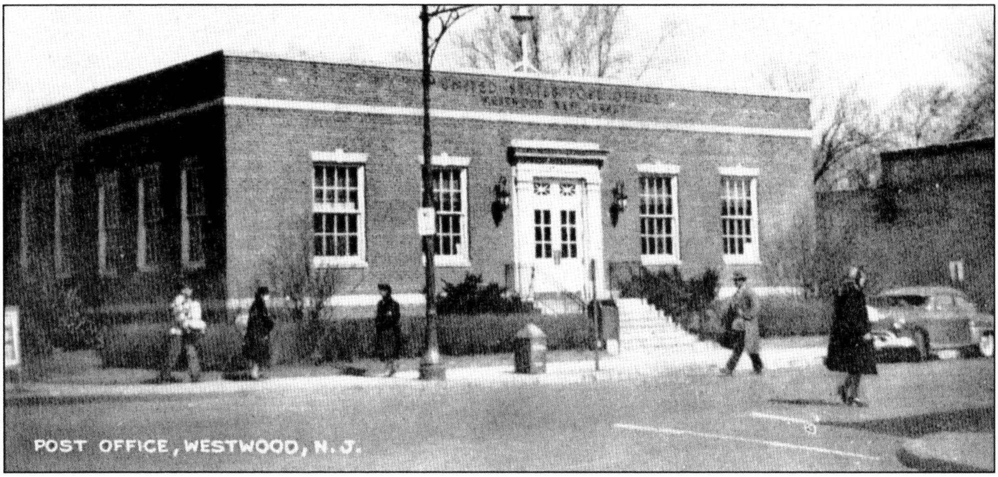

In 1935, the present post office was built at the corner of Westwood and Fairview Avenues. By this time, Main Street had been renamed Westwood Avenue and most of the houses had been squeezed out to make room for commercial businesses. The dirt road, horses, and hitching posts were replaced with asphalt, parked cars, and light poles.

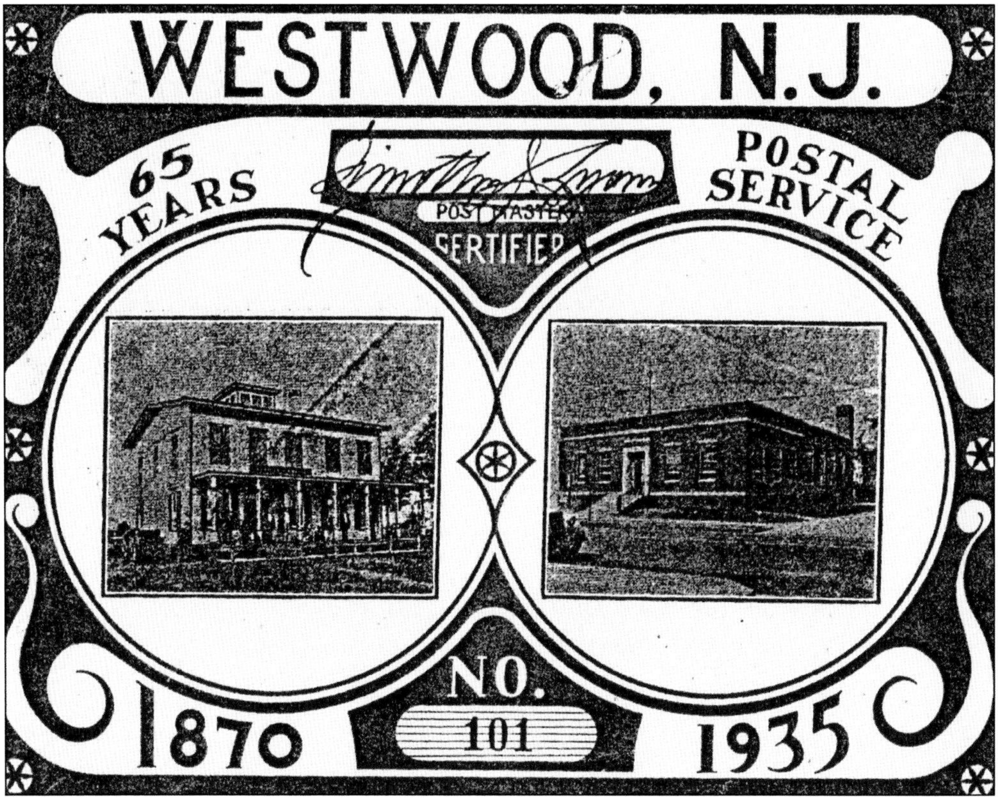

This commemorative card, circulated in 1935, celebrated the new post office building and its historical beginning. The card bears the signature of Timothy Lyons, who served as postmaster in 1935. When the post office was officially established in Westwood on June 21, 1862, Pres. Abraham Lincoln was in office and there were only 15 other post offices in Bergen County. At that time, mail was delivered by stagecoach from the Northern Railroad.

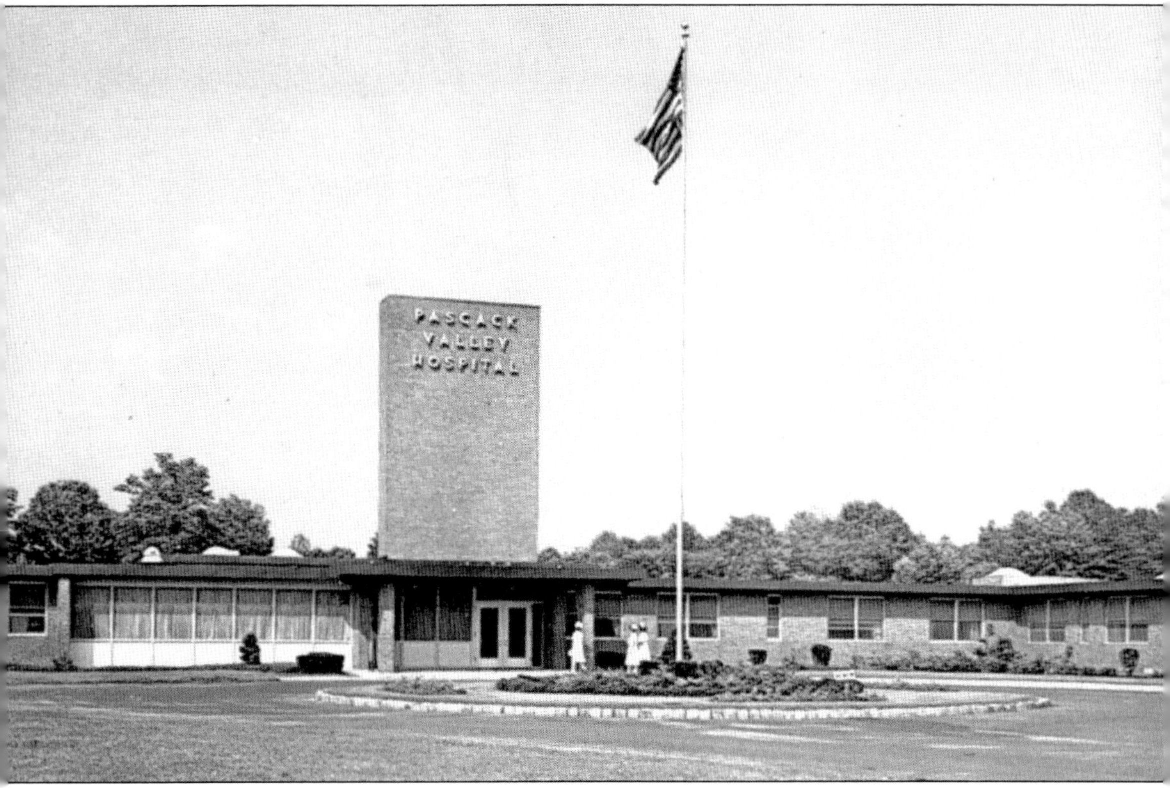

The first hospitals in Bergen County were not established until the late 1800s. Prior to that time, all illnesses were treated by local doctors or, in most cases, by family and neighbors. Dr. Simeon Zabriskie was Westwood's first doctor. Beginning in 1869, he practiced from his home, at 289 Broadway (where the Seville Diner now sits), and made house calls by horseback or buggy from River Edge to Spring Valley, New York. In 1888, Hackensack Hospital was opened, with a capacity for just 30 patients. Hospitals were overcrowded with long waiting lists and limited options for treatment. Westwood led the Pascack Valley in health care. The Pascack Valley Hospital began as a one-story cinder block building with 86 beds and a staff of 130. It was the inspiration of Westwood resident Louise Bohlin, who formed the Pascack Valley Hospital Association in 1941, determined to create an outstanding medical facility for the people of Pascack Valley. The association continued to gain community support and was able to raise funds to purchase 20.5 acres of land on Old Hook Road in the early 1950s. After several more years of fund-raising, construction began in 1957, and the hospital opened its doors to patients on May 30, 1959. A four-story addition was constructed in 1966 at the back of the hospital, and further expansion is currently taking place.

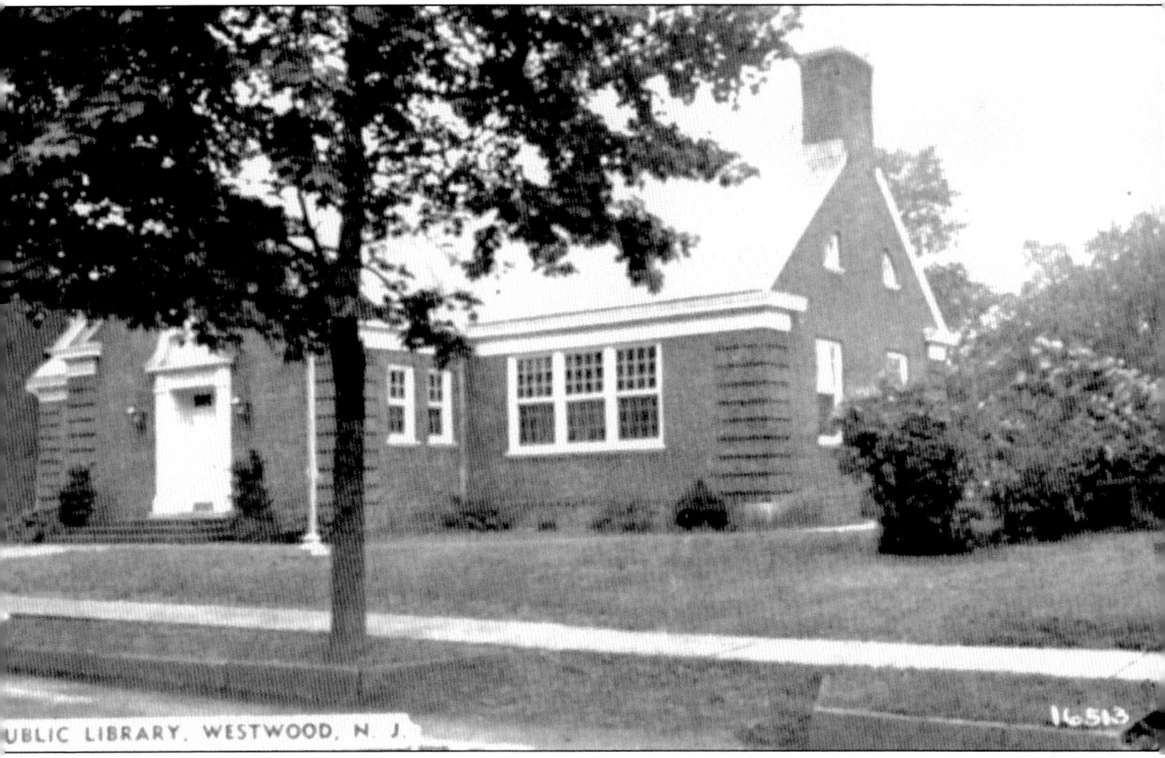

Westwood had the first library in the Pascack Valley. Fund-raising efforts for Westwood's library date back to newspaper articles printed in March 1904. The library was formed by a group of volunteers who had also organized the Girls Patriotic League to aid the war effort during World War I. Following the war, the volunteers shifted their focus to collecting books and funds for a public library. The Westwood Free Circulation Library originally opened on Main Street but moved on June 7, 1919, into three rooms rented from the Demarest family in a Victorian house on Center Avenue (where Heck Realty is located today). The library's name was changed to the Westwood Free Public Library in 1924. After being relocated to the Veterans of Foreign Wars building on Center Avenue and then to the corner of Broadway and Westwood Avenue, it opened at its present location on Park Avenue in 1939.

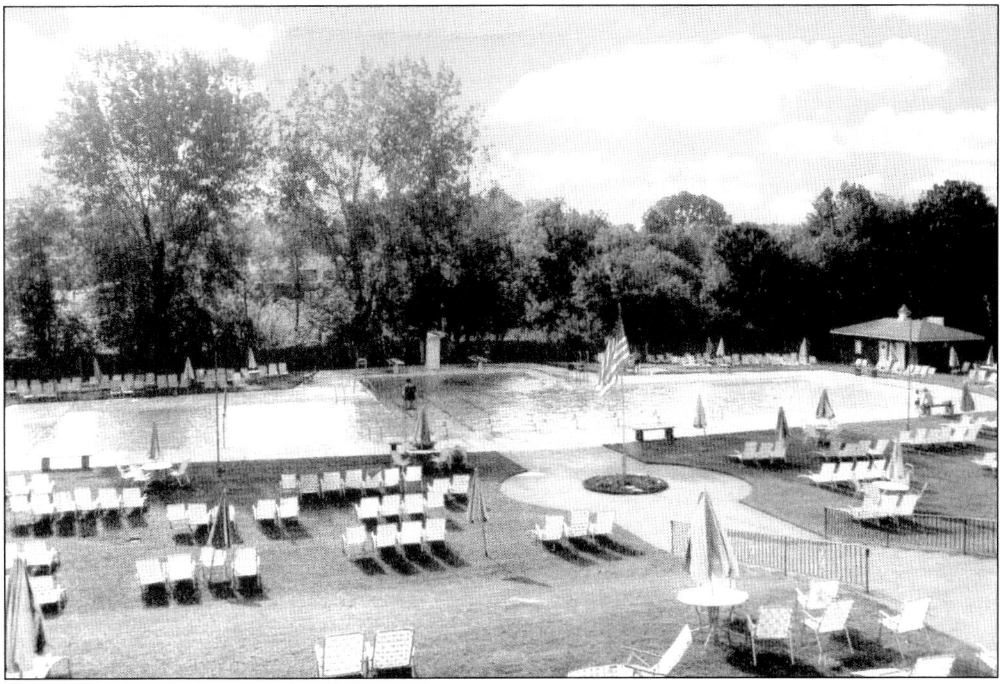

The Westwood Swim Club was formed in 1963 as a nonprofit company providing an affordable local spot for exercise, socializing, and good old-fashioned fun in the sun. Countless local children learned to swim in this pool, and many went on to become lifeguards and staff at the pool.

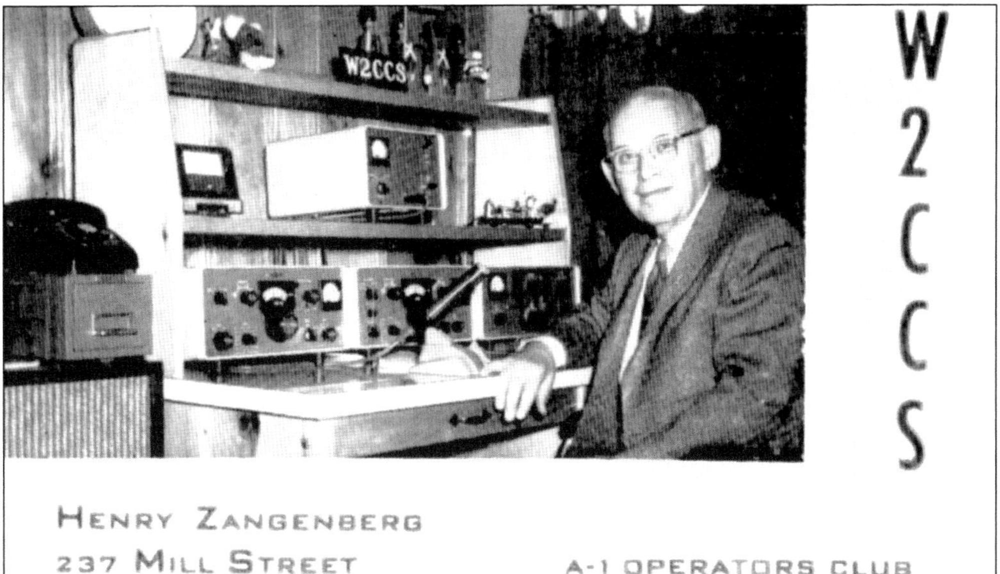

Ham radio enthusiasts commonly used personalized postcards to correspond with people they met on the radio. Like e-mails and Internet chat rooms of today, ham radio allowed them to communicate and socialize with people all over the world for free. They would often collect hundreds of cards memorializing conversations with other radio operators worldwide.

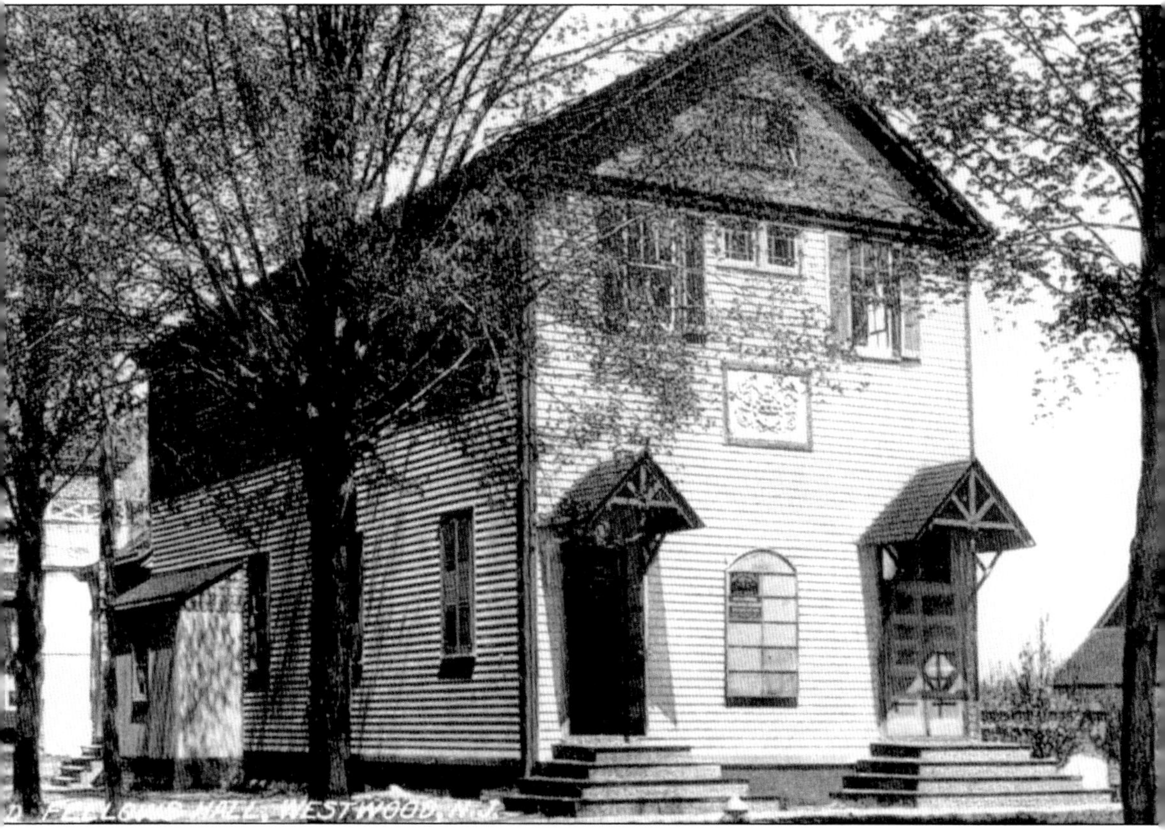

The place for meetings and social gatherings in the early days of Westwood was known as Odd Fellows Hall and was run by a social club akin to a Rotary Club or Masonic Lodge. Each of the early churches met at the hall until money could be raised for their own building, and the founders of Westwood met there to organize the town's secession from the township of Washington. The hall was also used as a community theater. Odd Fellows Hall originally rented space in the Volz Building, on Railroad Avenue (now 313 Broadway). In 1897, the group rented the second floor of the building at the corner of Center Avenue and Main Street (now Westwood Avenue). On January 31, 1900, Odd Fellows Hall then relocated to its own building, shown here, at the corner of Jefferson and Center Avenues, where the firehouse parking lot exists today.

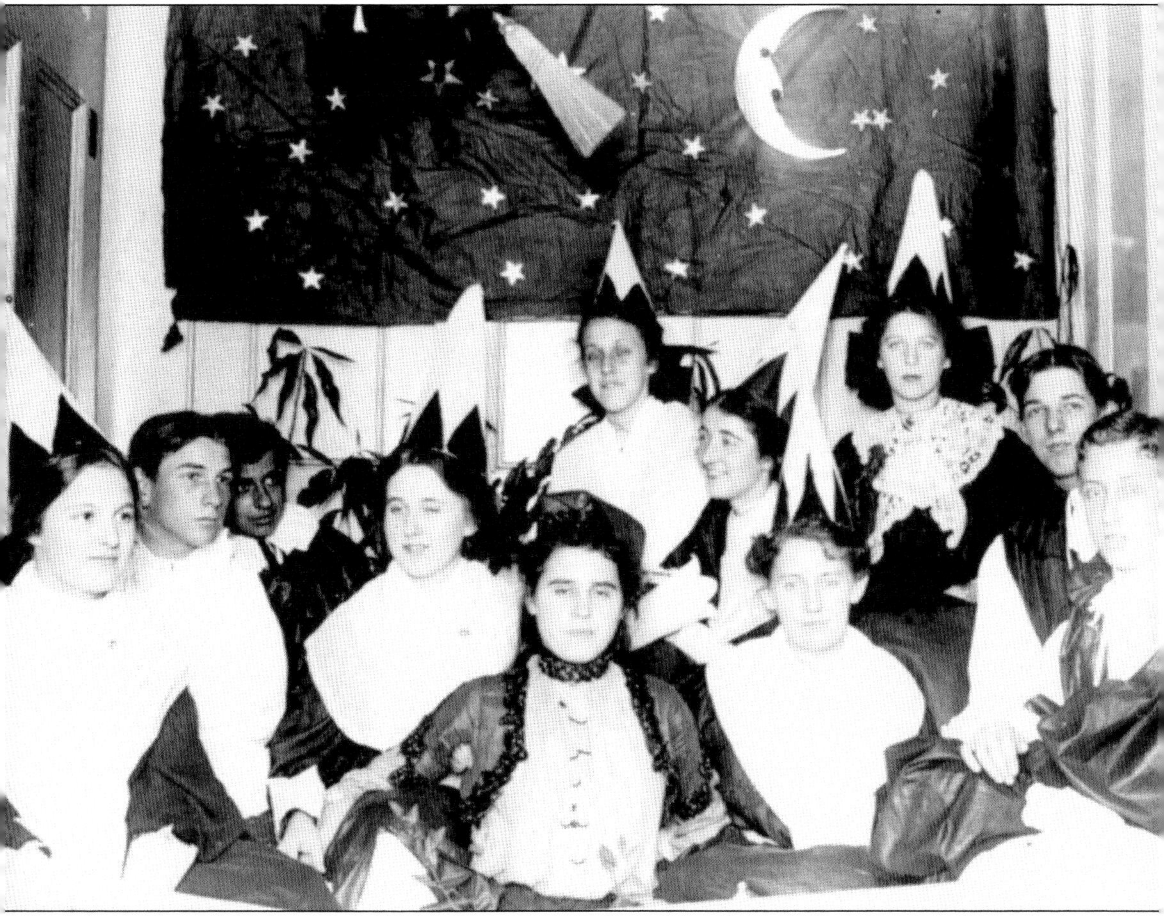

Odd Fellows Hall hosted many festive parties and dance events. Records of newspaper articles reveal that the Westwood Athletic Club held an annual masked ball at Odd Fellows Hall to raise money. Florine Ponton, one of Westwood's most senior residents, recalls that schoolchildren would meet at the hall many days after school to spend the afternoon dancing and listening to music.

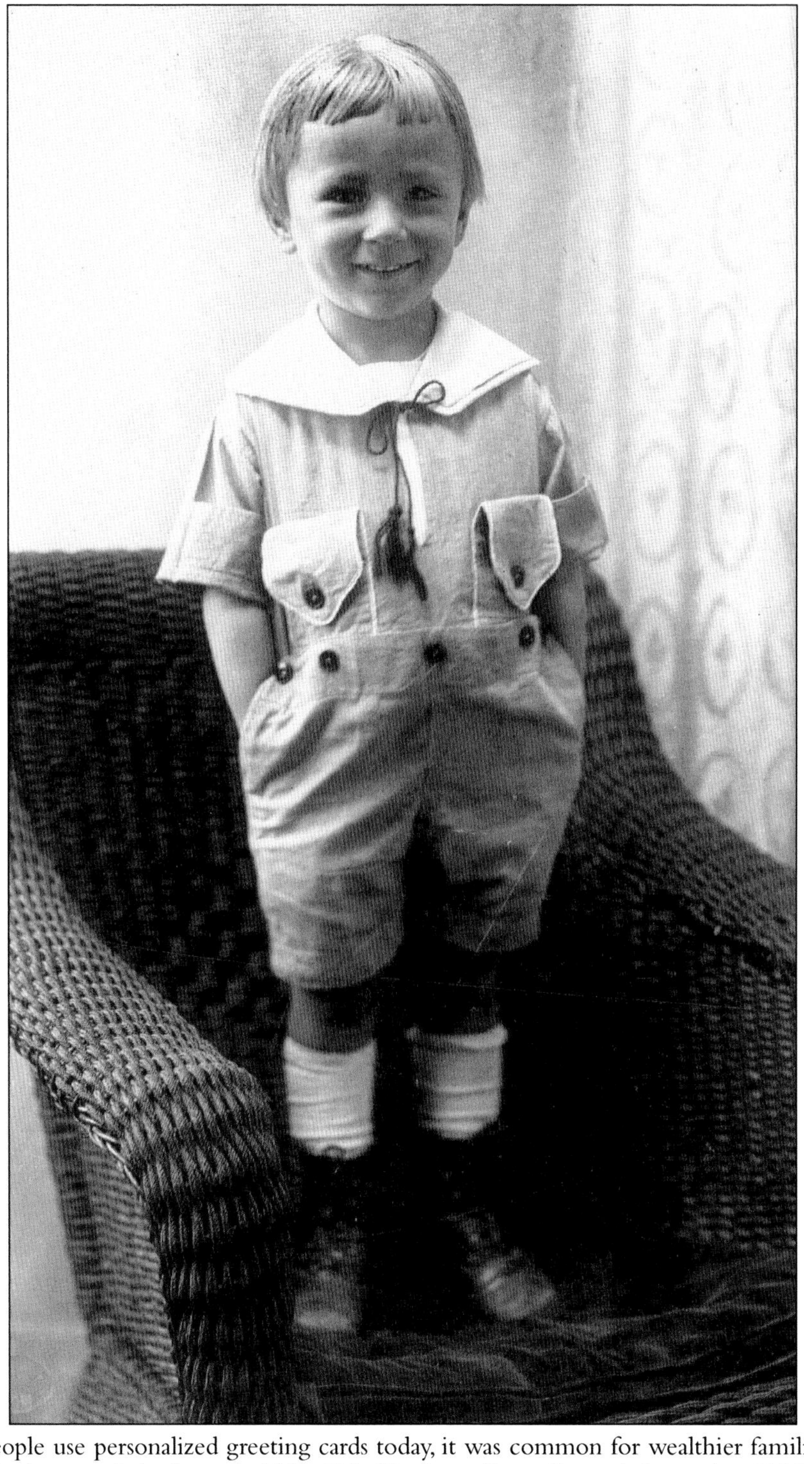

Just as people use personalized greeting cards today, it was common for wealthier families to use personalized postcards in the early 1900s. Volz Hardware Store, formerly located at 313 Broadway, made the Volz family well known in Westwood beginning in the 1890s. This card depicts Robert Volz as a child *c.* 1927.

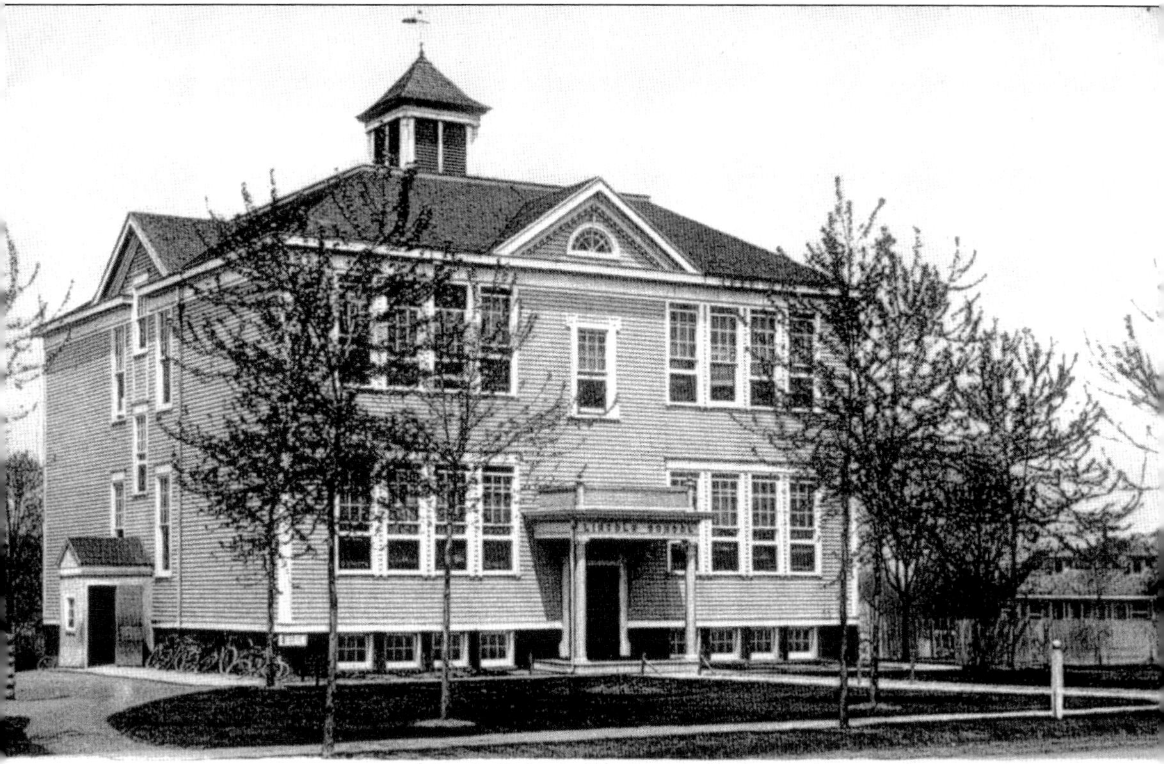

Lincoln School, Westwood, N. J.

The first schoolhouse in Westwood stood at the corner of Old Hook and Sand Roads. It is unknown when the one-room school was first built, but it was expanded in 1840, 1860, and again in 1879. In 1900, the Lincoln School was erected facing Third Avenue, near the corner of Fourth Avenue and Mill Street. That marked the end of the Old Hook School, which was sold for $161, disassembled, and moved to the Old Hook Farm in Emerson, where it remains today. Another small, older two-room schoolhouse known as the Washington School once stood near the corner of Mill Street and Third Avenue. It was sold and moved to the corner of Third Avenue and Elm Street for use by the Calvary Baptist Church in 1902.

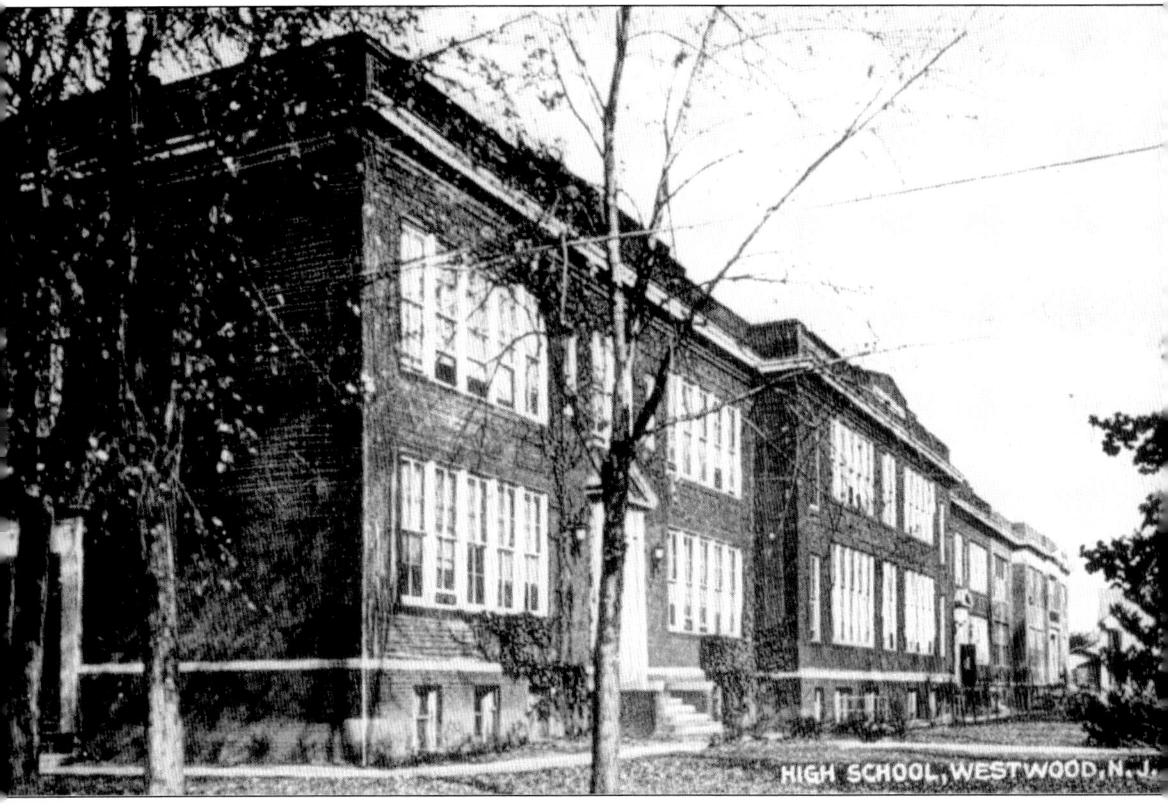

As the community grew, a larger brick building was built in 1913 just south of the Lincoln School. It stood facing Fourth Avenue, at the corner of Mill Street and Third Avenue. The brick school eventually became known as Westwood High School and later was used as the middle school. Today, modern townhouses have replaced the long string of schools that stood at the corner of Mill Street and Third Avenue. Westwood schools had always been attended by children from surrounding towns. In 1964, Westwood formally joined school systems with Washington Township, and Westwood Consolidated High School opened in Washington Township.

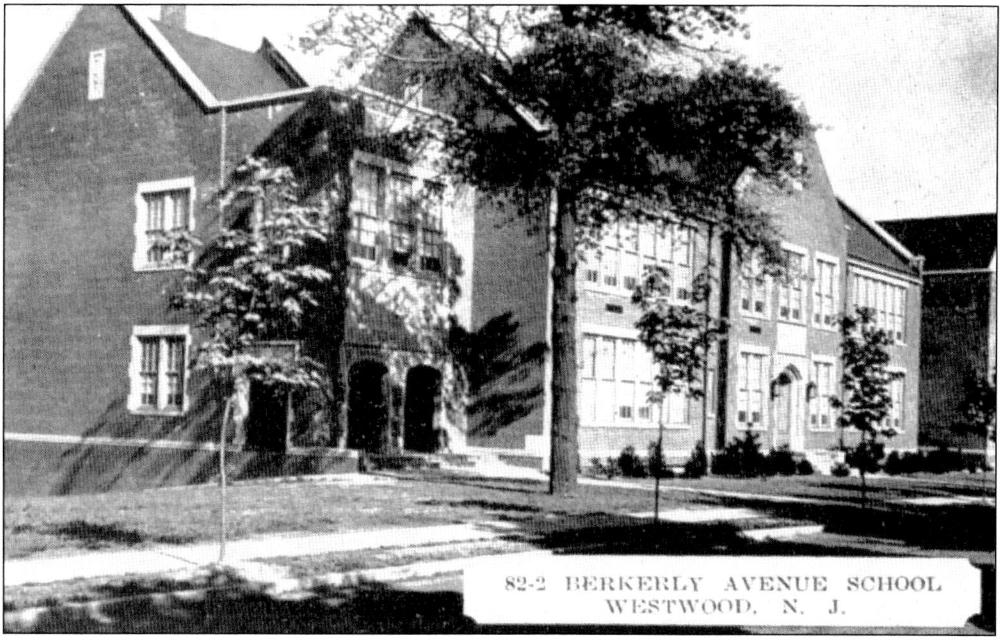

Until 1929, all students from kindergarten through high school were housed in one building. At that time, the Berkeley School added a second school for children living on the east side of town. Although the interior has been updated over the years, the Berkeley School building remains largely the same today as it was in 1929.

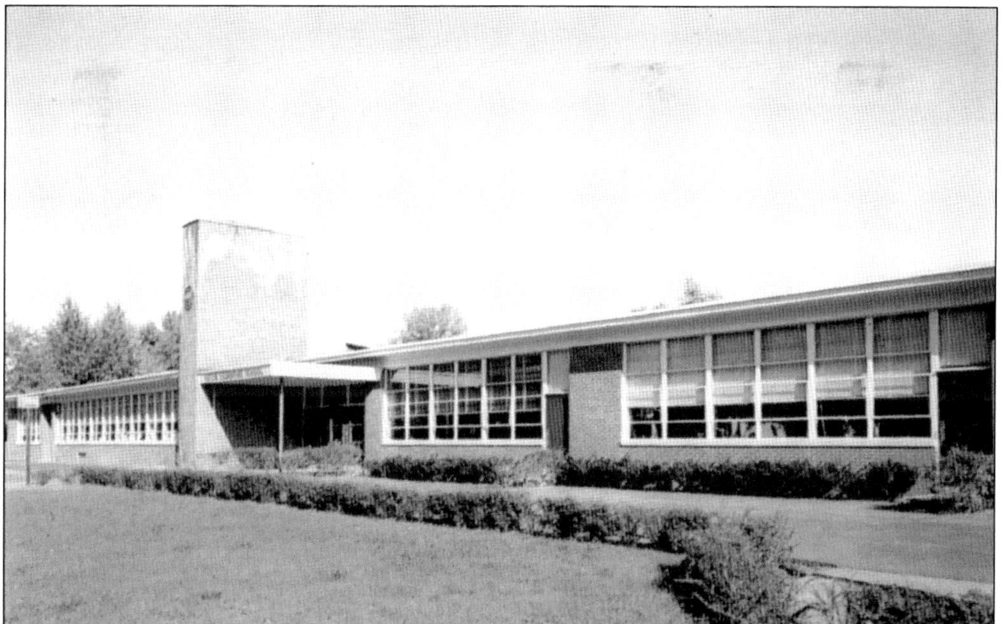

Ketler Elementary School was opened in 1952 in response to the rapidly growing school population following World War II. The school was named after C. Wesley Ketler, who was a member of the board of education.

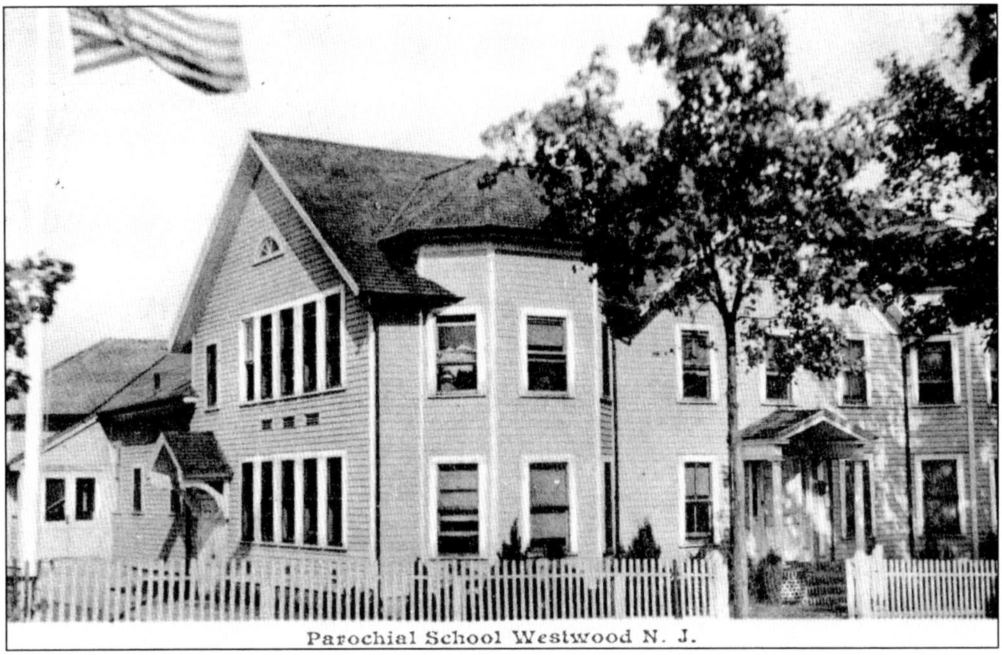

The original St. Andrew's Parochial School opened on Washington Avenue in September 1923. It was used for classes until 1931, when the new St. Andrew's School was built next door. The original building was then used as the parish house for the nuns who taught in the school.

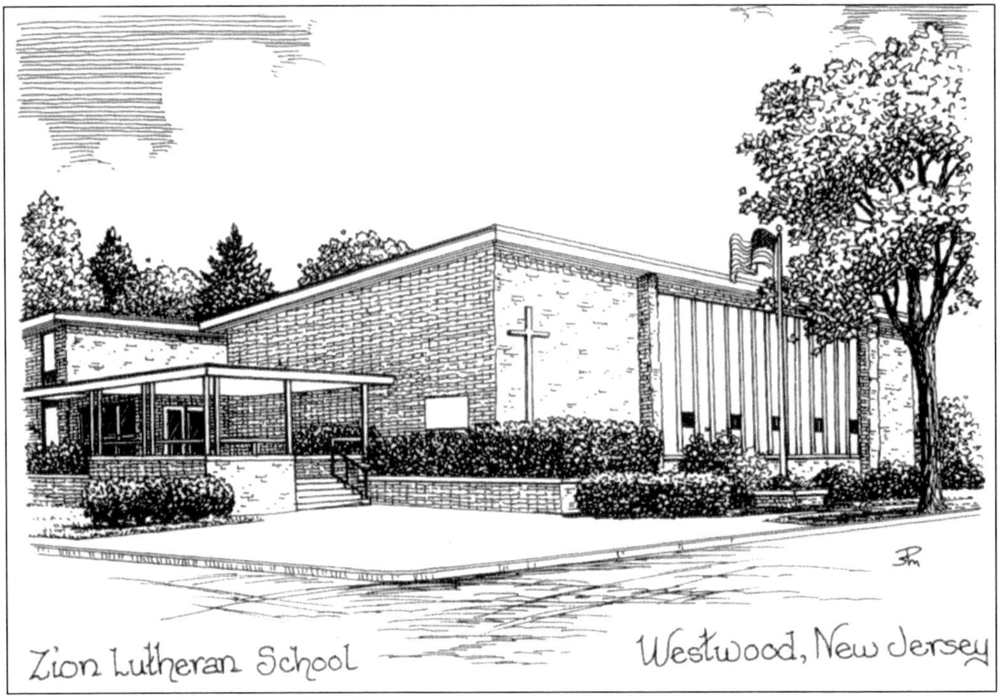

Zion Lutheran School is located at the corner of First Avenue and Elm Street. It was opened in 1963, providing a highly rated education for children in prekindergarten through eighth grade.

Three

The Old Mills

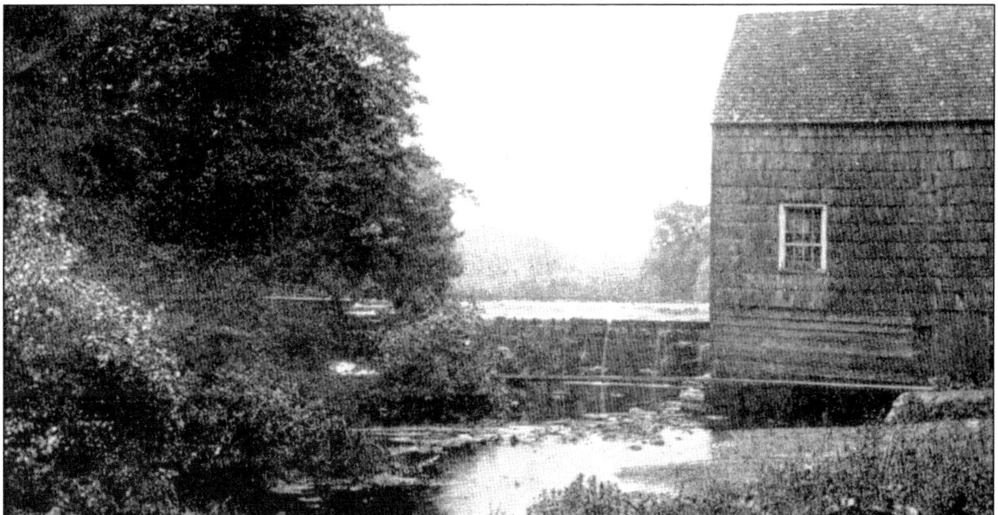

As in most towns, Westwood's businesses grew around the train station, but Bogert's Mill, centrally located on First Avenue, was the town's early attraction. The original dam and mill were built by Lutheran Rev. Johannes Van Dieren before 1734. The mill attracted early settlers from throughout the Pascack Valley. People visited the mill to have their grains milled or to buy flour and other ground grains. The mill also served as a resting place for Gen. George Washington and his troops in October 1780 as they passed through Westwood. The mill burned down in 1910.

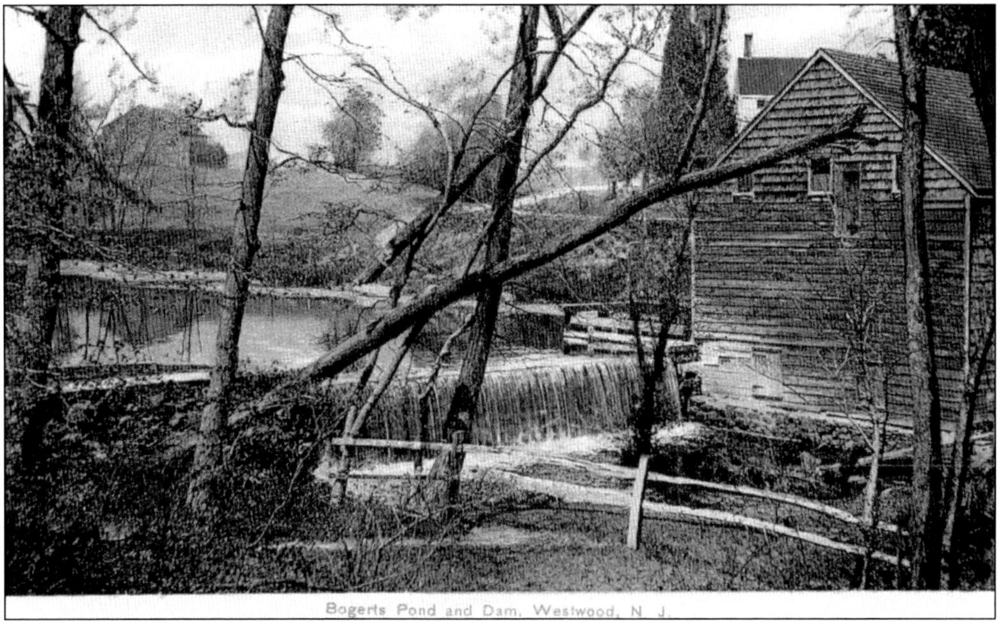

Bogert's Mill and Dam were located on the Musquapsink Brook, at the corner where First Avenue turns into Mill Street. The dam created a waterfall that powered the grain mill and created a picturesque scene.

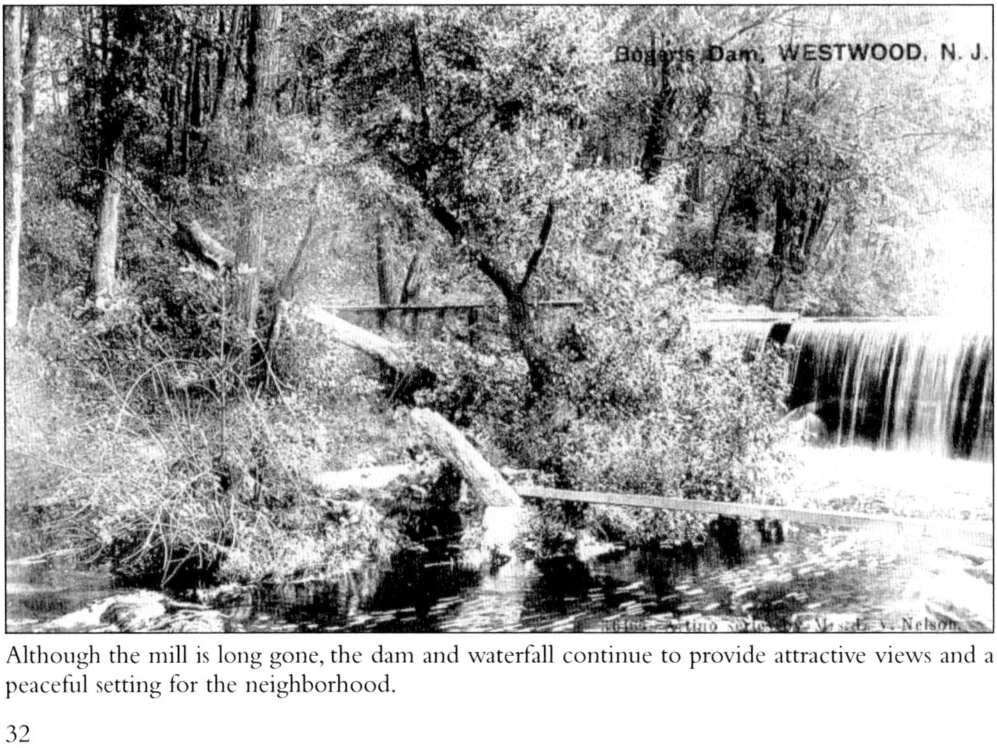

Although the mill is long gone, the dam and waterfall continue to provide attractive views and a peaceful setting for the neighborhood.

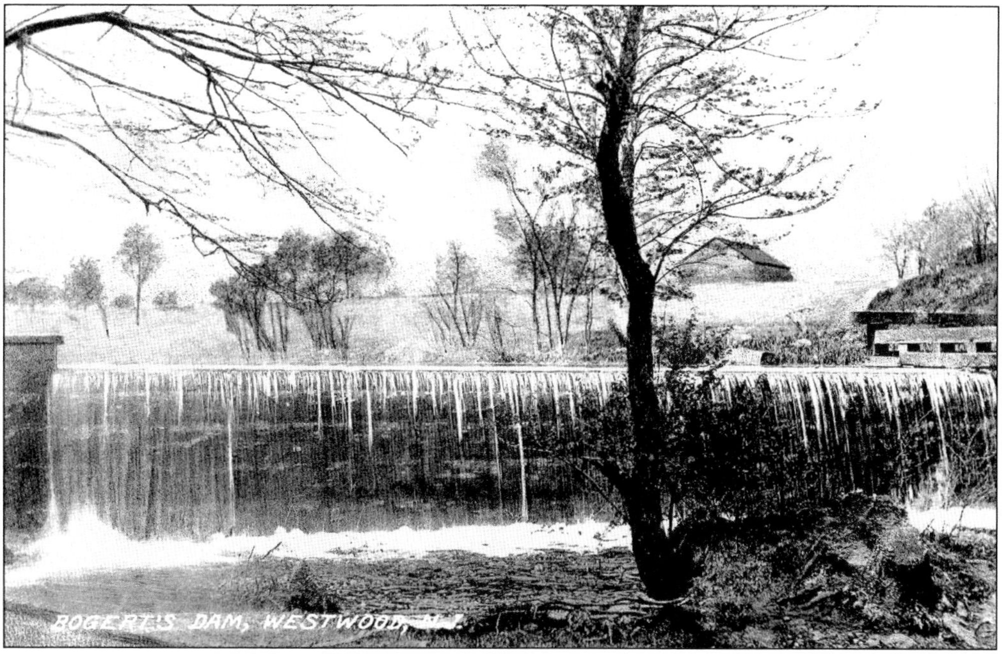

Of course, Bogert's Dam also created a large pond that has been a popular spot for boating, fishing, and skating.

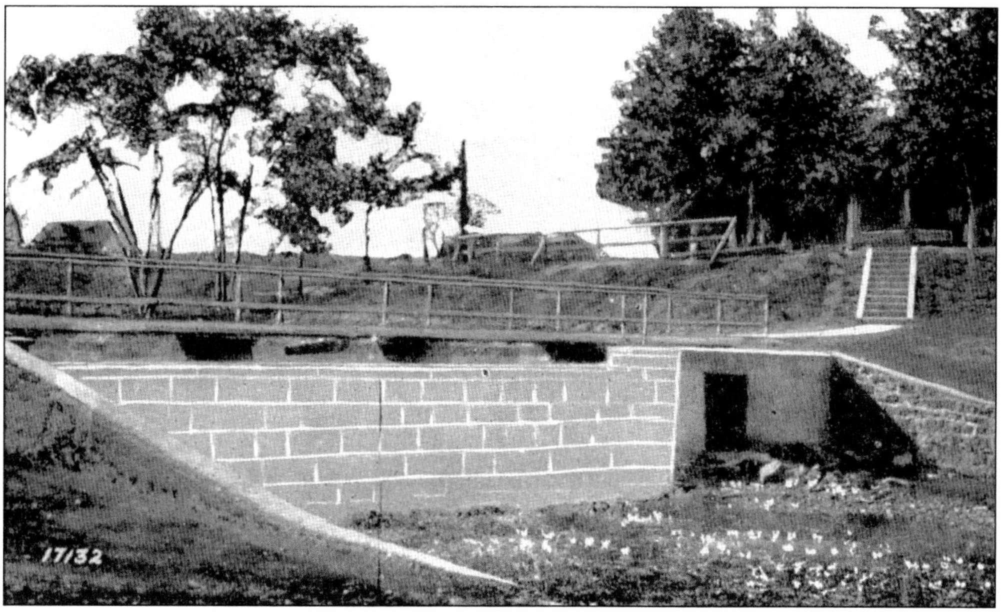

Property owners along the east side of Second Avenue and the west side of Goodwin Terrace own the pond and enjoy the view from their backyards.

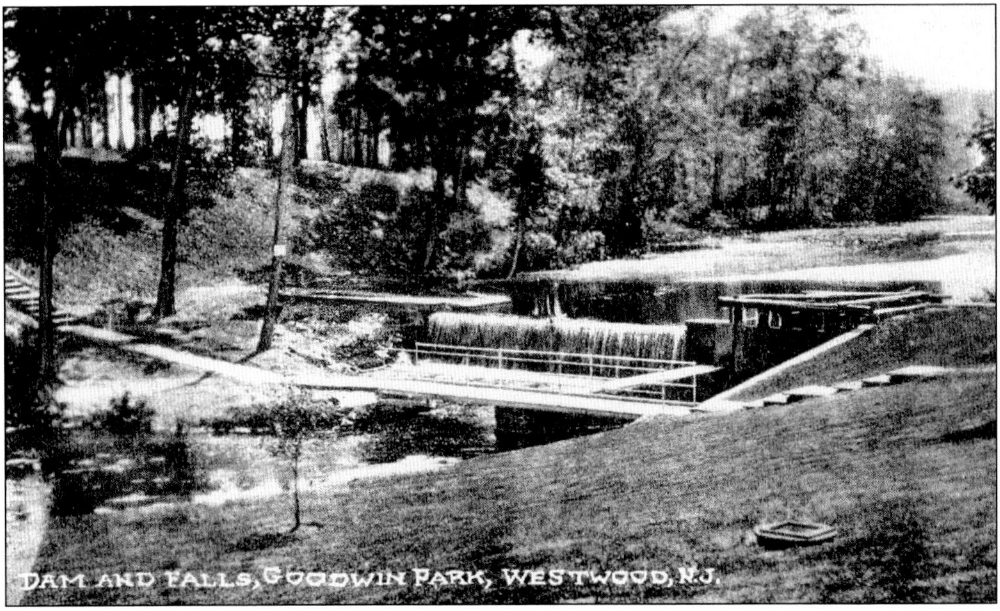

A footbridge spanned the brook near the location of the mill and provided residents in the Goodwin Park neighborhood with a shortcut to Mill Street. The bridge was originally below the dam but was later rebuilt over the dam.

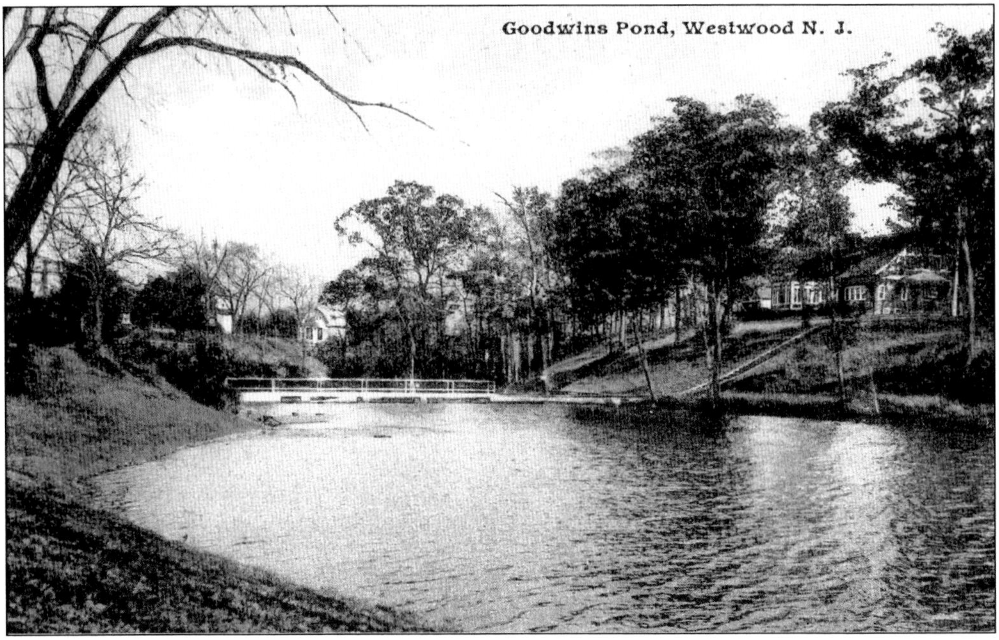

Although the dam is privately owned, a longstanding easement allows the public to cross the bridge. At the time of this writing, the bridge is being rebuilt by the borough. Beautiful homes have been built all along the pond.

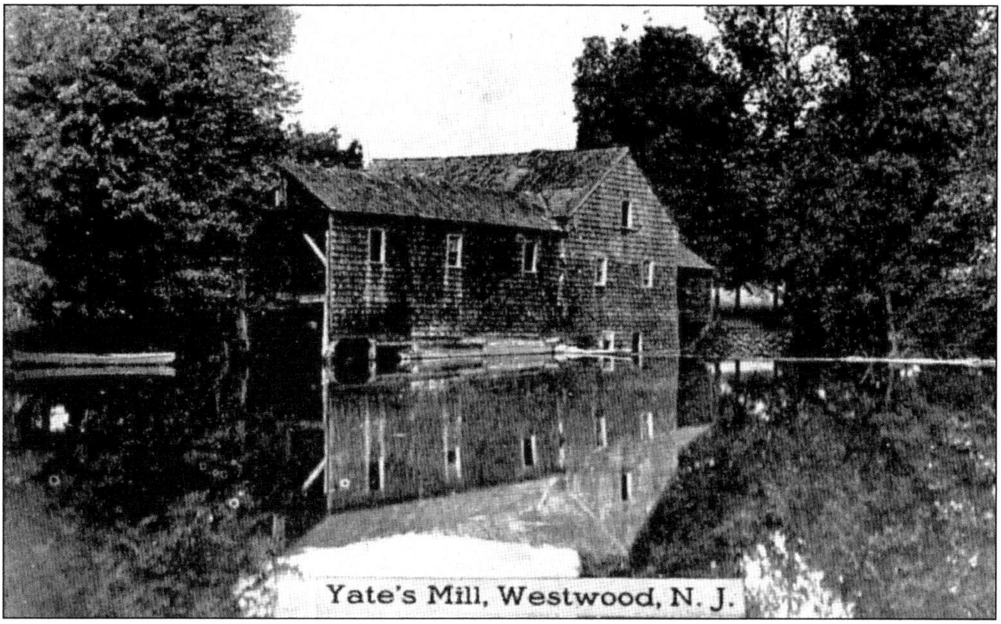

Yates Mill was also a major contributor to Westwood's early commerce. It was on the Pascack Brook, near the corner of Westwood Avenue and Dean Street. Not much information is available about Yates Mill—probably because it was already in ruins by the time this postcard was made in 1907.

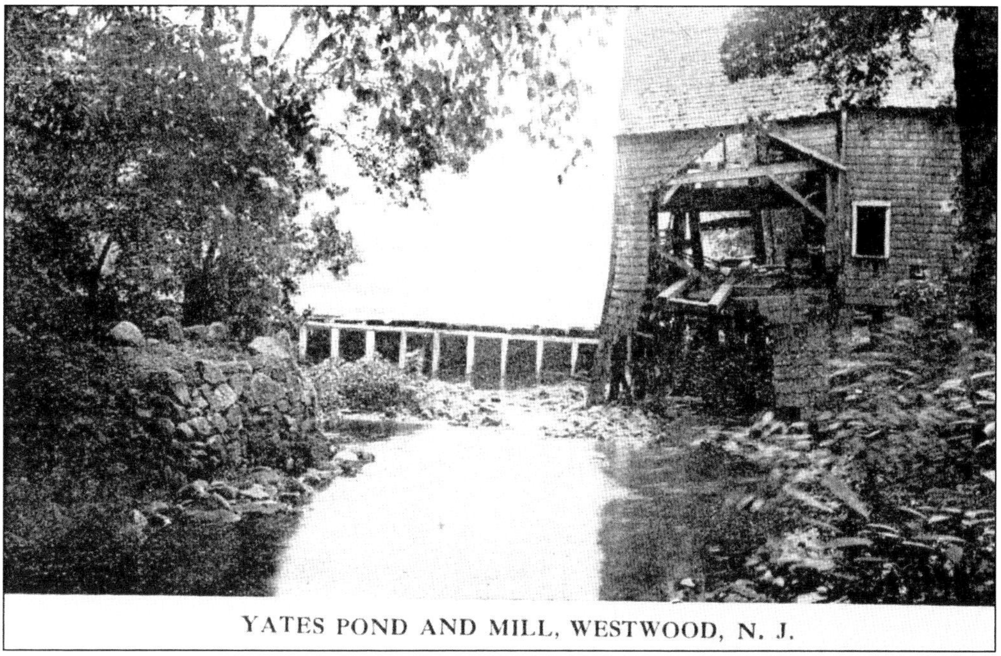

As explained by Katherine Randall in *Pascack Valley Tales,* published by the Pascack Historical Society, Garret Demarest constructed a mill at this site prior to 1789. The dam powered a sawmill, as well as a gristmill, and the Demarests also operated a store. The bridge located below the dam has been rebuilt twice to keep pace with modern traffic.

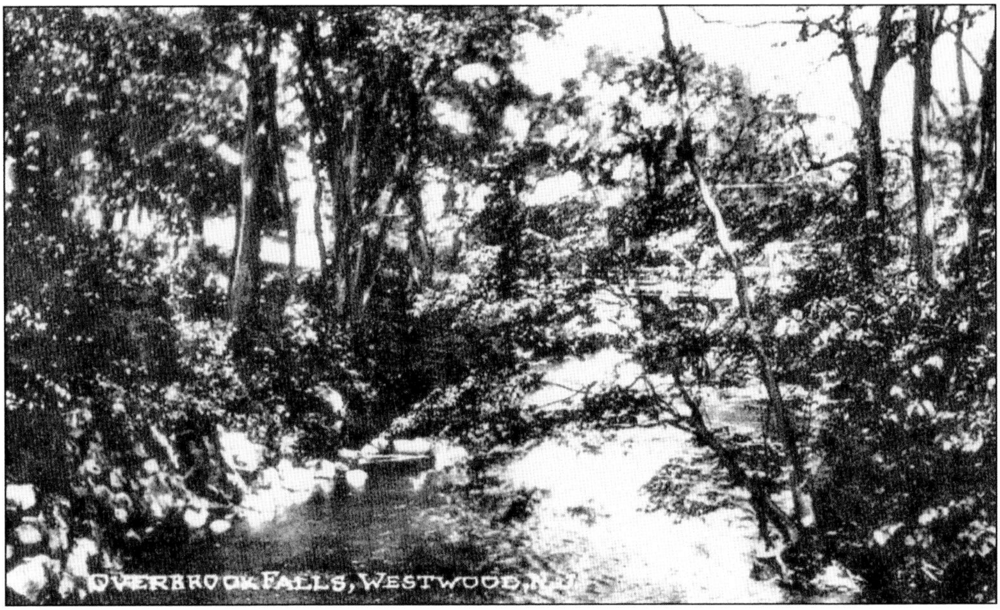

The mill was operated by the Demarest family until 1864, when it was sold to Robert Yates. It is unknown how long the Yates family operated the mills.

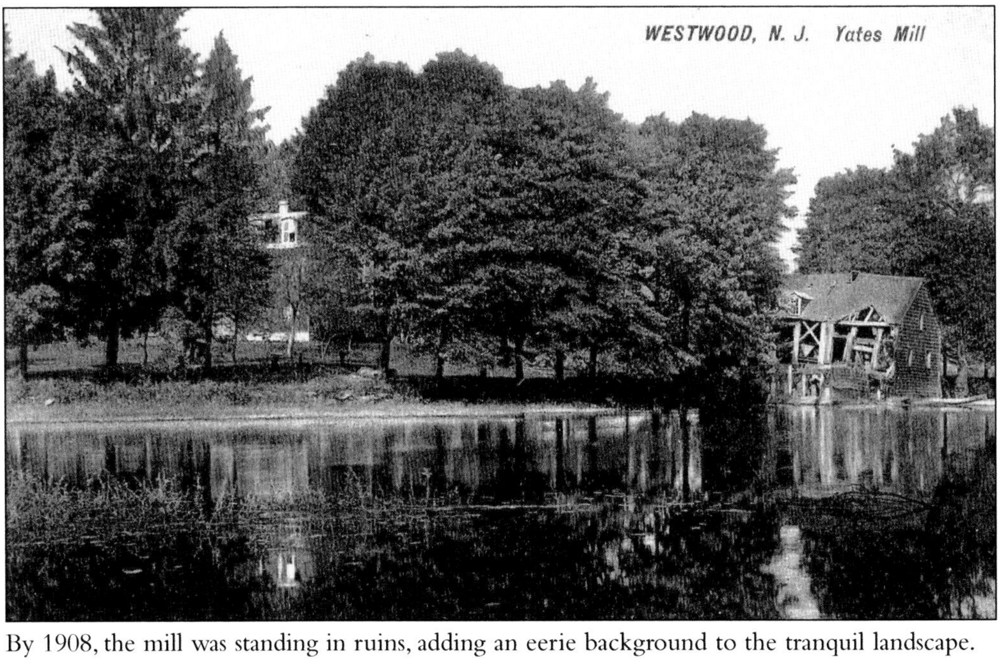

By 1908, the mill was standing in ruins, adding an eerie background to the tranquil landscape.

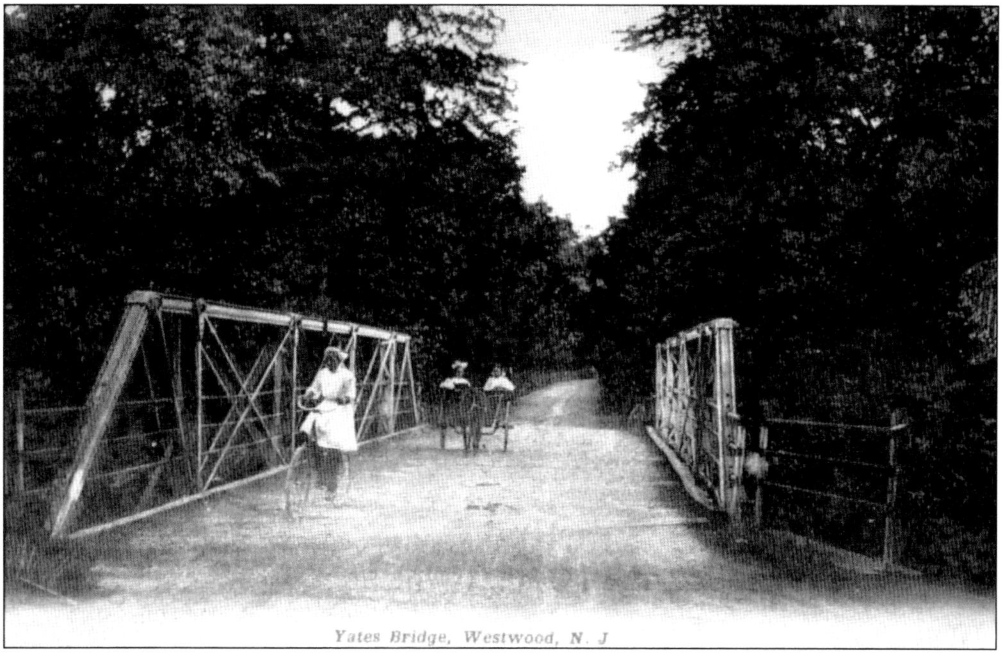

Yates Mill included a bridge over the Pascack Brook that provided a critical crossing from Westwood Avenue to Demarest Avenue in Hillsdale. Since Kinderkamack Road originally ended at Five Corners, this bridge provided the only access into Westwood from the bordering Hillsdale neighborhoods.

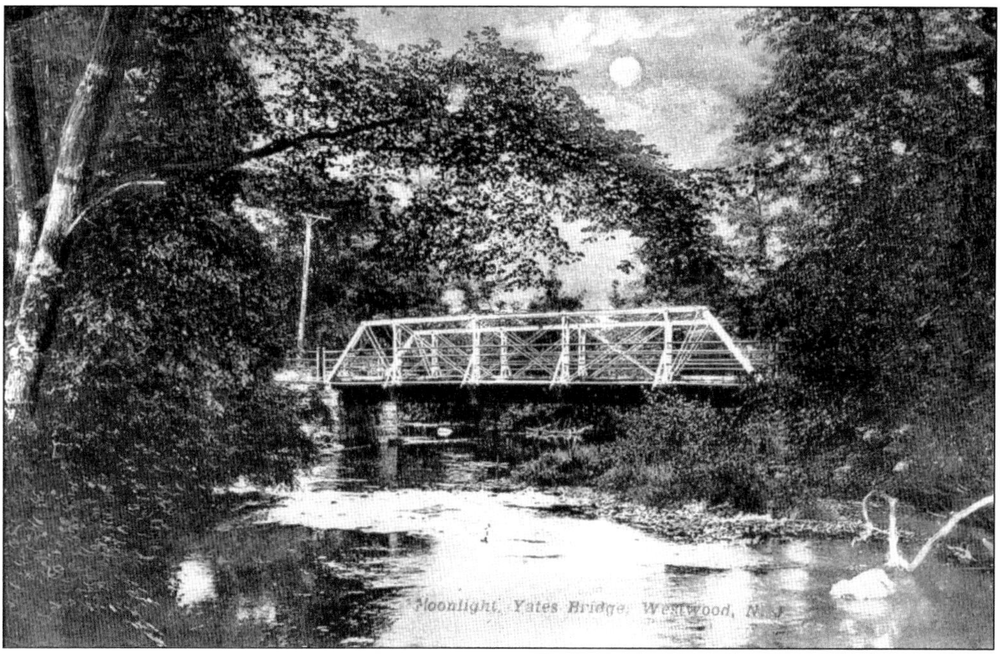

The bridge has been known as Yates Bridge and Overbrook Bridge. The bridge and pond created an attractive view for the houses along Terrace Avenue (featured on page 114).

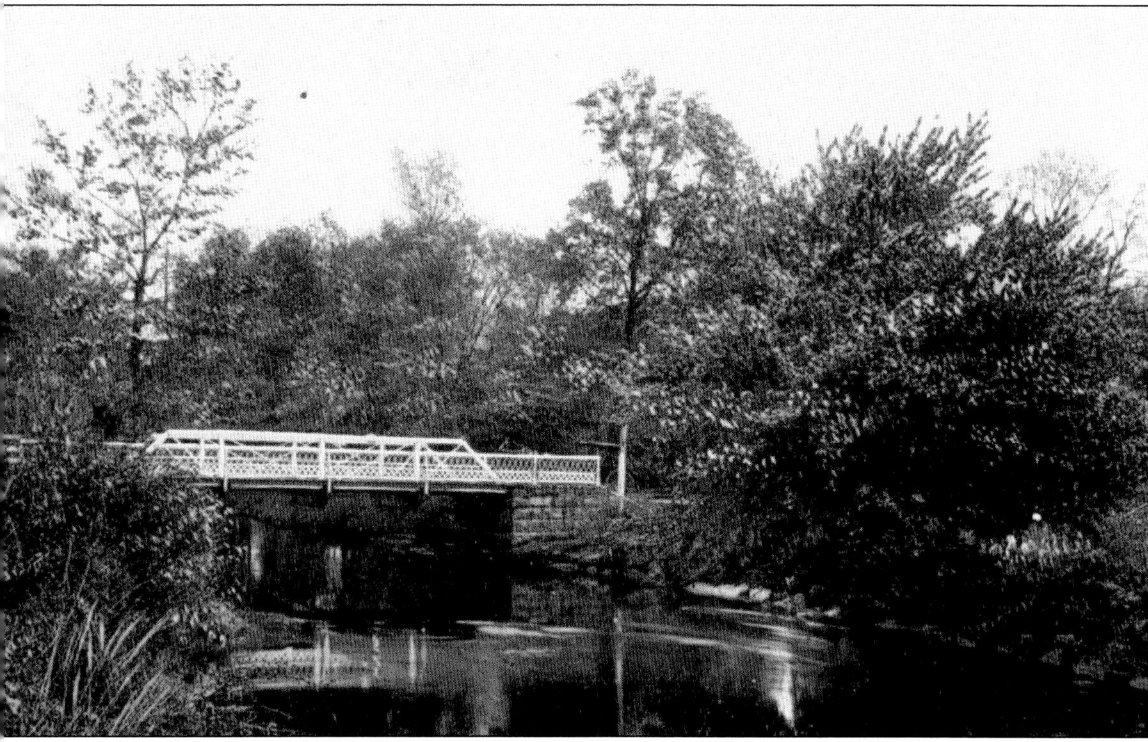

The dam that powered the mill widened the Pascack Brook into an attractive pond. The dam was destroyed when Westwood built its sewer system in the 1920s.

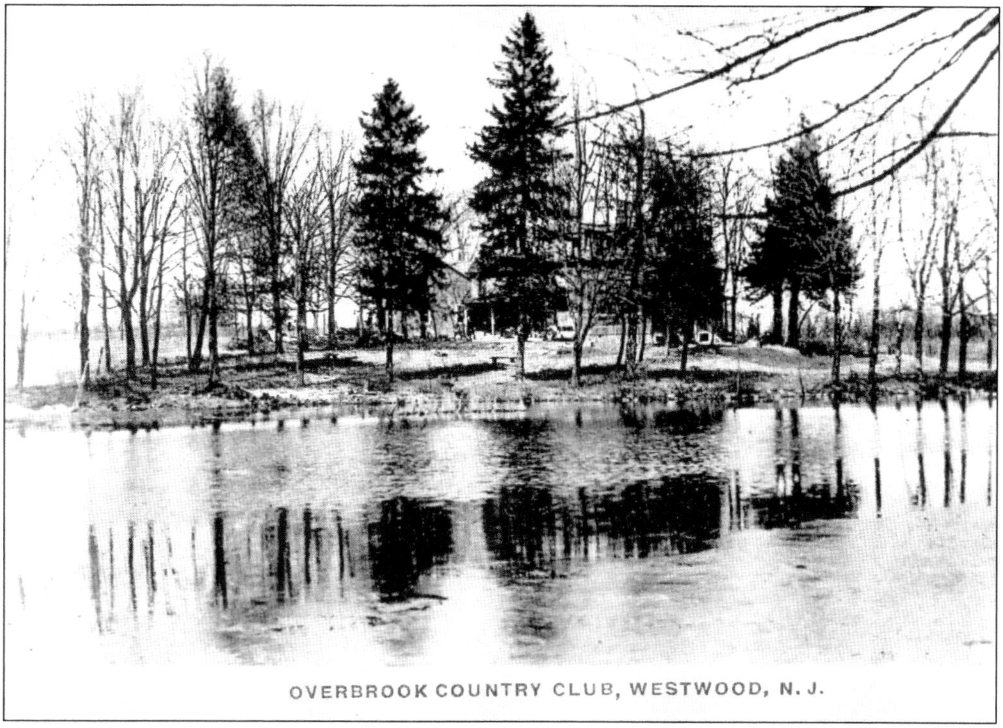

In 1915, Yates Mill became the site of the Overbrook Country Club. The club included the pond, a new running track, tennis courts, bowling lanes, and a baseball field in which the legendary "Shoeless Joe" Jackson once played.

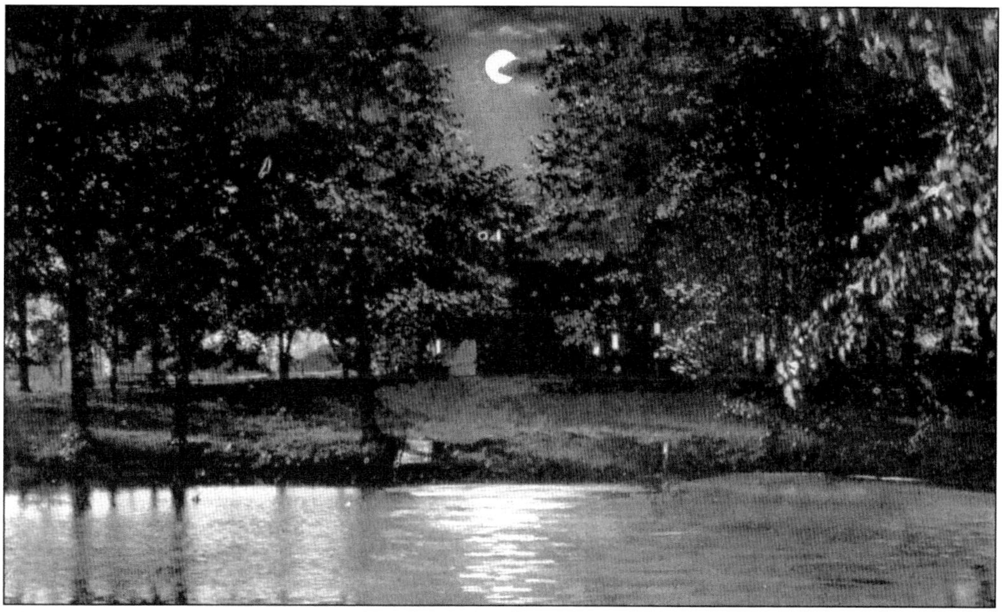

The Overbrook Country Club prospered though the Roaring Twenties as a popular location for parties, card games, dancing, and sporting events, but it began to falter as the Great Depression approached. On the night of August 7, 1931, three arsonists burned down the country club. One of the culprits was reported to be a Westwood police officer.

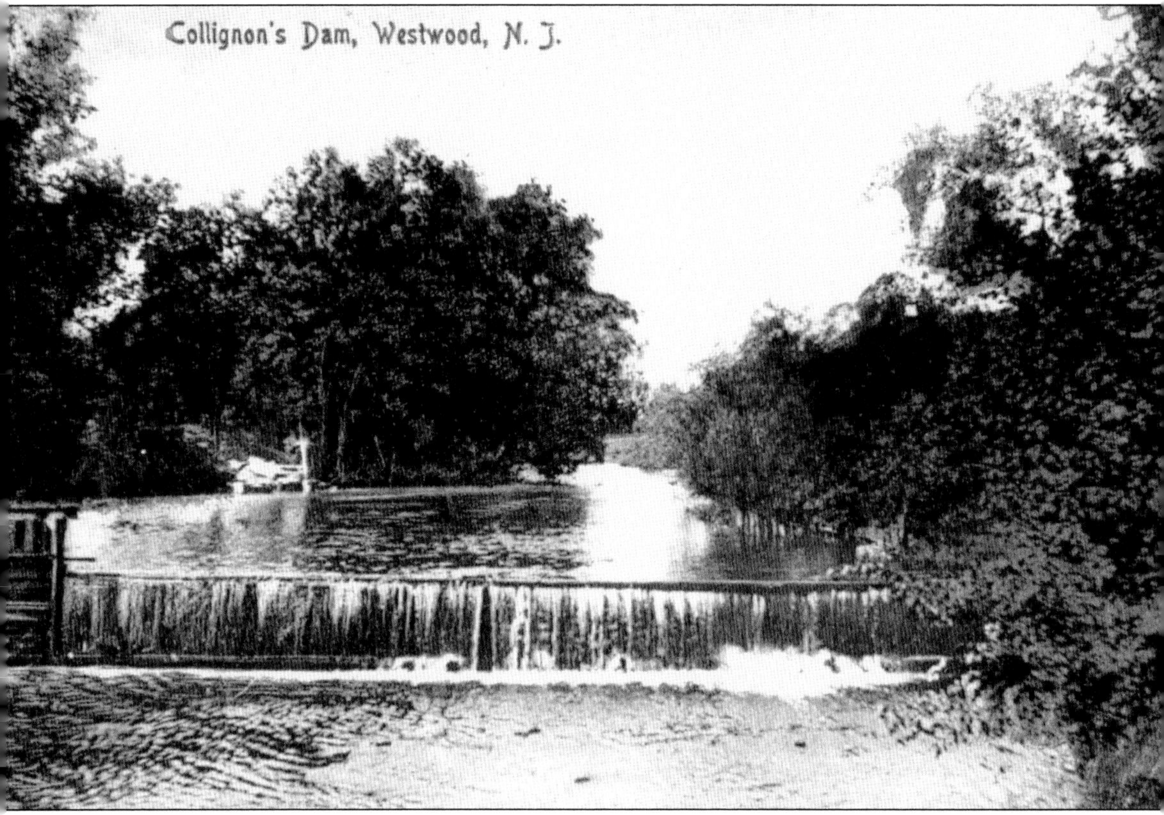

Collignon's Mill was located on the Hackensack River in what is now known as River Vale. At the beginning of the century, Collignon's Mill used power from the river to mill grains and saw lumber. All of that experience with wood led Nicholas Collignon to invent the first folding chair. The Collignon Folding Chair was very popular for a period of time and was authorized by Queen Victoria for use on the Cunard Steamship Line. The structure on the left was used to store bodies during winter months until the ground thawed enough to allow burials.

Four

The Business District

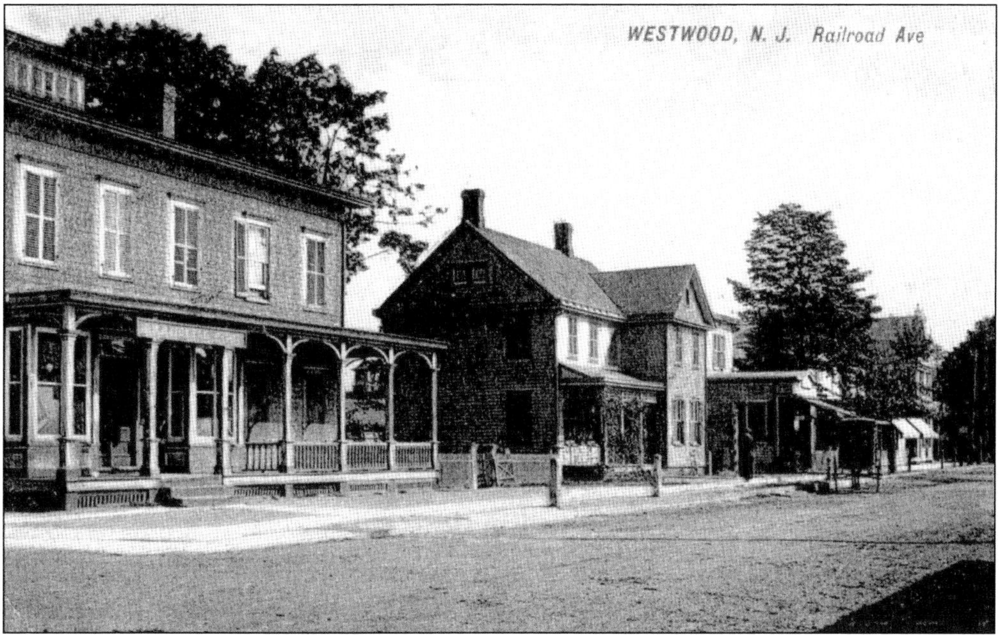

In 1869, Isaac D. Bogert and Z. B. Van Emburgh built the town's first general store on the corner of Westwood Avenue and Railroad Avenue (now Broadway), across from the train station. The store provided everything, including eggs, meat, lumber, coal, cake, and shoes. It even included a smokehouse and served as a post office. Eventually, George Brickell took over the store and ran it for many years. This corner, having both the train station and general store, was the local hot spot. Locals congregated here to pick up their mail and supplies at the general store, to wait for the train, or to catch up on local news. The town was still very small. A 10-minute walk in any direction led to complete wilderness, where hunters and trappers roamed.

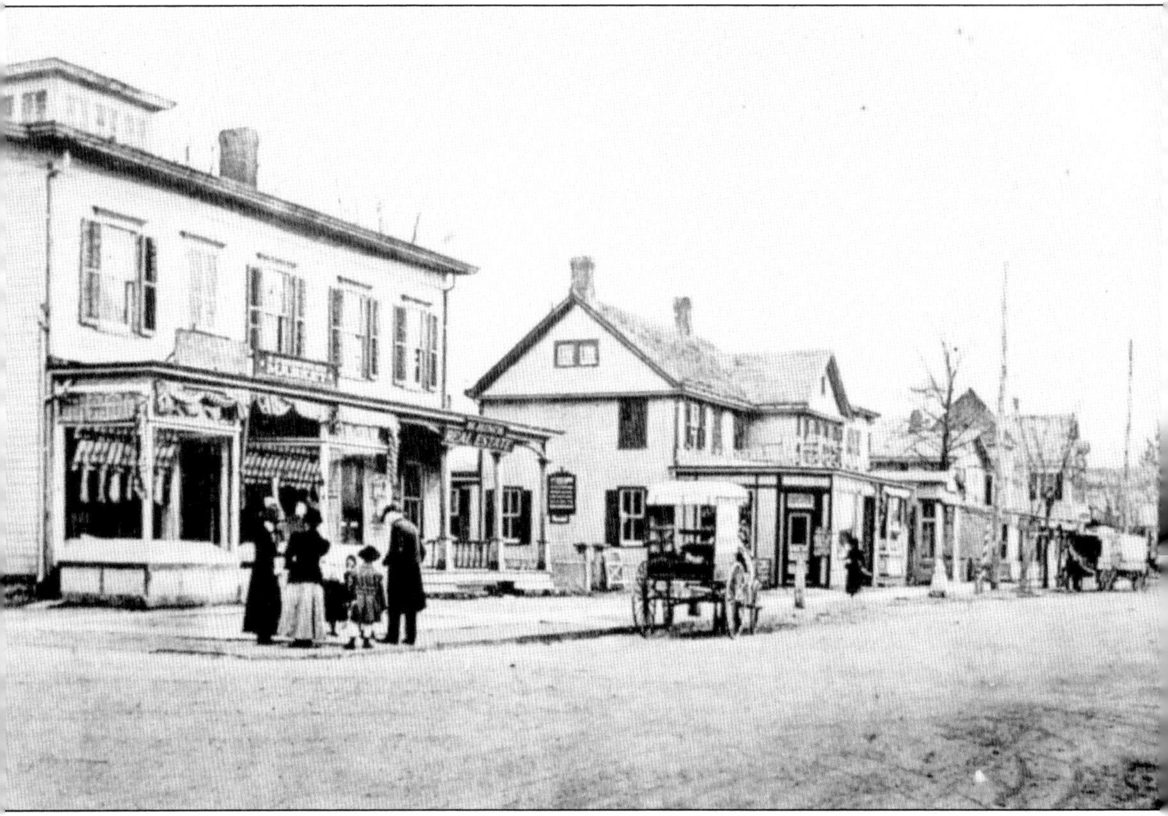

Railroad Avenue (now Broadway) was not paved *c.* 1900, when these postcards were mailed. The dirt roads and hitching posts create the appearance of an Old West cowboy movie. In 1932, the general store was replaced by the bank building at the corner of Broadway and Westwood Avenue.

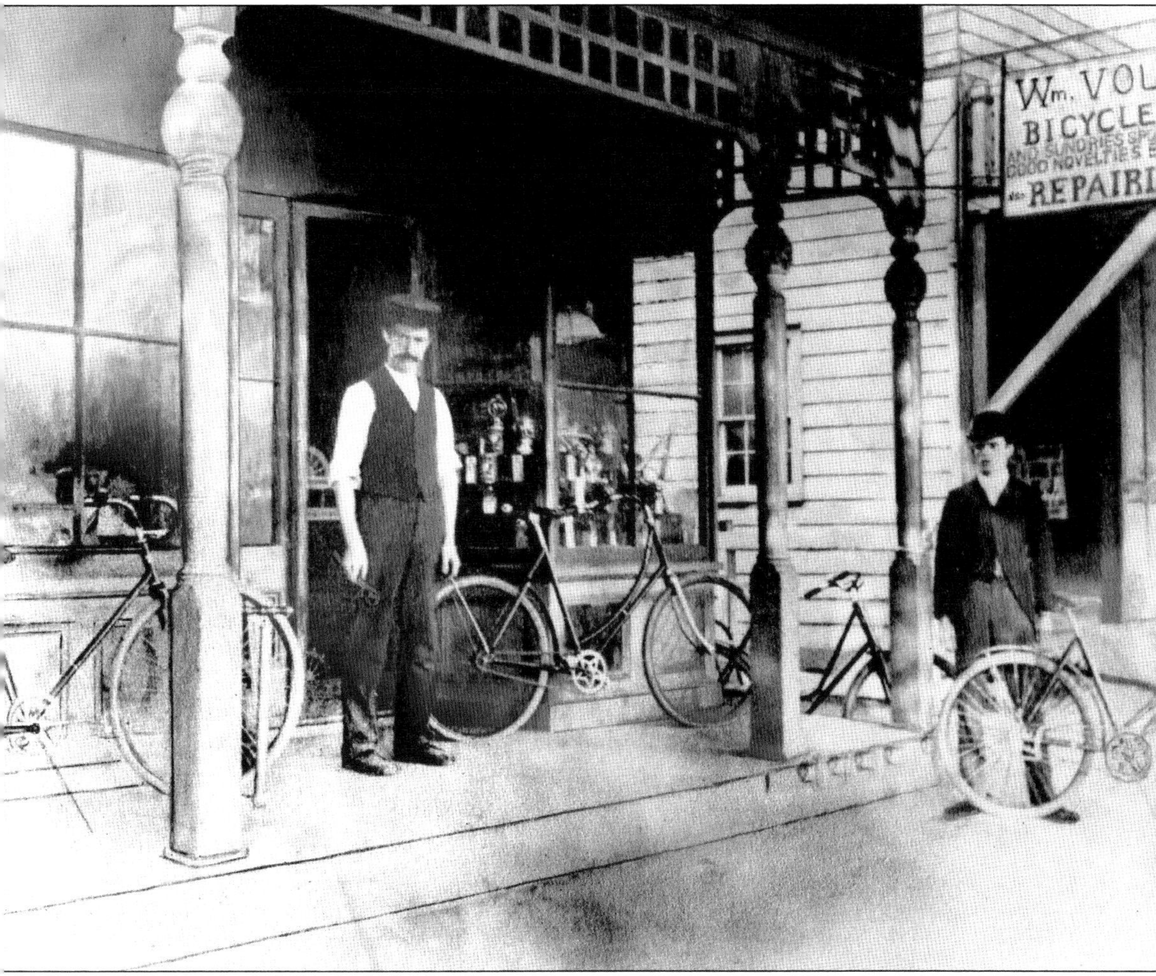

Dating back to the 1890s, William Volz's Bicycle and Sports Shop was one of Westwood's early businesses along Railroad Avenue. It started out at what is now known as 341 Broadway and moved to 313 Broadway, where it remained for most of the 20th century.

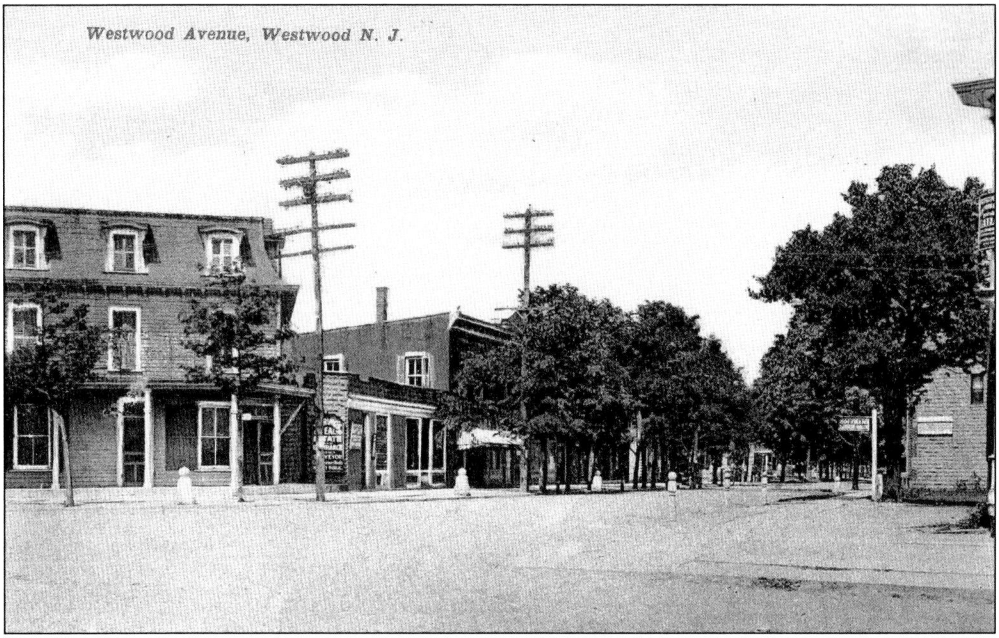

The Westwood House Hotel sat on the other corner of Main Street and Railroad Avenue (now Westwood Avenue and Broadway) from 1869 to 1921. It was built by A. B. Bogert and was operated by Genest Ottignon. Ottignon owned land directly across the tracks on Madison Avenue that later became part of Veterans Memorial Park. He wore large muttonchop sideburns, and served in the 22nd Infantry Regiment during the Civil War with A. B. Bogert and I. D. Bogert.

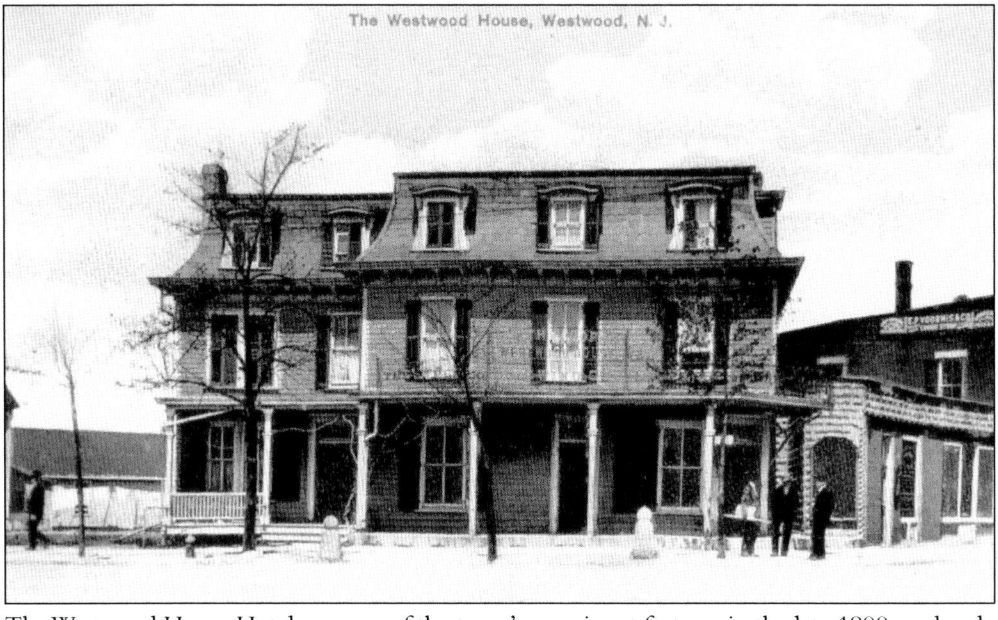

The Westwood House Hotel was one of the town's prominent features in the late 1800s and early 1900s due to its size, architecture, and location across from the train station. A century later, in 1980, the senior housing facility at 100 Madison Avenue was named after this historic hotel. In 1880, A. B. Bogert sold the Westwood House to J. B. Speth, who operated it until 1899 and then sold it to Ernest Grabedunkel.

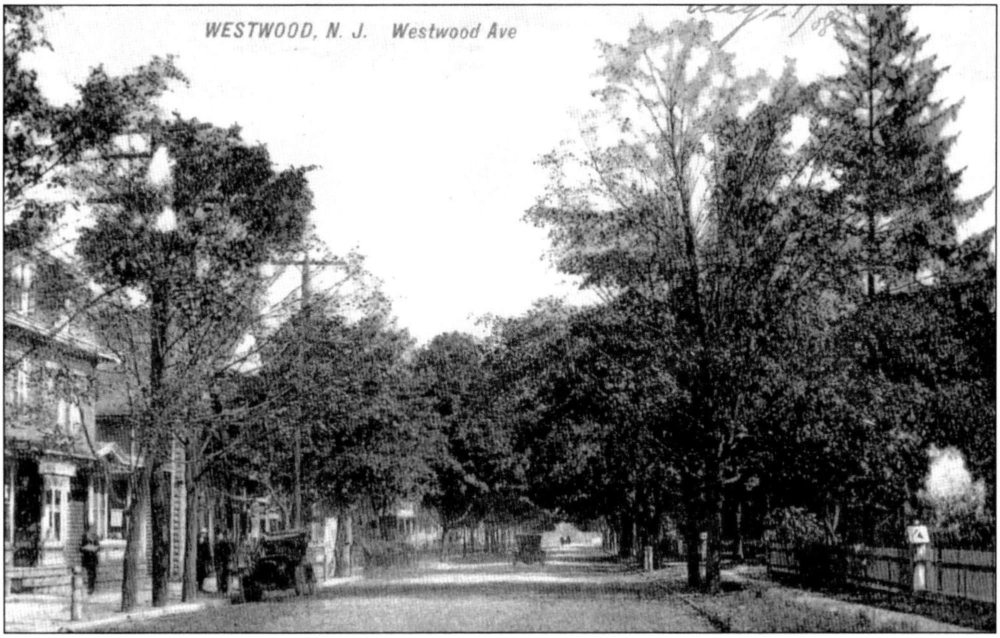

Although this corner was established as the center of town, this postcard, mailed in 1908, reveals that Broadway and Westwood Avenue were still tranquil, tree-covered lanes. Residents of that time would surely be surprised by the appearance of this corner today.

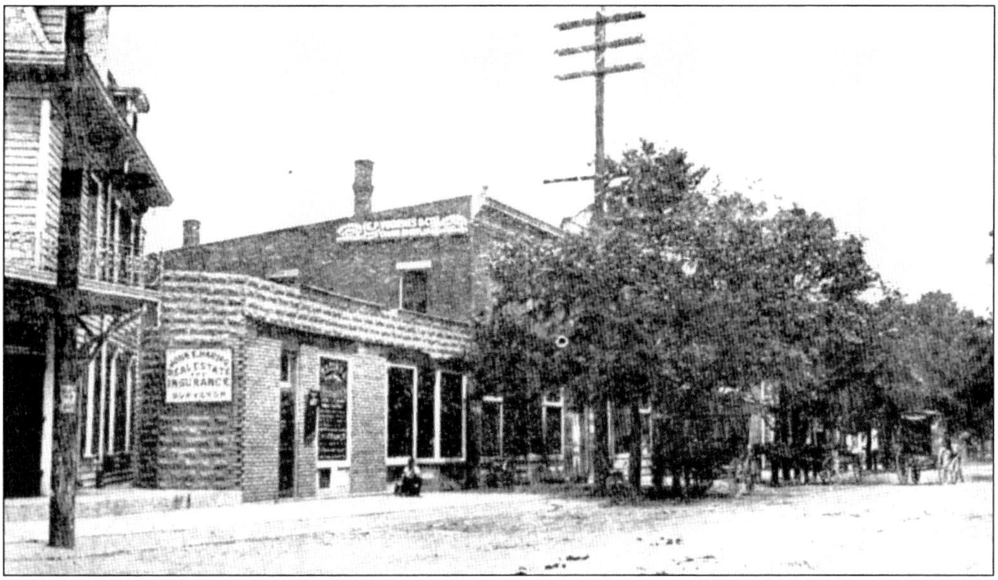

The corner of Westwood Avenue and Broadway across from the train station has been the center of Westwood's commerce since Westwood was settled. When this card was mailed in 1911, all of Westwood's houses were within a few blocks of this intersection, and businesses extended only about a block in each direction.

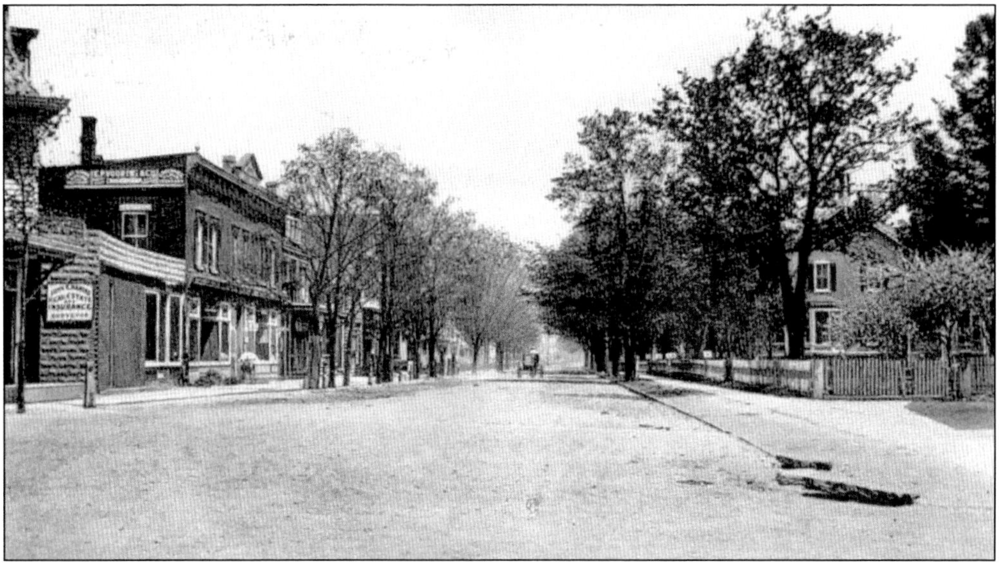

Prior to *c.* 1915, the south side of Westwood Avenue was entirely residential and was lined with large trees and picket fences.

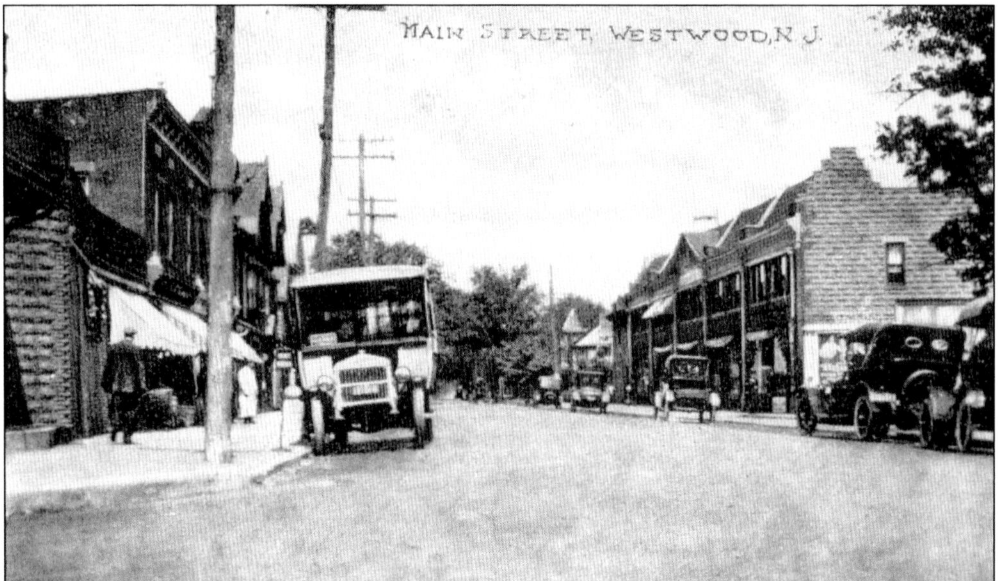

Businesses gradually spread out in each direction from the train station, as Westwood increased from a population of just 500 in 1894.

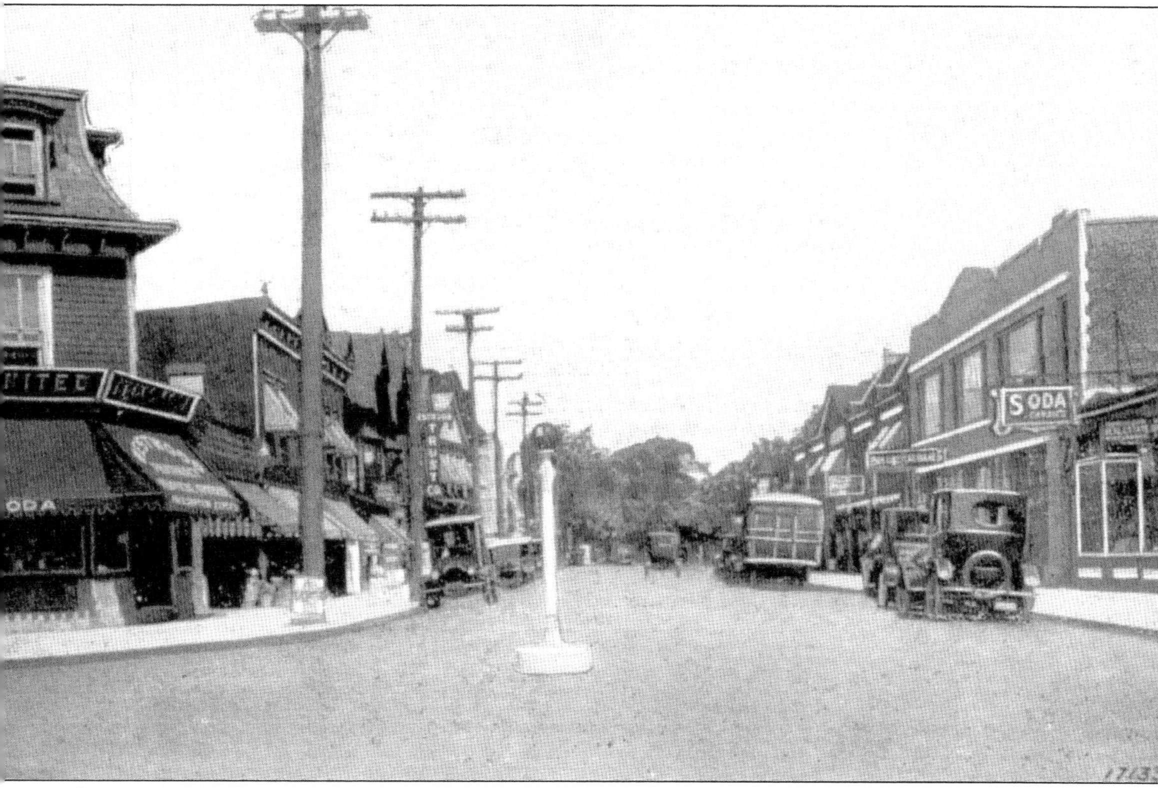

This *c.* 1925 postcard illustrates how quickly the corner of Westwood Avenue and Broadway developed. The Westwood House Hotel has been converted to stores, and the south side of Westwood Avenue has been developed with new brick storefronts. All of the added traffic apparently necessitated a traffic signal.

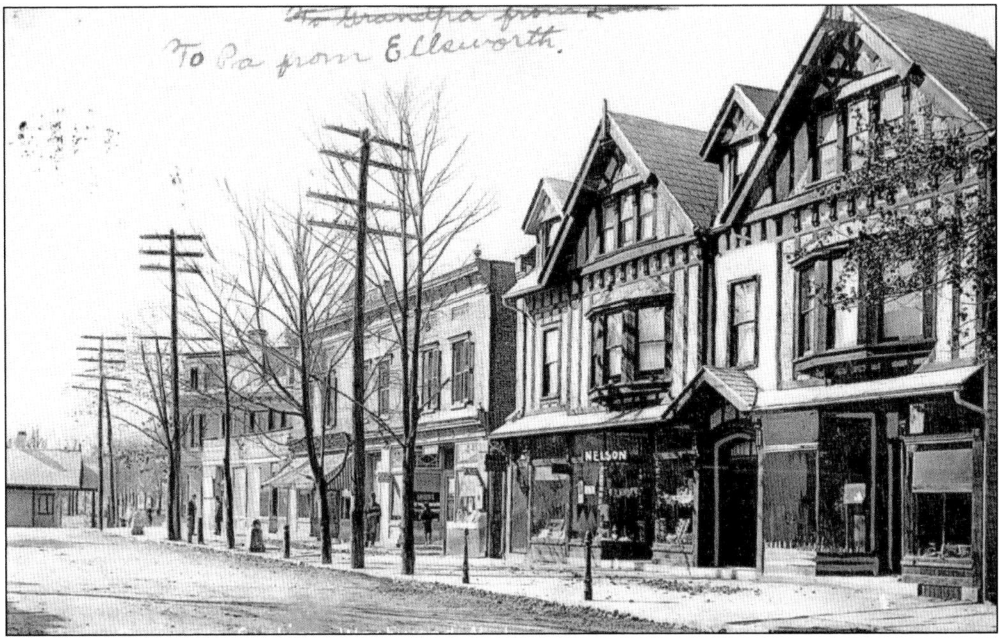

This 1913 view of Westwood Avenue looks west toward the train tracks. The old train station in the background was located on the east side of the tracks, at the end of Westwood Avenue. The peaked roofline of 58–68 Westwood Avenue remains the same today.

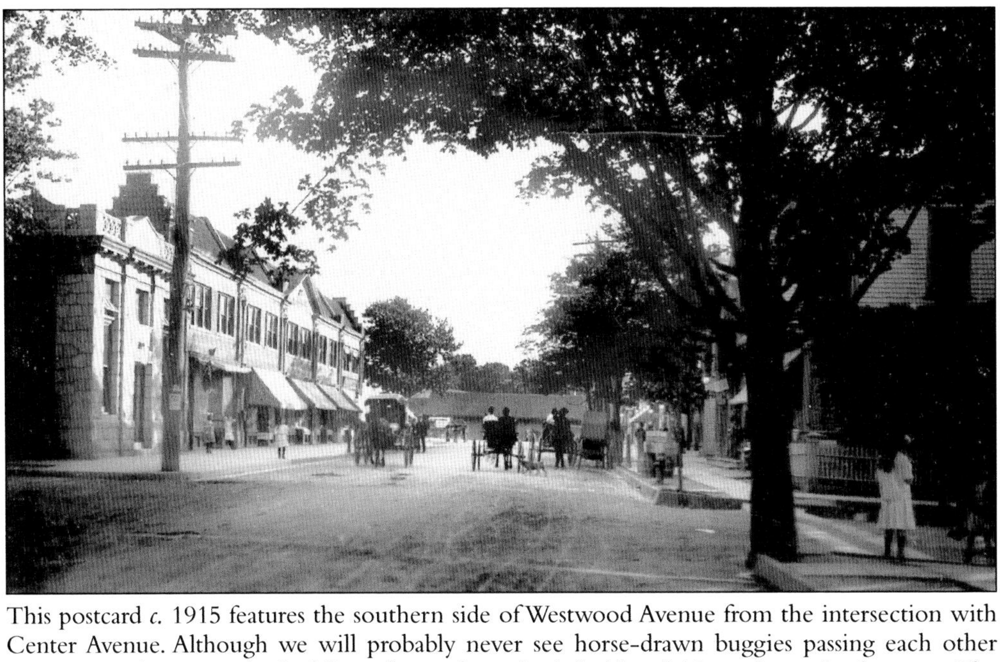

This postcard *c.* 1915 features the southern side of Westwood Avenue from the intersection with Center Avenue. Although we will probably never see horse-drawn buggies passing each other on Westwood Avenue, the buildings featured on the left side of this card remain the same. The four-story bank building is noticably missing at the far corner of the block because it was not built until 1932.

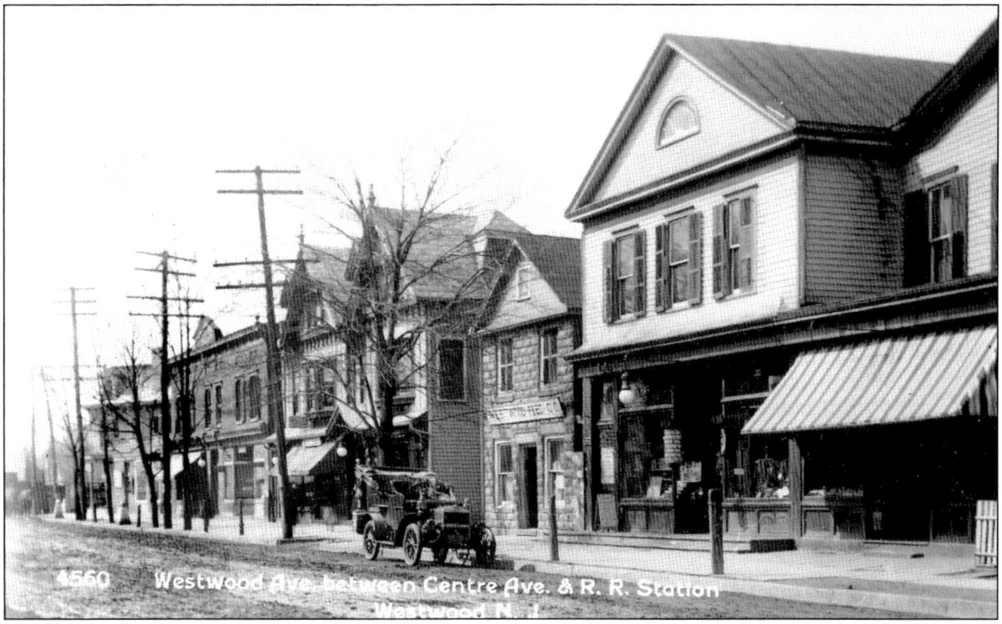

Although many aspects of everyday life have obviously changed, many of the same things that are sold on Westwood Avenue today could have been found in the stores of 100 years ago. Banks, insurance salesmen, hardware stores, and shoe stores have always found their place along Westwood Avenue.

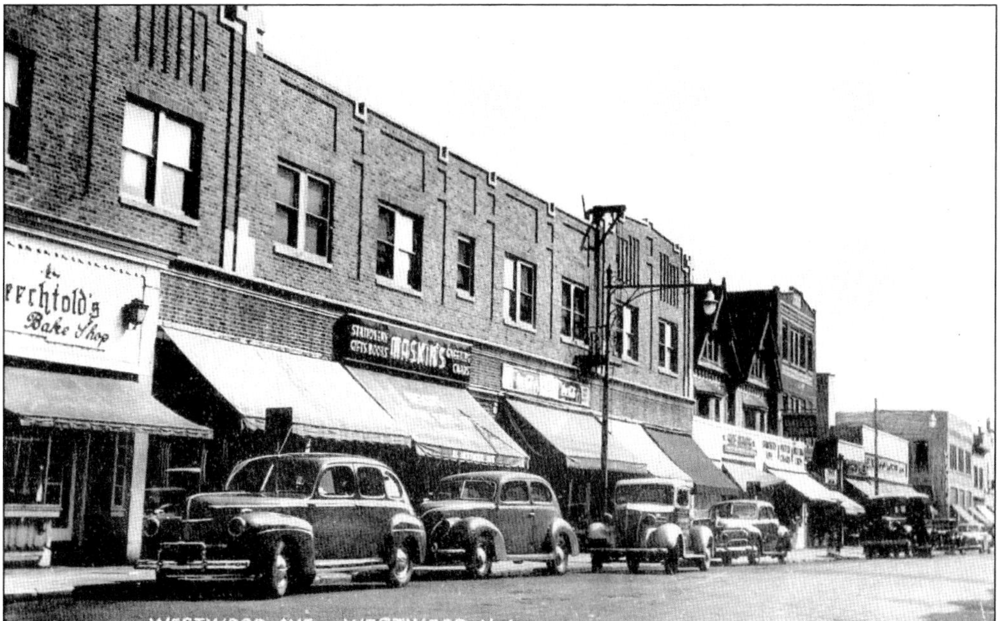

You would not have found any shops selling video games or latte, but Westwood Avenue was lined with stores selling familiar products and services. In this *c.* 1940 card, a bakery, a stationery store, F. W. Woolworth's, and a department store can be seen.

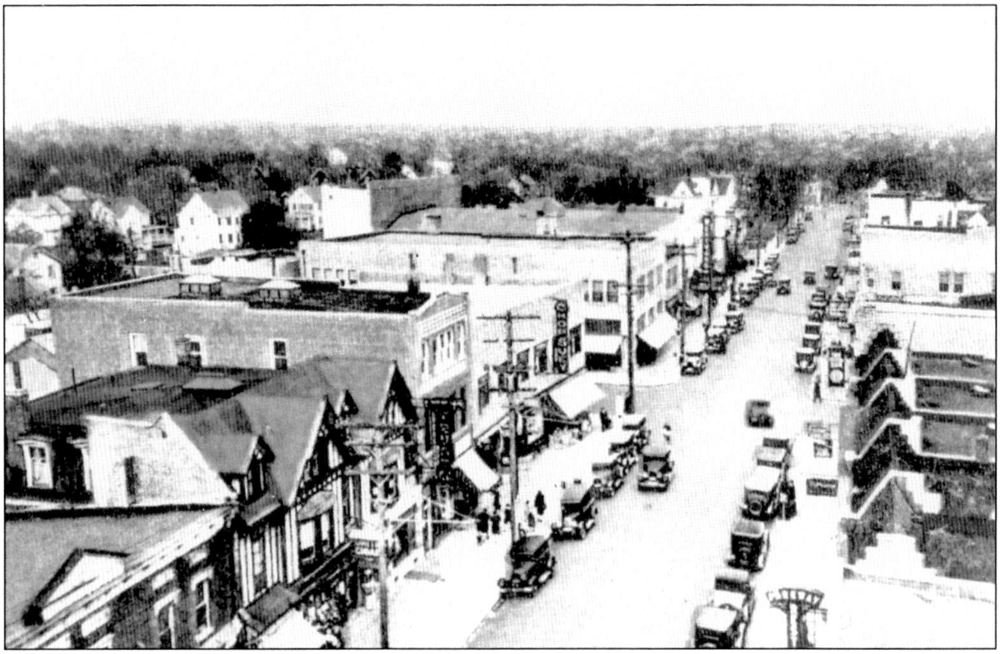

This aerial view of Westwood Avenue from the top of the bank building at the corner of Broadway appears to date back to the late 1920s. It illustrates how Westwood Avenue extended all the way to Kinderkamack Road. Most of the roofline architecture remains the same today. The Parkway Restaurant, at the lower right, was at located 45 Westwood Avenue (where Tyrrell's Florist is today). With its grand opening in 1929, the restaurant was doomed by the Great Depression, and by 1932, it had closed.

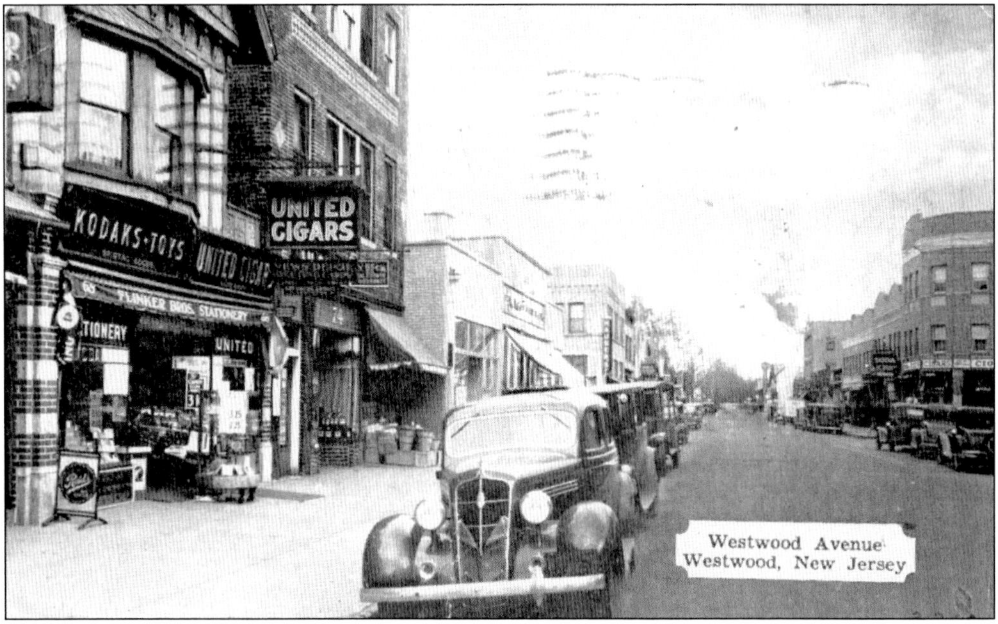

Flinker Brothers Stationery, located at 68 Westwood Avenue, answered the public's demand for paper and smoking products from 1932 through the 1950s. Many of the postcards featured in this book undoubtedly were sold in this store.

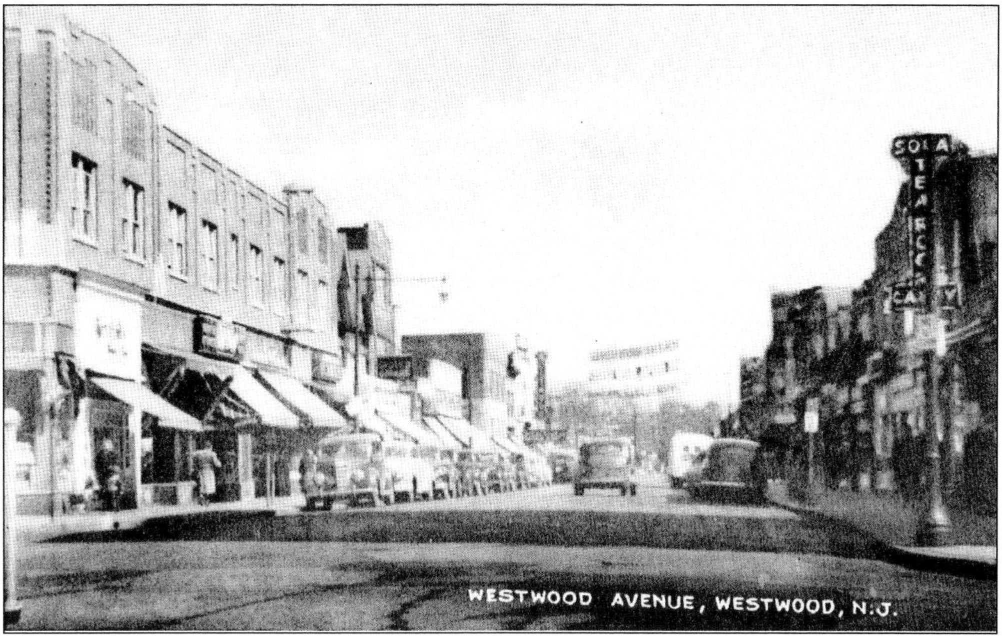

By the 1930s, the corner of Westwood Avenue and Broadway had largely been rebuilt and was beginning to look more familiar, with automobiles lining each side of the avenue. The Terminal Tea Room, on the far right, was located at 15 Westwood Avenue (where Westwood Pets is now) from 1935 to 1941.

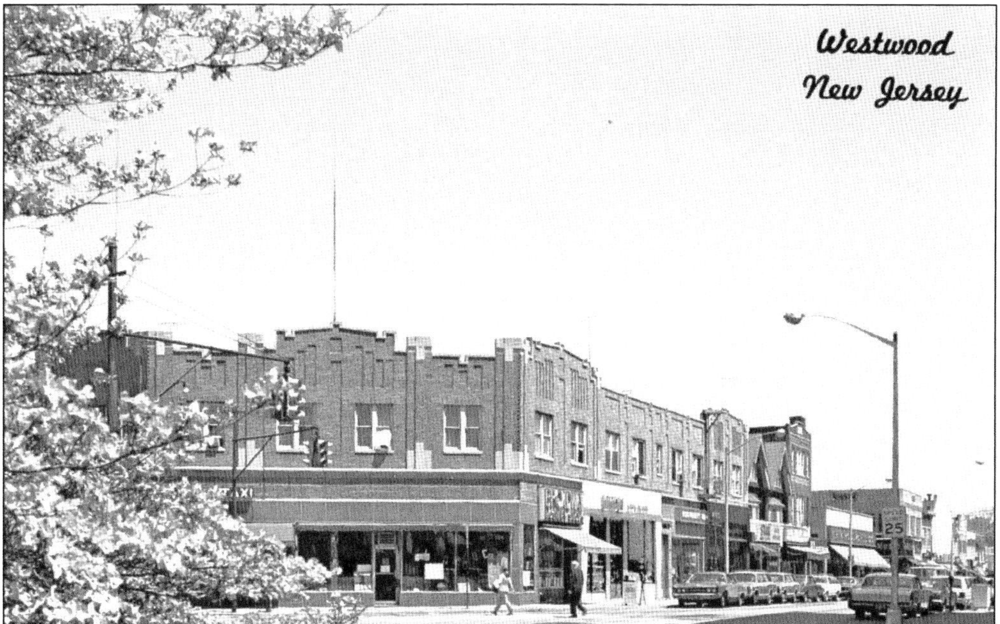

The cars in this postcard of the same corner date it to the late 1960s or early 1970s. This corner of Broadway and Westwood Avenue remains the center of Westwood's business district, just as it has been since the 1870s.

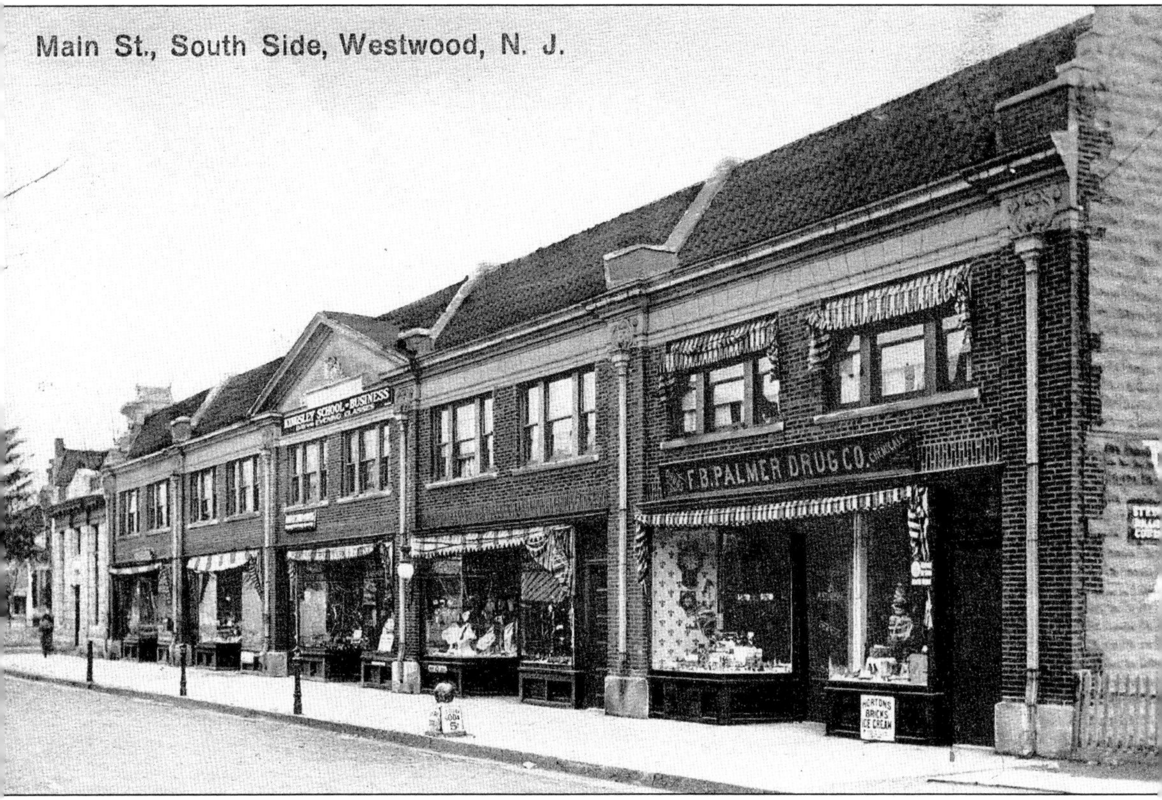

The A. B. Bogert Building was built in 1908 along the south side of Westwood Avenue. Its first tenants included a jeweler, a grocer, a tailor, and a paint store. This view looks east toward Center Avenue.

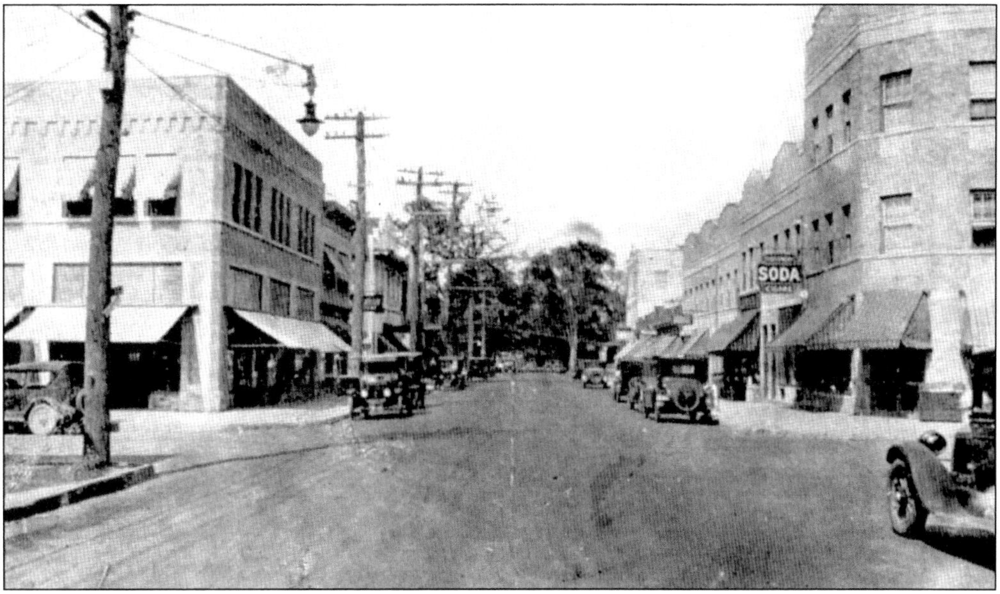

This corner of Westwood and Center Avenues is now occupied by CVS Pharmacy, New World Coffee, the Stationery Store, and Parian Jewelers. Although the storefronts have changed since the 1930s, the architecture of the buildings is still apparent on Westwood Avenue today.

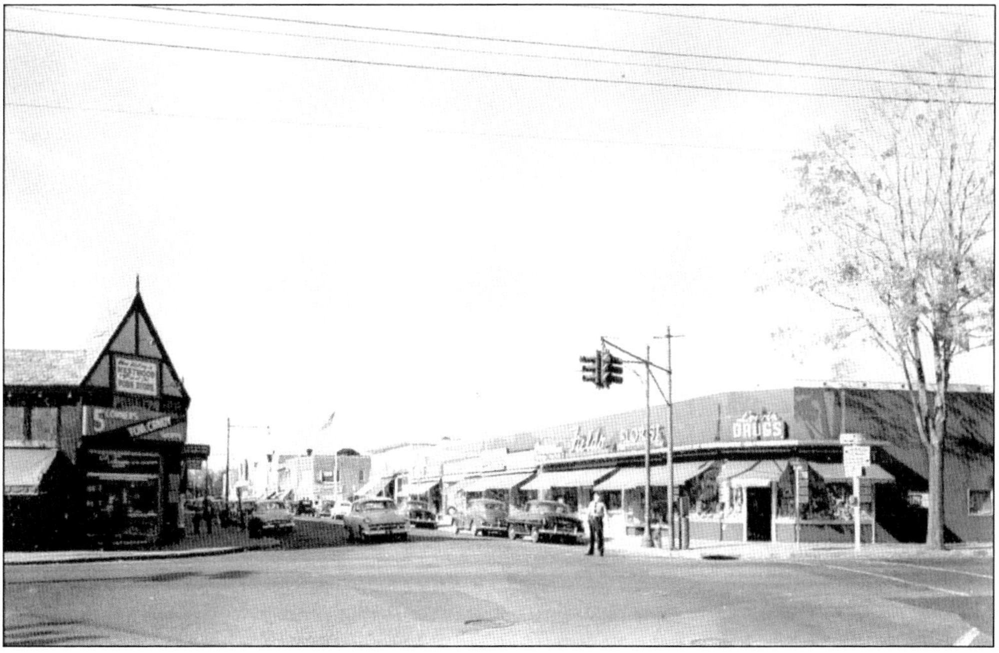

Eight stores on the corner of Kinderkamack Road and Westwood Avenue, known as Five Corners, were destroyed by fire on May 14, 1982. Some 200 firefighters from 12 departments fought the fire. This image was created after the corner had been rebuilt.

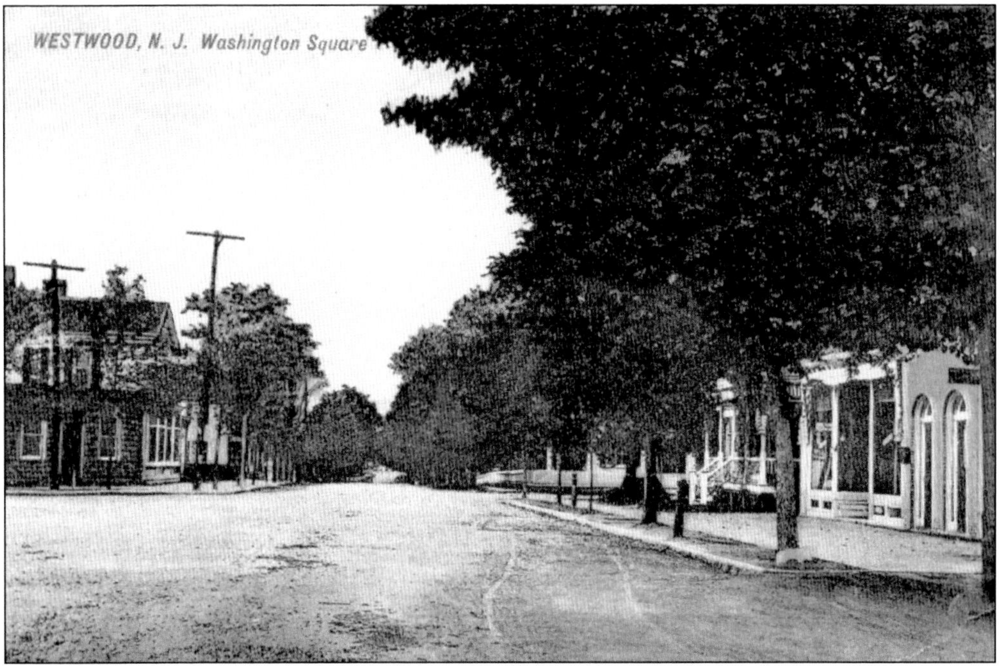

The streets surrounding Veterans Park formed what was known as Washington Square. Mailed in 1909, this card includes the Meyer's Park Hotel, which is now occupied by the Iron Horse Restaurant.

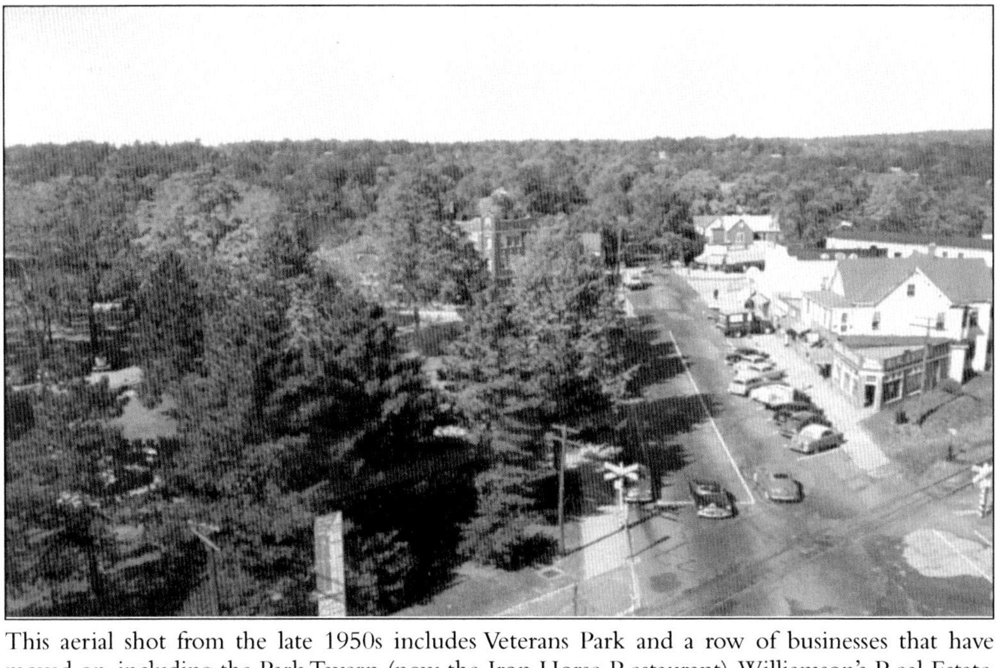

This aerial shot from the late 1950s includes Veterans Park and a row of businesses that have moved on, including the Park Tavern (now the Iron Horse Restaurant), Williamson's Real Estate, and Tyrrell's Florist, which moved farther east on Westwood Avenue. The white rectangular sign in the lower portion of the picture showed the progress of a fund-raiser for the planned construction of Pascack Valley Hospital.

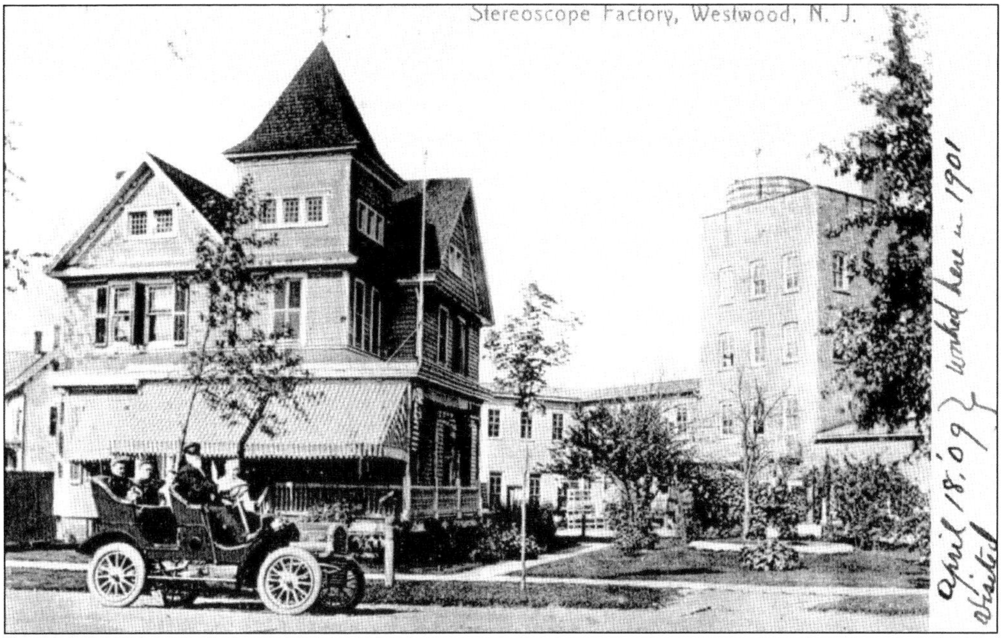

The four-story stereoscope factory, in the background, was Westwood's highest building and was famous for producing Underwood & Underwood stereoscope viewers and slides, which were the predecessors of the popular View-Master toys. The two water tanks on top of the factory provided water pressure for the town from 1894 to 1898. The top stories of the factory were removed in 1912. Today, the building is occupied by the Valley Ford dealership. The C. S. DeBaun house stands in the foreground. Early newspaper records indicate that C. S. DeBaun may have been the first Westwood resident to own an automobile, having purchased one in October 1900. DeBaun must have been very proud to send this postcard displaying his new high-tech vehicle, his stately house, and the large factory in the background.

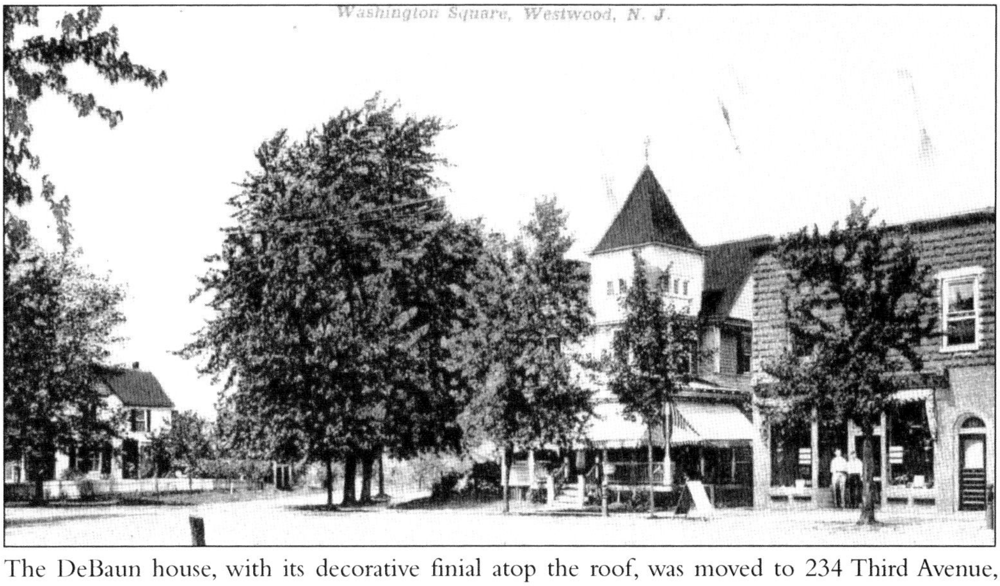

The DeBaun house, with its decorative finial atop the roof, was moved to 234 Third Avenue, where it remains today. The building to the right of the DeBaun house, 48 Washington Avenue, was occupied by the Westwood Hardware Store when this card was mailed in 1912.

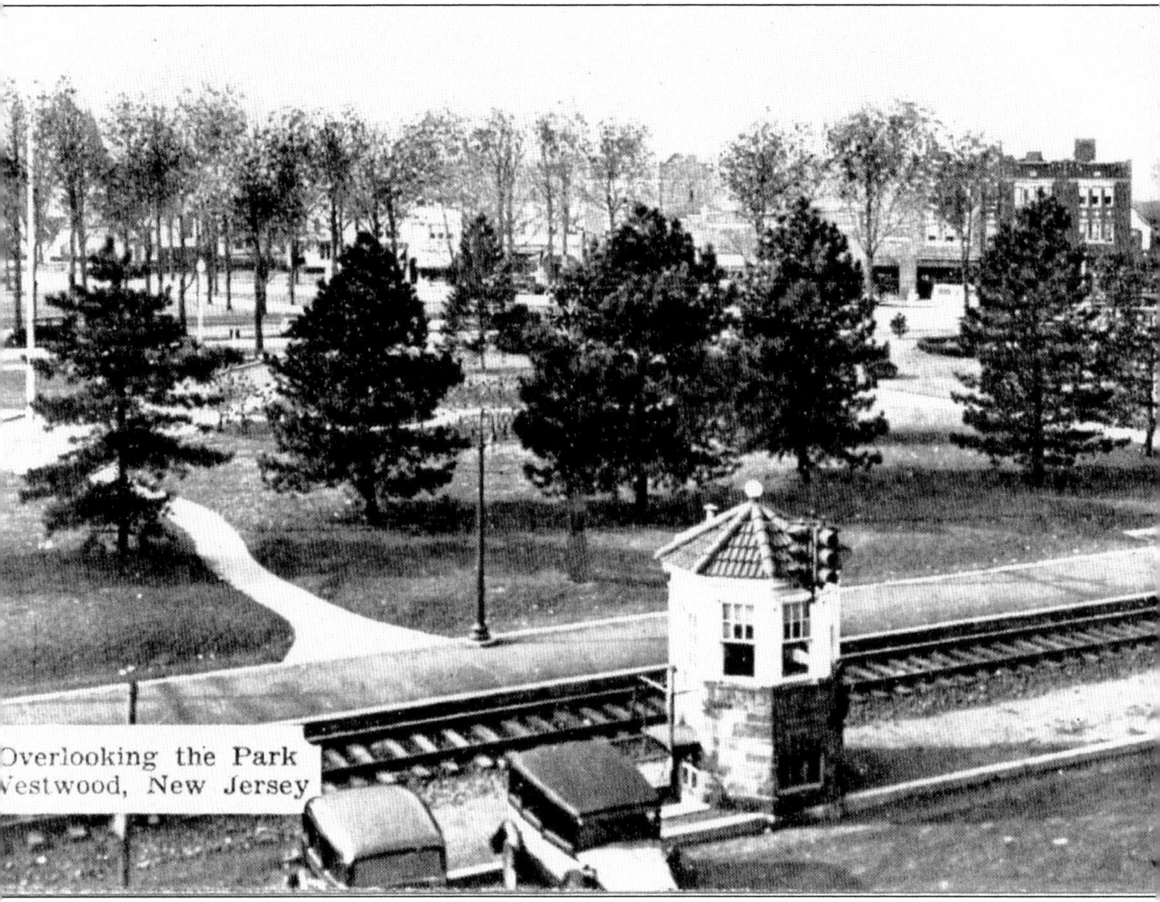

This view of Veterans Memorial Park *c.* 1940 includes the row of businesses that line the park along Third Avenue. The police booth in the foreground was common at that time. The police were alerted to a call by a flashing light at the peak of the roof.

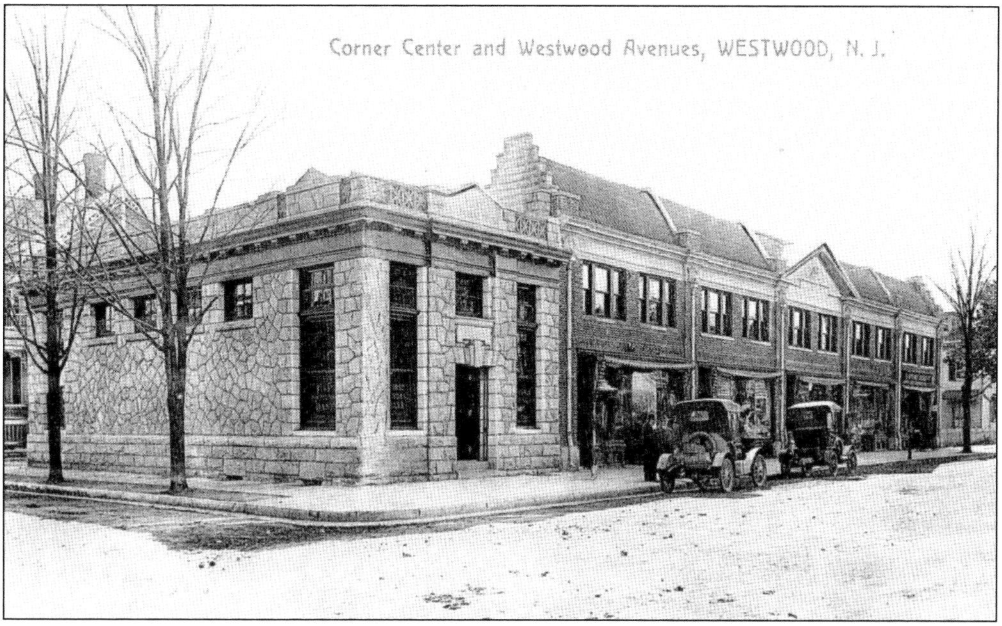

The first bank to open in the Pascack Valley was located in Westwood. In 1907, the First National Bank of Westwood received its federal charter and opened at the corner of Westwood and Center Avenues (where Parian Jewelers stands today). The A. B. Bogert building was built next to the bank at the same time, and the architectural detailing can still be seen along the roofline. The establishment of a local bank was big news in town. Prior to its opening, residents had to travel to Hackensack or another larger city to do their banking. Because of this inconvenience, a lot of business was done through barter, and the general store ran accounts, which reduced the need for local residents to exchange cash.

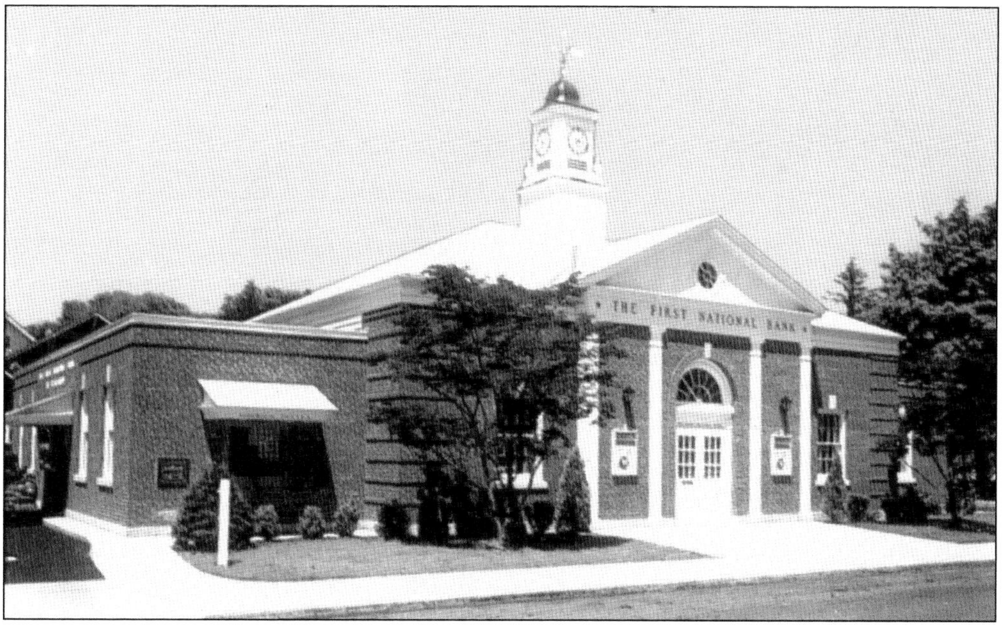

The First National Bank of Westwood later moved to a modern building at 36 Bergen Street, where it continues to stand today, although it is now part of a larger national bank.

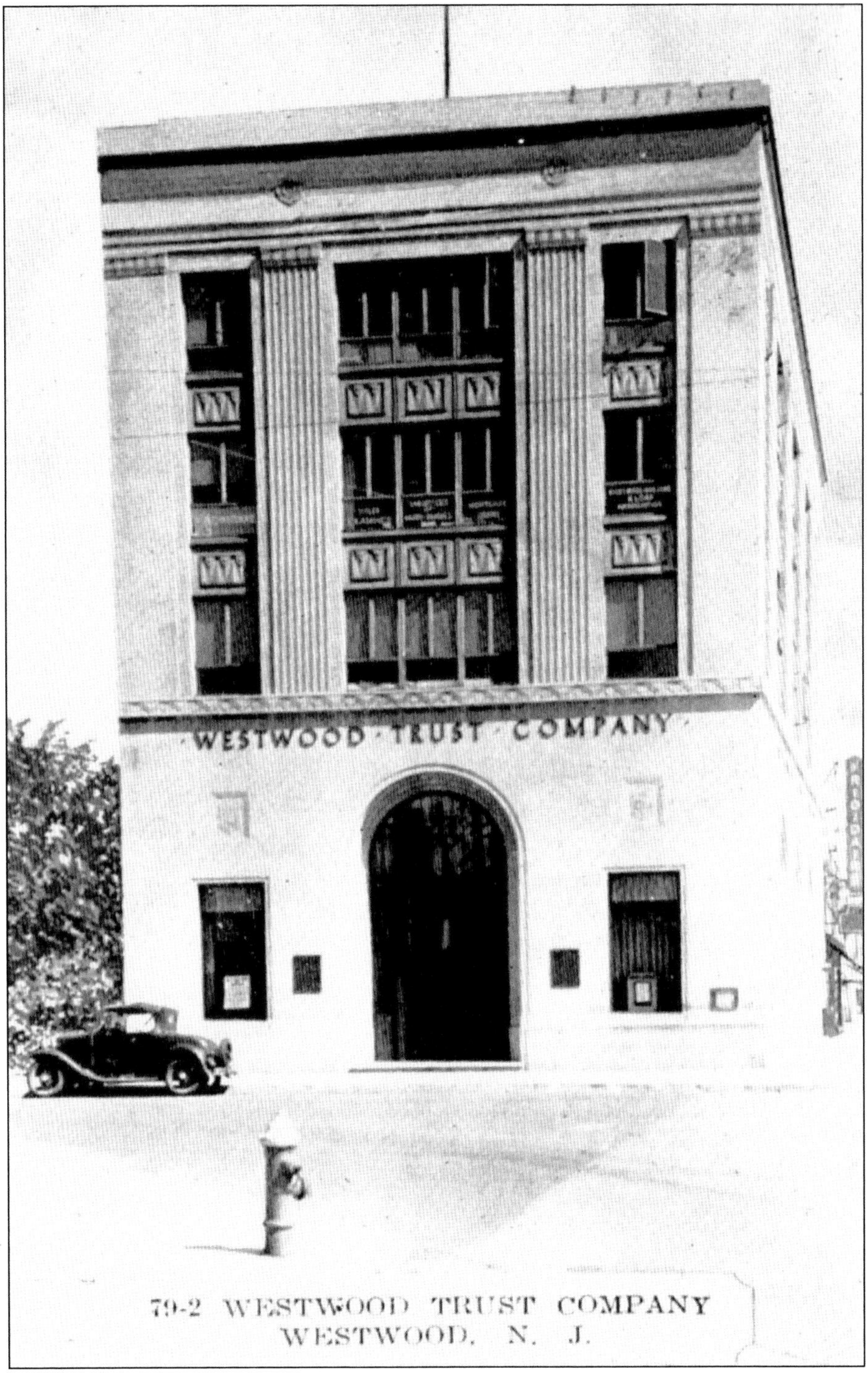

As Westwood's population and business activity grew, more banks were established. The Trust Company of Westwood opened in 1932 at the corner of Westwood Avenue and Broadway. Although the bank has changed its name several times, the bank building has remained the most prominent structure on Westwood Avenue.

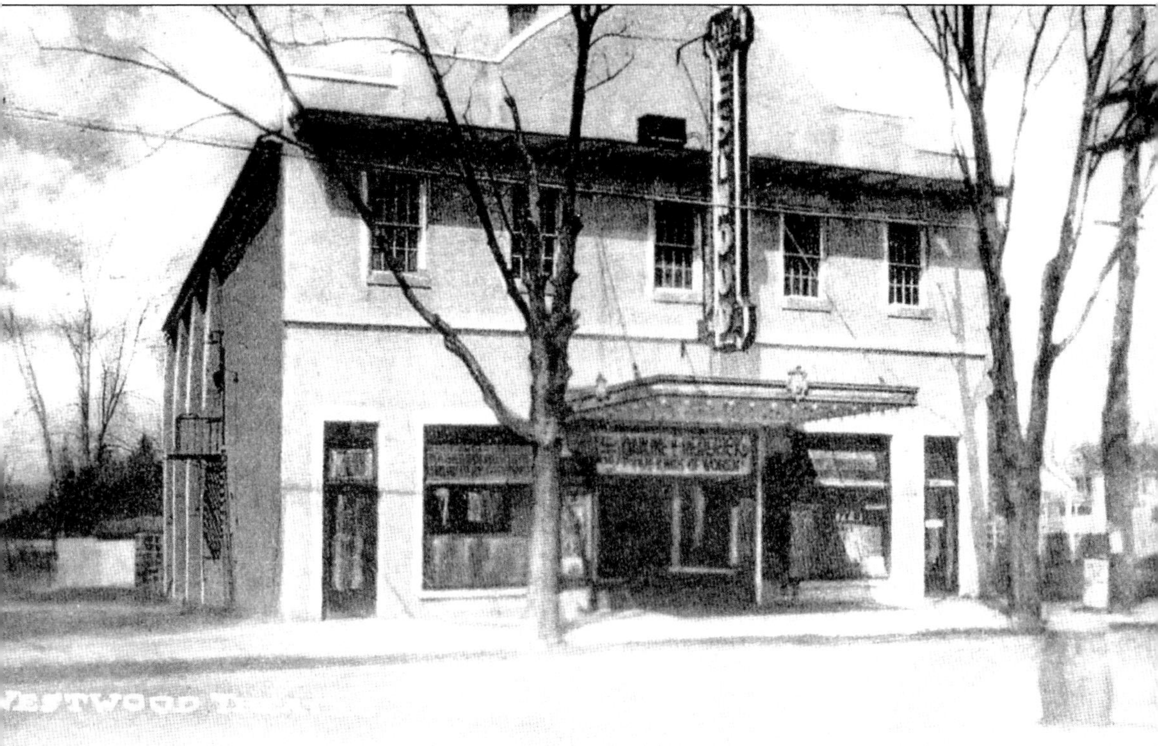

Westwood's entertainment attractions kept pace with its growth, and in 1919, the Westwood Theatre opened at 142 Westwood Avenue (where the Gap is today). In addition to movies, the theater offered vaudeville acts and community plays. In June 1922, the Westwood was the subject of a local scandal that made the front page of the *New York Herald Tribune.* E. Alan Meyer, who owned the theater and served as Westwood's justice of the peace, scheduled a Sunday showing of a motion picture. Seven local ministers reportedly urged their congregations to demonstrate against the theater, and they convinced the municipal council to have the police shut down the theater and arrest the proprietor for illegally conducting business on a Sunday. Some 18 months later, on December 27, 1929, residents voted 869 to 609 in a special election to repeal the prohibition of movies on Sundays. The theater was also the site of many Westwood High School graduations. It closed in 1943, and the building has been used for retail ever since.

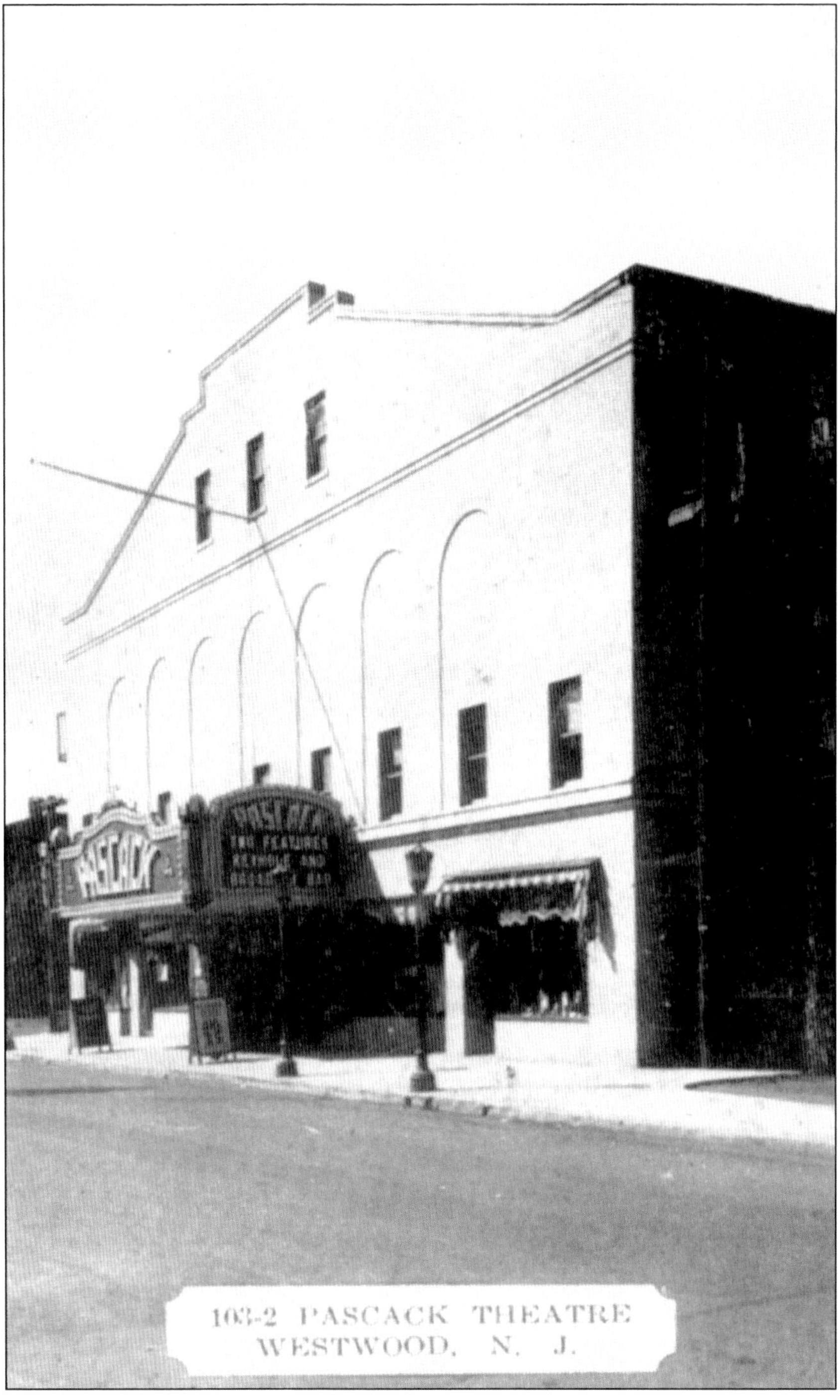

For some 14 years, Westwood was home to two movie houses. The Pascack Theatre opened *c.* 1929 at 172–186 Center Avenue, where it remains today. The availability of entertainment was always a Westwood attraction. Before these theaters, the Canvas Theatre presented vaudeville and moving picture shows in a canvas tent erected in Veterans Park *c.* 1900 and the Casino briefly opened in 1915 as a small theater at the corner of Broadway and Irvington Street.

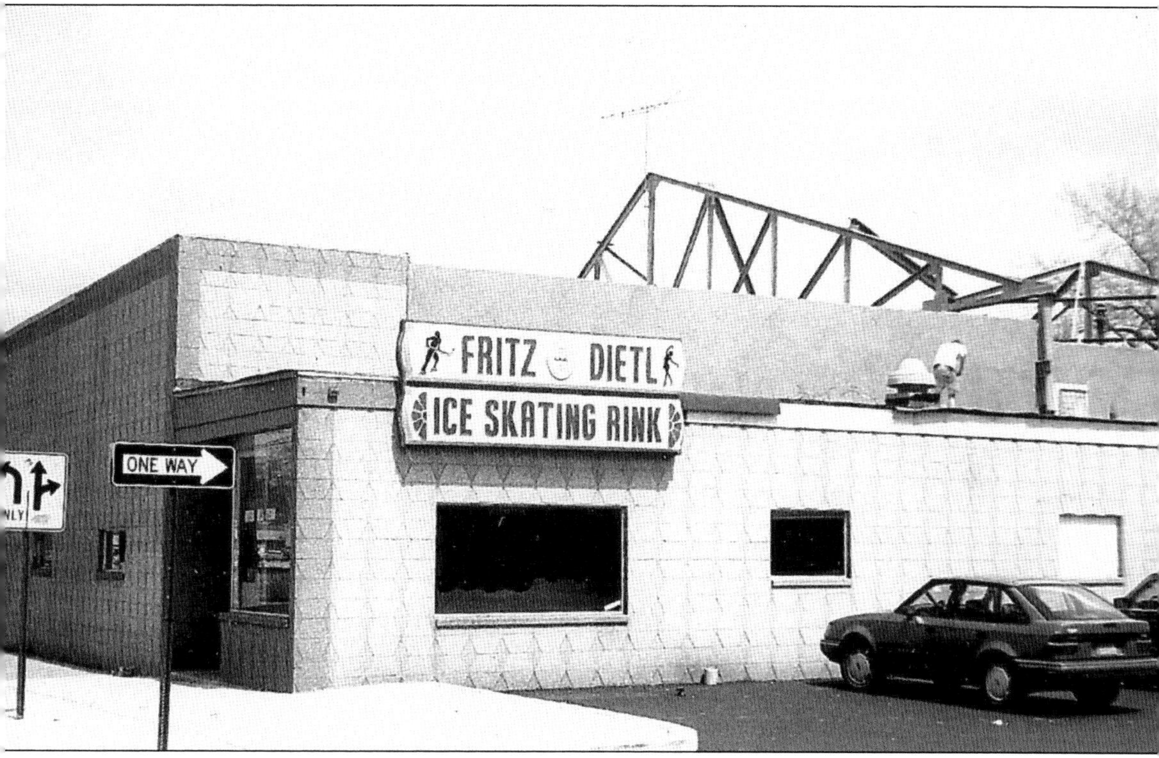

The Fritz Dietl Ice Skating Rink opened in 1957 on the corner of Broadway and Lake Street. Fritz Dietl, who died in 2003, was a renowned figure skating coach who coached several Olympic skaters. The rink is home to the oldest operating Zamboni machine. This building was originally an automobile showroom.

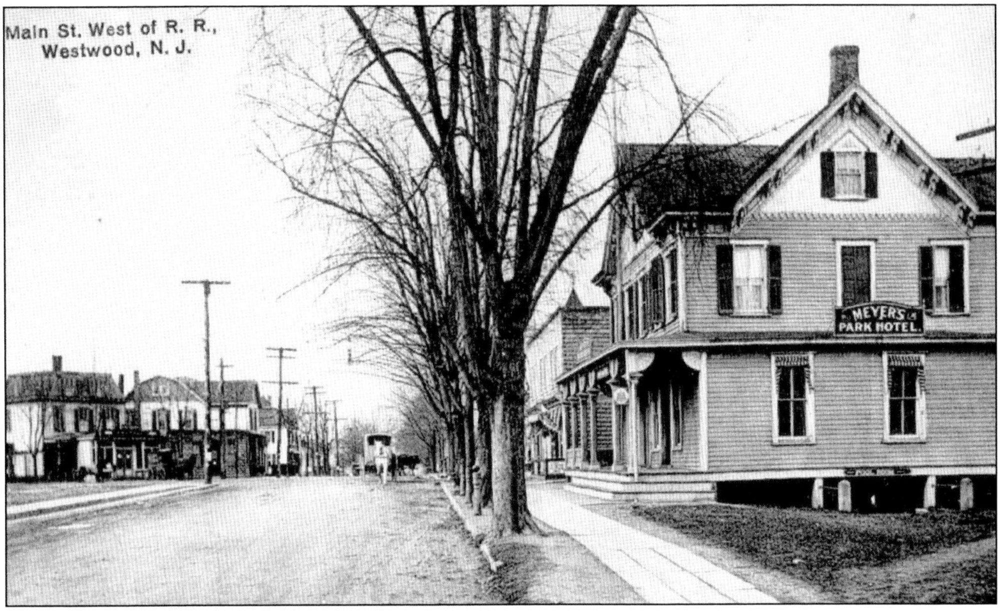

For more than 150 years, Westwood has attracted visitors to its many restaurants. The list of Westwood eateries is far too long to include, but at least six of them have found their way onto postcards. The Iron Horse Restaurant, named for the railroad that it borders, is known for its stuffed cheeseburgers, but back in 1910, the building was Meyer's Park Hotel. Established in 1877, the hotel provided meals and accommodations to visitors arriving on the train.

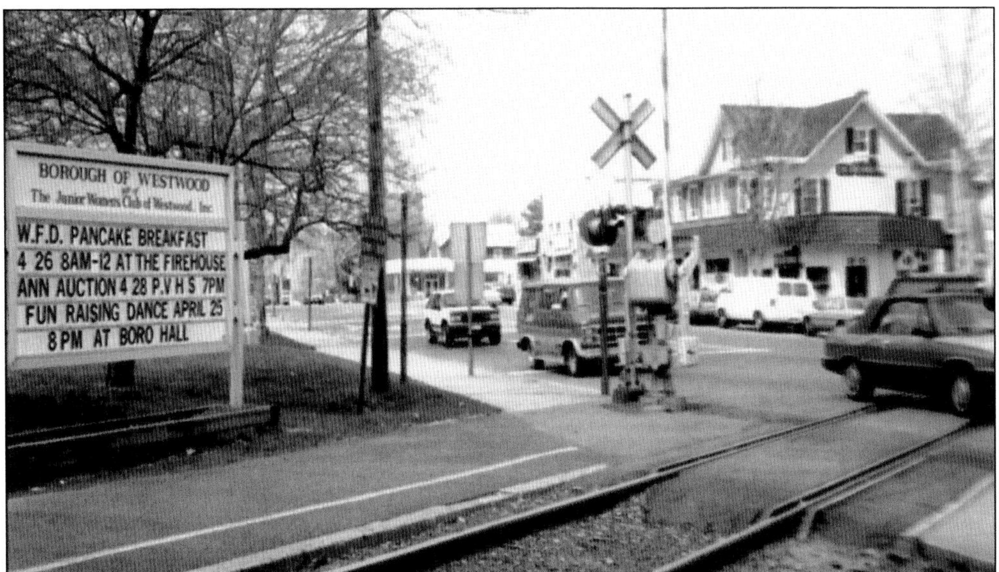

Although the front porch has been enclosed, the building has maintained the same appearance and remains a popular family restaurant today.

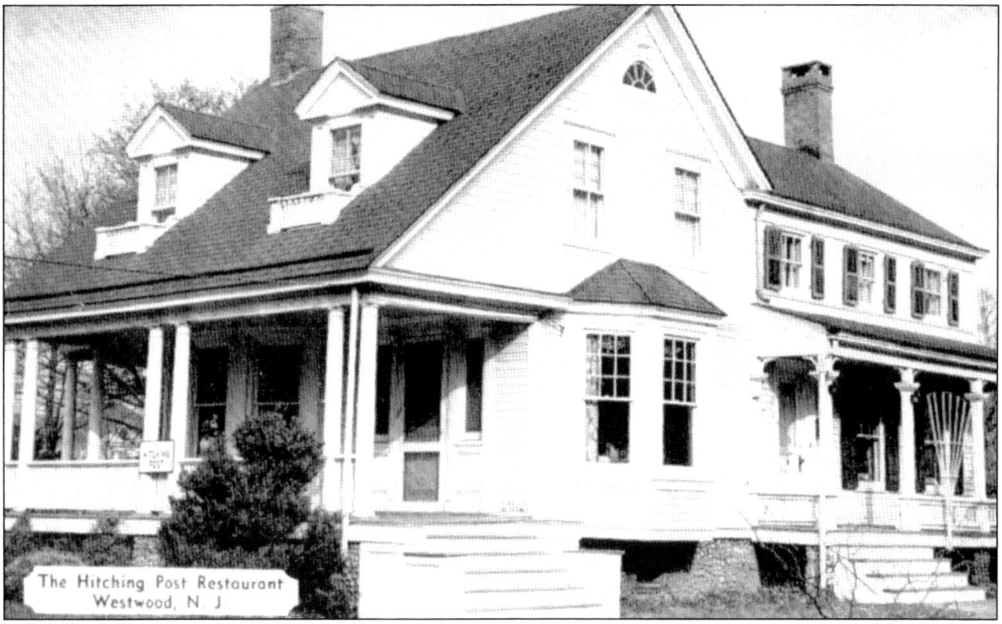

The Hitching Post Restaurant opened *c.* 1947 at 231 Kinderkamack Road, a house that dated back to the late 1800s. The restaurant and was aptly named for the hitching post that stood at the curb.

Phone Westwood 5-2467 **Paul Henning**

THE HITCHING POST

GOOD FOOD — PLEASANT SURROUNDINGS

Specializing in Small Parties

231 Kinderkamack Road **Westwood, N. J.**

Opposite Esso Station

Now occupied by a dentist, the building is still recognizable today, across from the Exxon Station, but the hitching post is long gone.

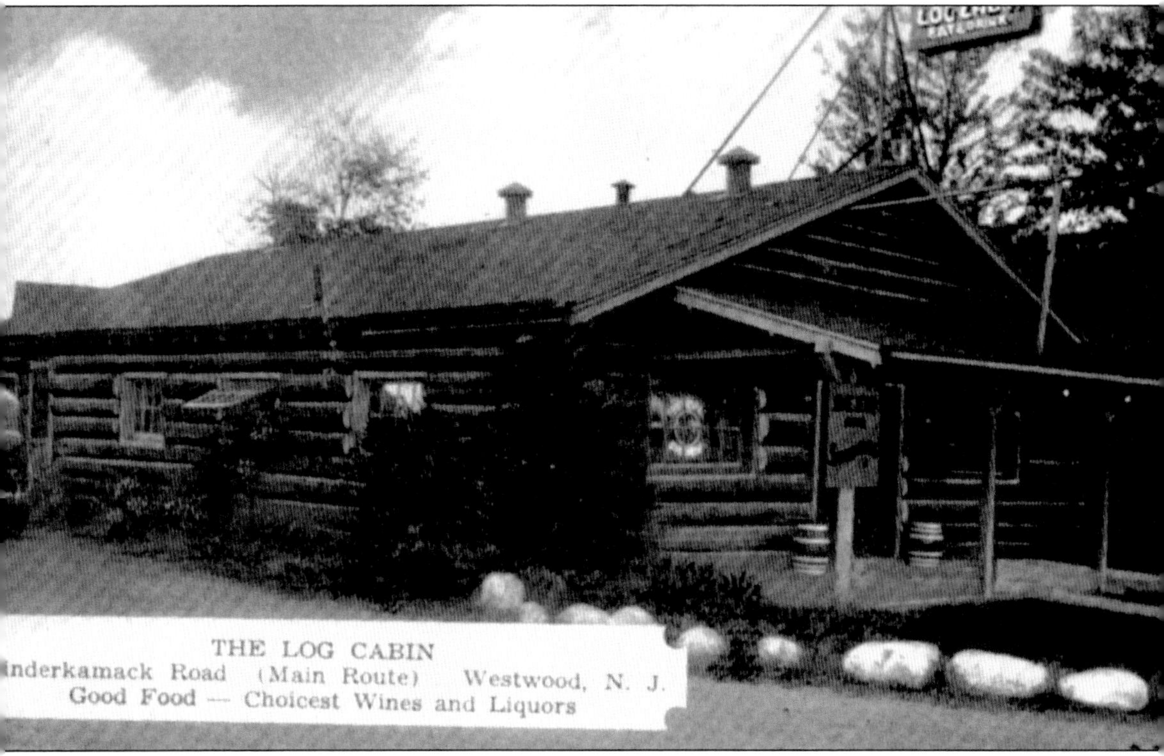

The Log Cabin was located on Kinderkamack Road at the corner of Lester Avenue, close to the Emerson border. The restaurant served family-style meals. It closed some time in the 1940s or 1950s.

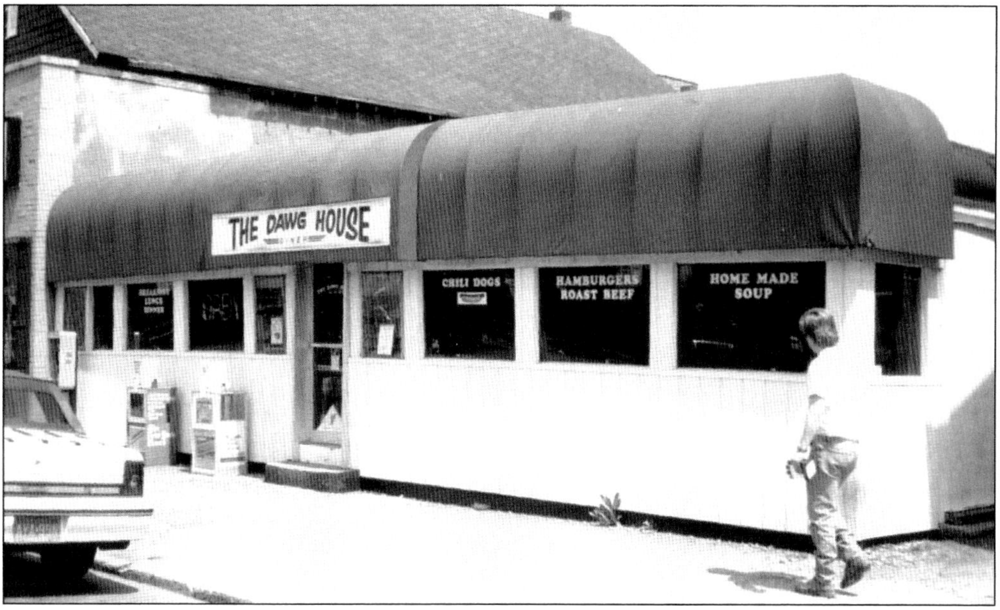

The Dawg House served a wide variety of custom hot dogs at 325 Broadway from 1989 through 1993. Chock Full of Nuts is now at this location. This site has been used for diners and cafes since *c.* 1910. The current structure was ordered through a catalogue and shipped preassembled.

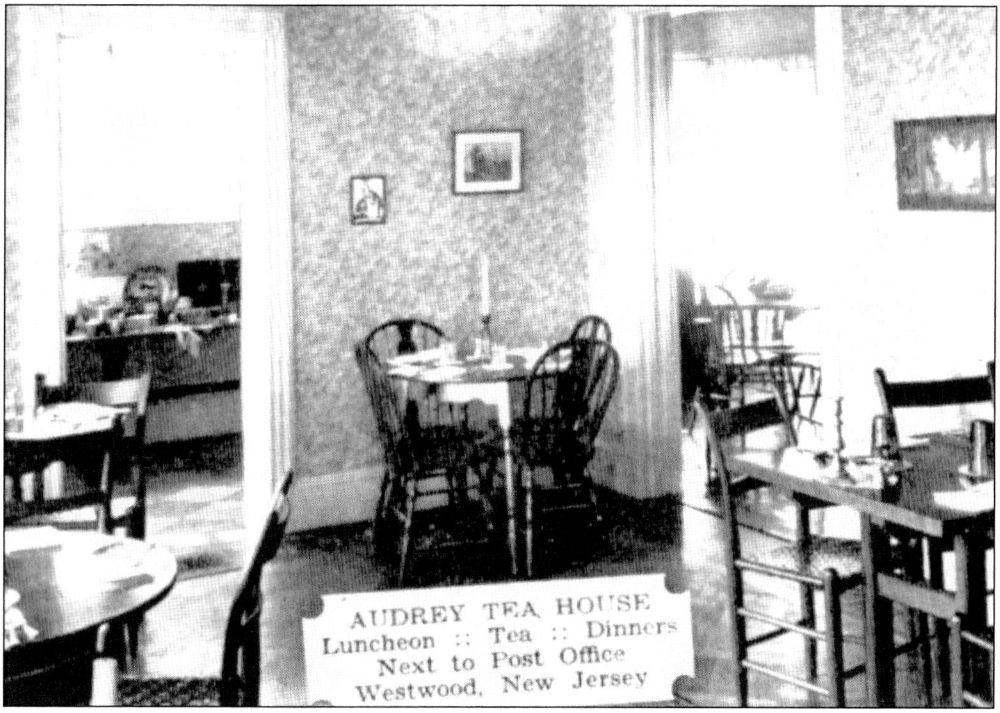

From 1902 through the 1940s, this quaint teahouse stood next to the post office at 234 Westwood Avenue. Today, it is a hair salon.

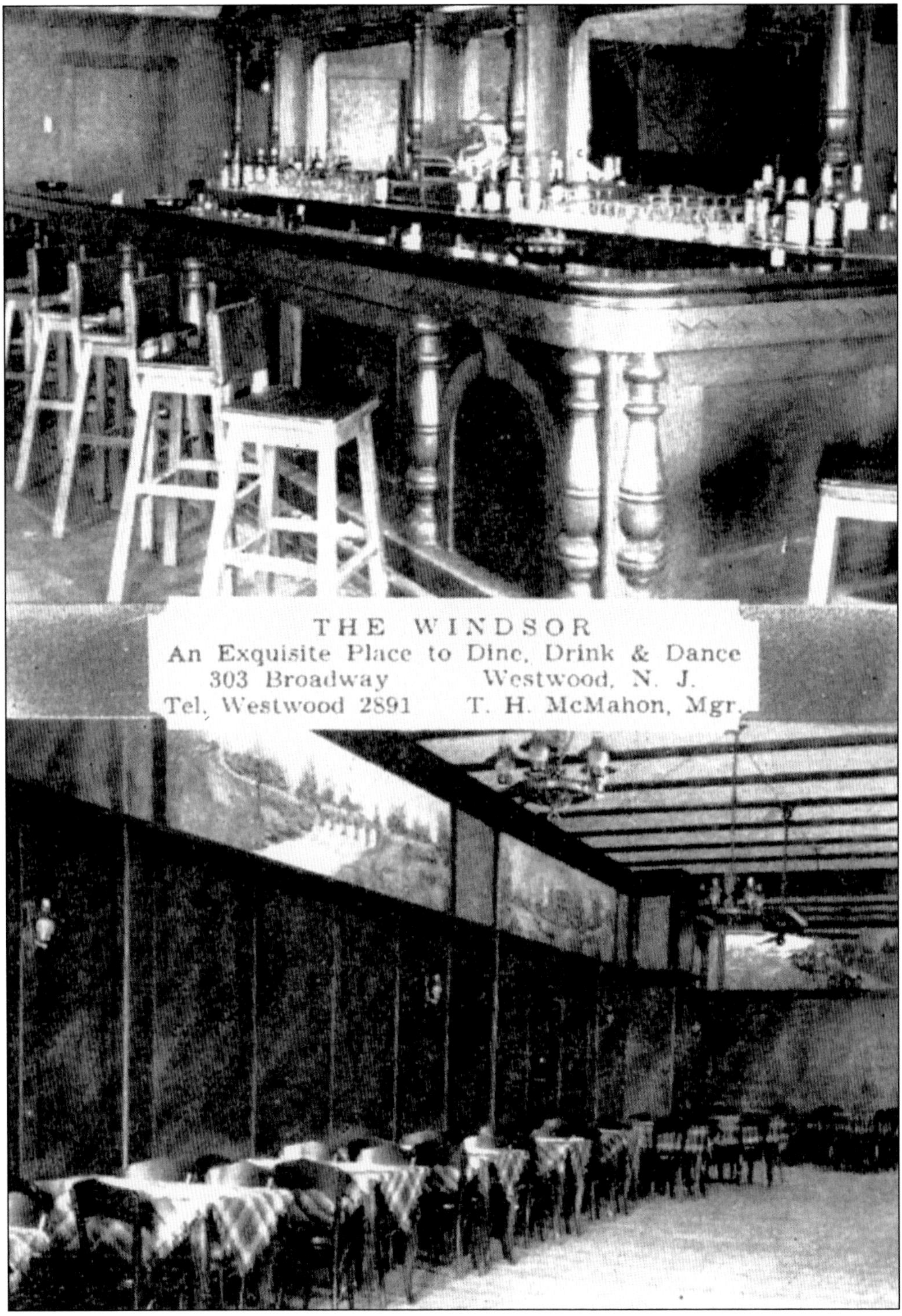

The Windsor was a bar and restaurant with a dance floor and bowling alley. It was in operation from the 1940s into the 1970s and was located at 467 Broadway, which is still the location of a restaurant today.

Five

Commercial Postcards

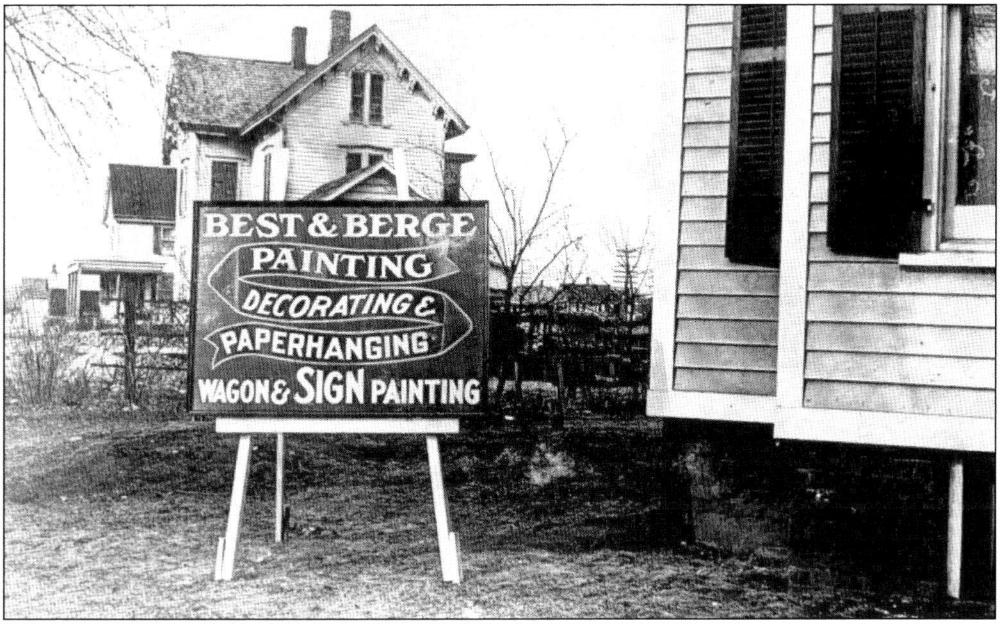

As Westwood grew, contractors prospered, and many contractors and construction supply companies were located in Westwood's downtown area. The businesses, with the approximate year they began, included Westwood Construction Company *c.* 1928, Hering & Westphal Surveyors *c.* 1928, Adam's Glass House Glazier *c.* 1948, P.V. Green Painter *c.* 1924, Registered Floor Company *c.* 1976, Aztec Pools *c.* 1960, Randall Heating Company *c.* 1930, Registered Home Improvement Company *c.* 1930, Joe Newman Painting *c.* 1930, and Malcuit Floors *c.* 1950. The location of this painting and wallpapering business is uncertain, but the Best family lived on Third Avenue.

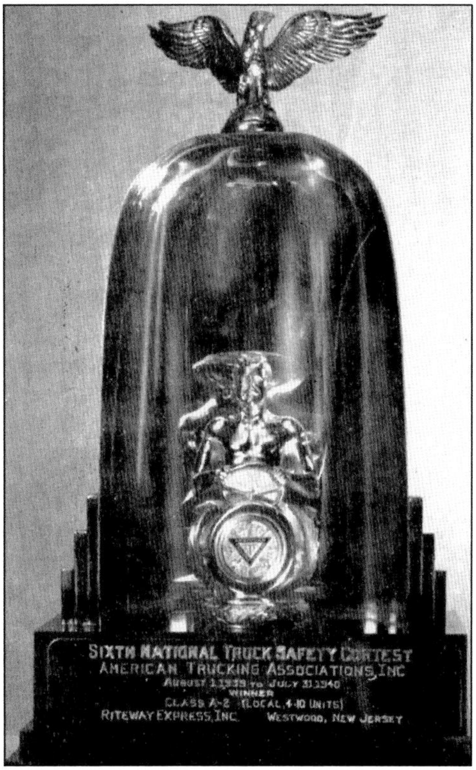

Riteway Express Trucking was located at 491 Broadway from 1929 to 1940. This postcard was used to celebrate an industry safety award the company received in 1940.

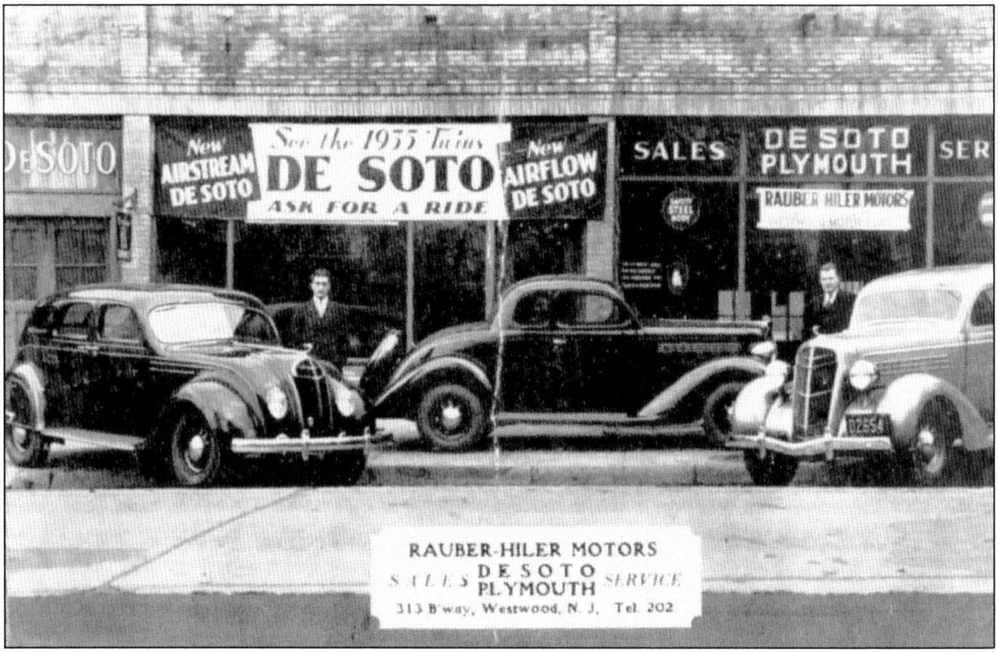

The Rauber-Hiler Motors Plymouth-DeSoto dealership was at the corner of Irvington Street and Broadway from 1935 through the 1950s. This postcard advertises the new twin Airstream and Airflow DeSotos.

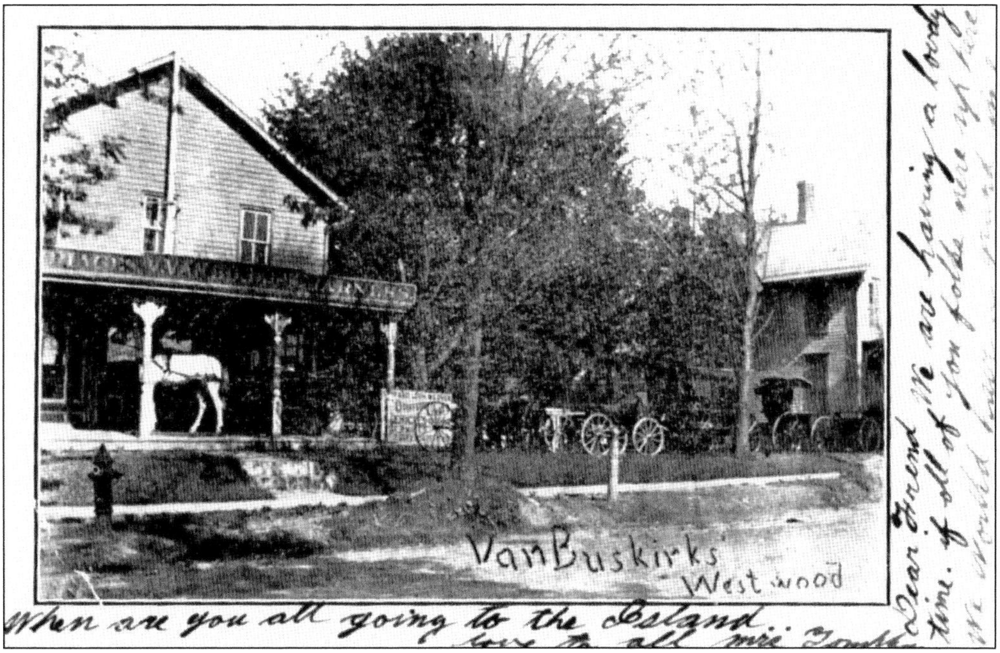

A carriage builder's shop stood at the southeast corner of Broadway and Irvington Street from the 1890s through 1914. Van Buskirk's Carriage Shop was an important local business back when horse-drawn wagons and buggies were the primary form of transportation. This card, mailed in 1908, features some of the new models of the day. Changing with the times, the carriage shop eventually became a Ford automobile dealership—Marsten's Motor Company.

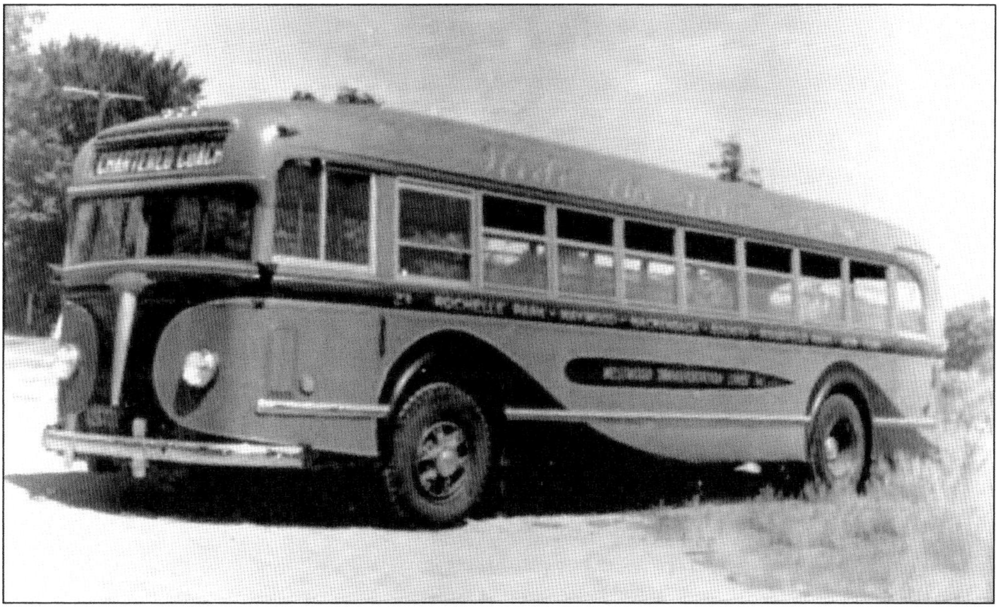
The Blue Coach Line, run by the Westwood Transportation Company, was based in Westwood from the 1930s through the 1950s. It provided full commuter service to and from New York City The bus terminal was located at 318 Third Avenue (now occupied by Mount Everest Ski Shop). The large arched garage door opening, in the middle of the building, is still recognizable.

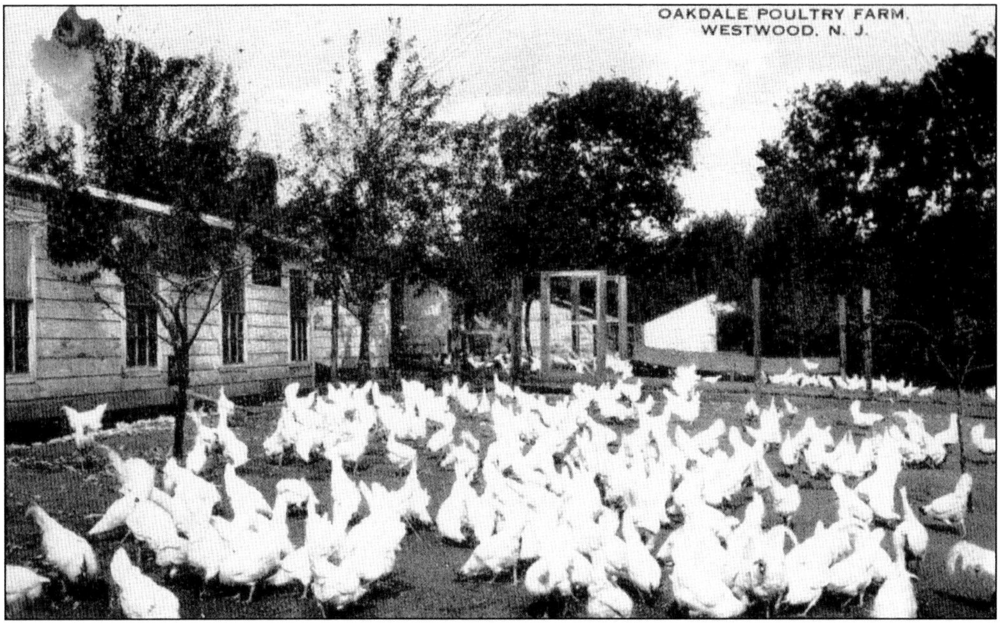

Westwood had its share of livestock, too. In 1922, the Oakdale Poultry Farm, owned by the Mouilleseaux family, was located on the south side of Mill Street, just west of Seventh Avenue. Although the chickens are gone, the farmhouse has recently been remodeled and remains at 155 Mill Street.

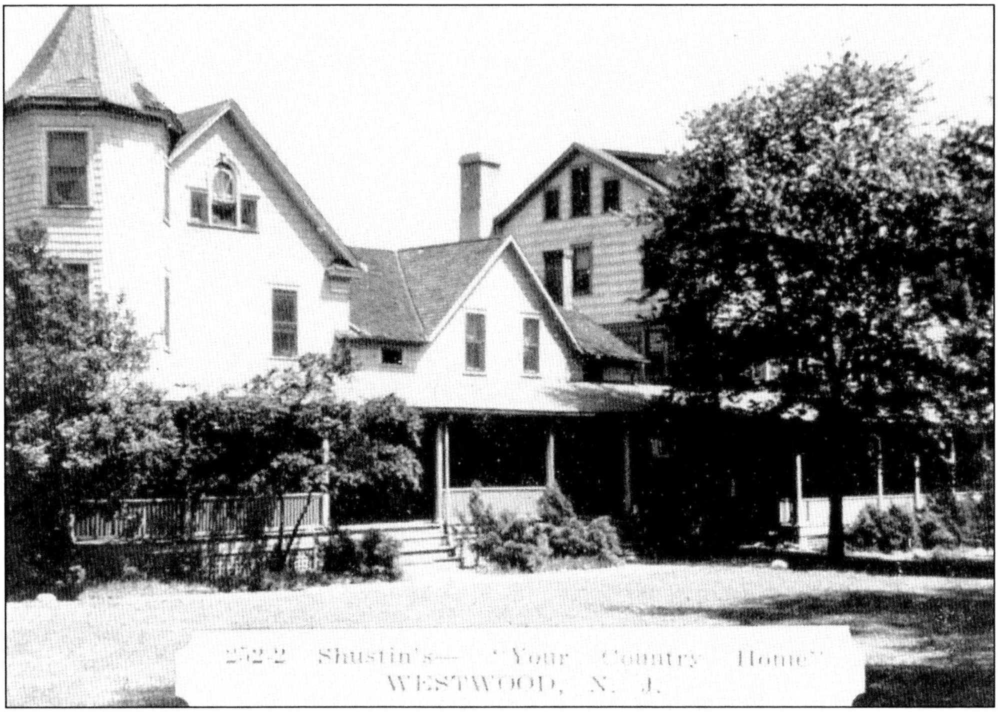

Shustin's is said to have been a hotel that was converted from a large old house in what is now River Vale. Unfortunately, this distinctive building no longer stands, and its location cannot be determined.

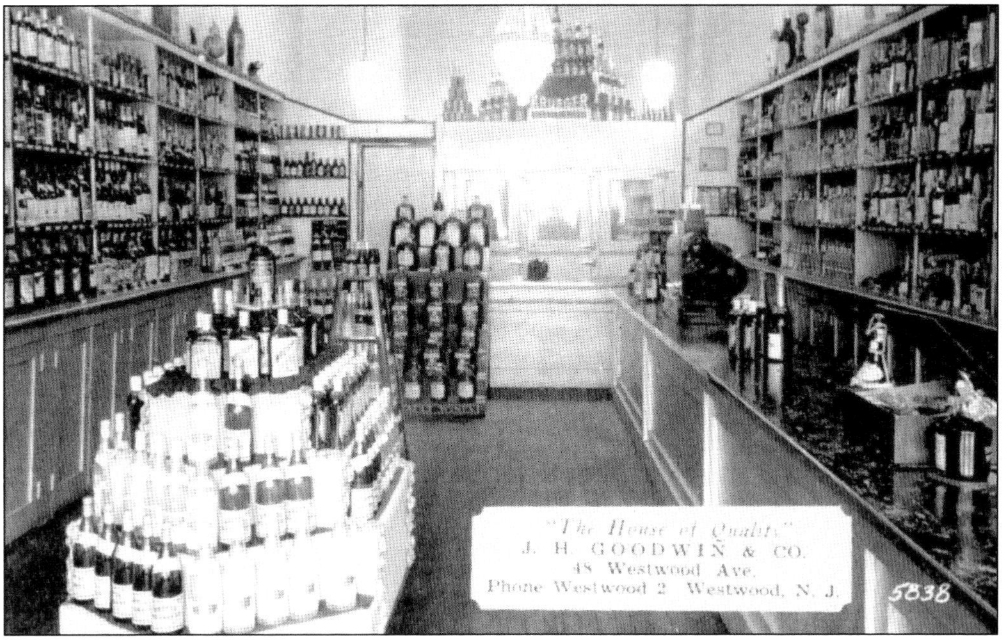

J. H. Goodwin & Company, "the House of Quality," sold liquor through the 1930s at 48 Westwood Avenue. The Goodwin family also developed the Goodwin Park neighborhood, on the east side of Bogert's Pond.

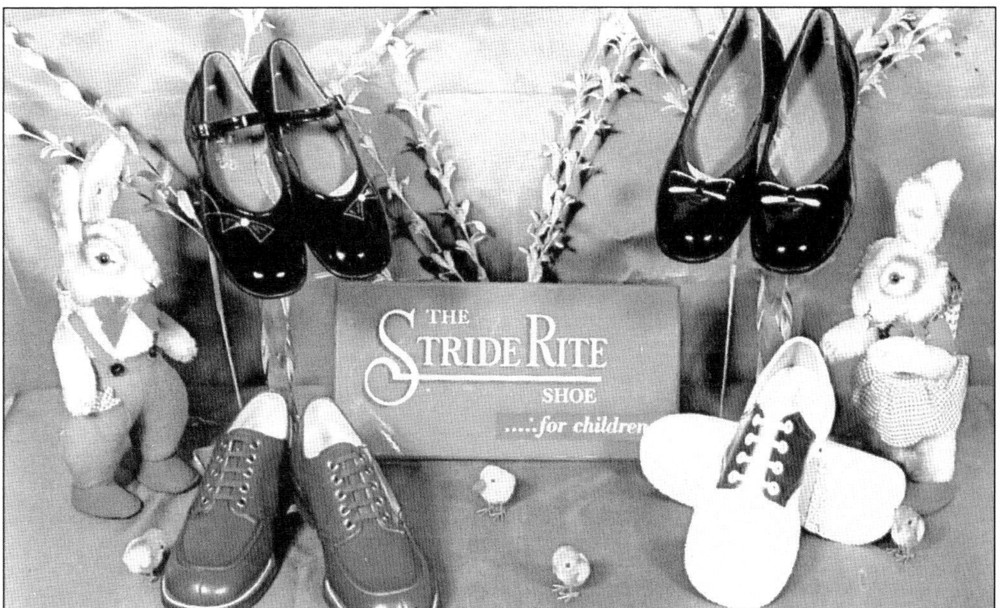

Martin's Stride Rite Shoes has been at 180 Westwood Avenue since 1982. This location has been used as a shoe store continuously since the 1950s.

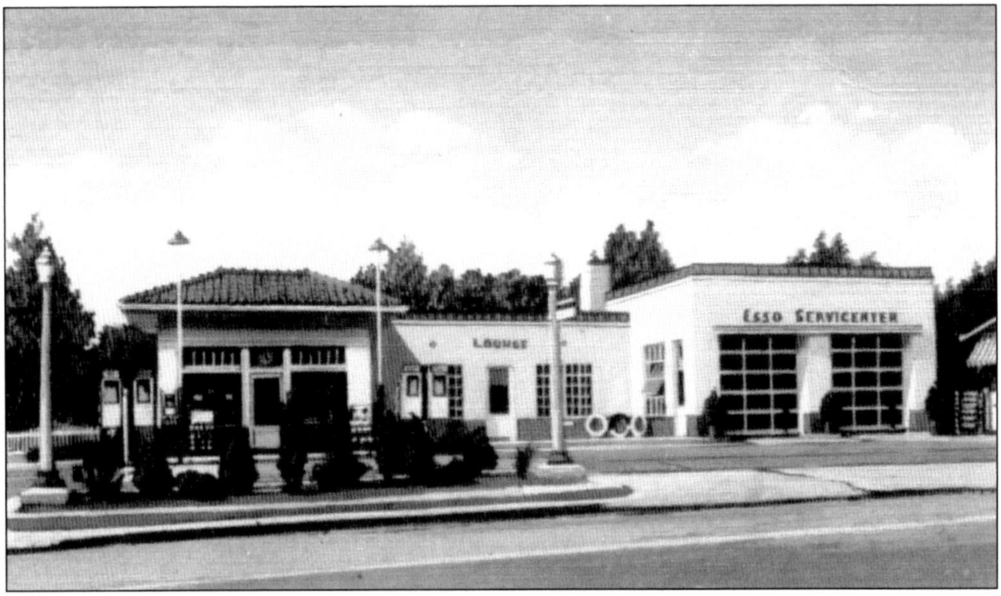

Westwood Esso station (now Ted's Exxon station) was located at the corner of Kinderkamack Road and Jefferson Avenue. At one time it was known as Pete's Esso station after the owner Peter Van Bouchaute.

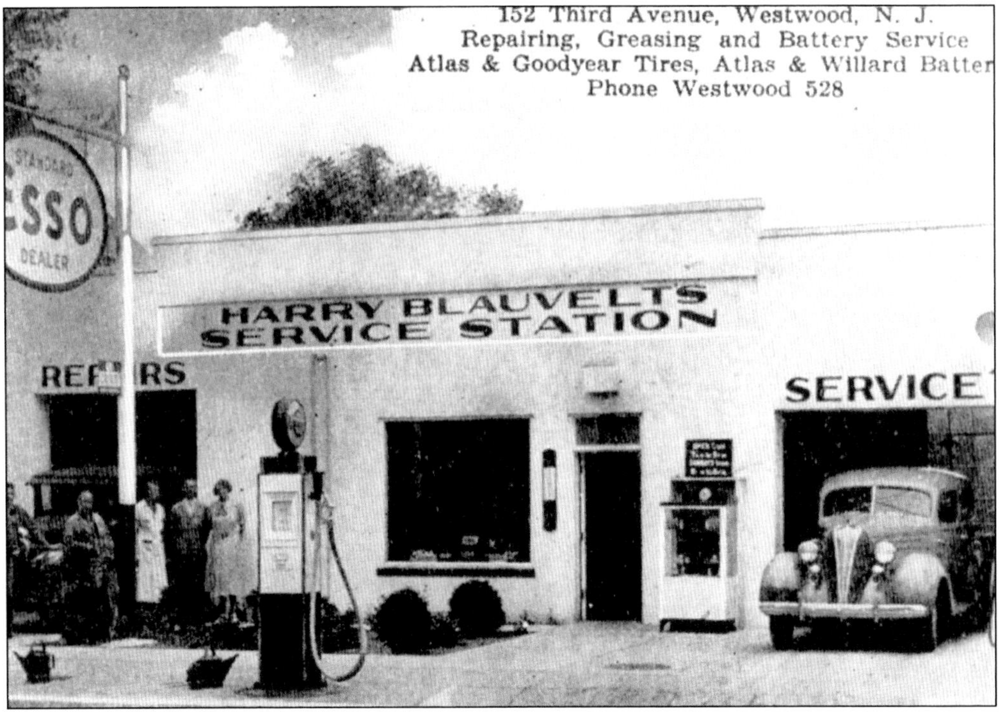

Blauvelt's Service Station was at 152 Third Avenue. The Blauvelt family is one of Westwood's earliest families, having settled here in the early 1800s. This station was later operated by Peter Van Bouchaute. Today, it is now the site of the Westwood Cycle Shop, pictured on the following page.

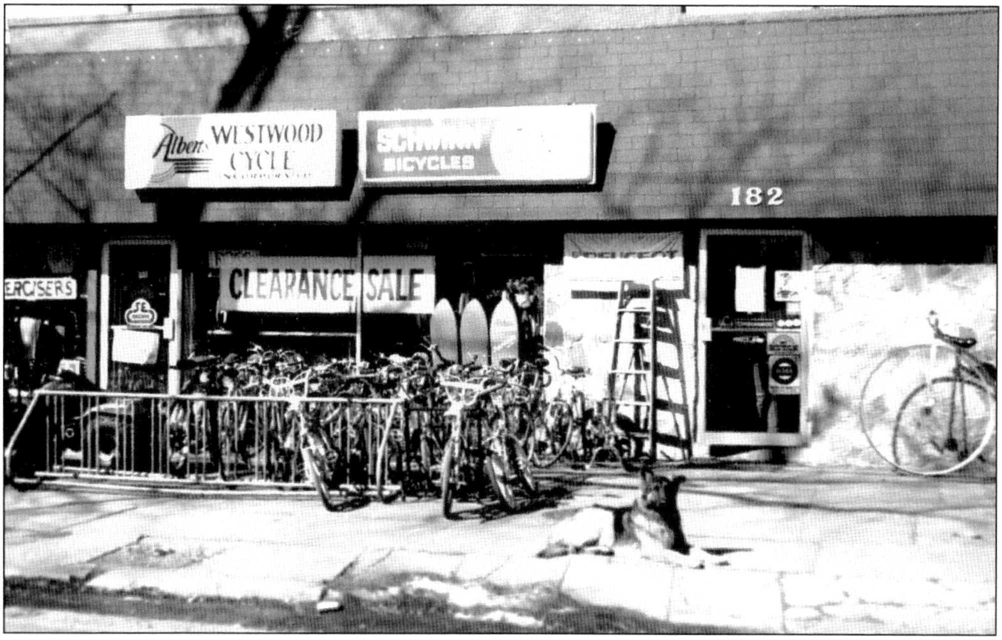

This postcard dates back just to 1990. The building is easily recognized as Westwood's local bicycle shop, located at 182 Third Avenue.

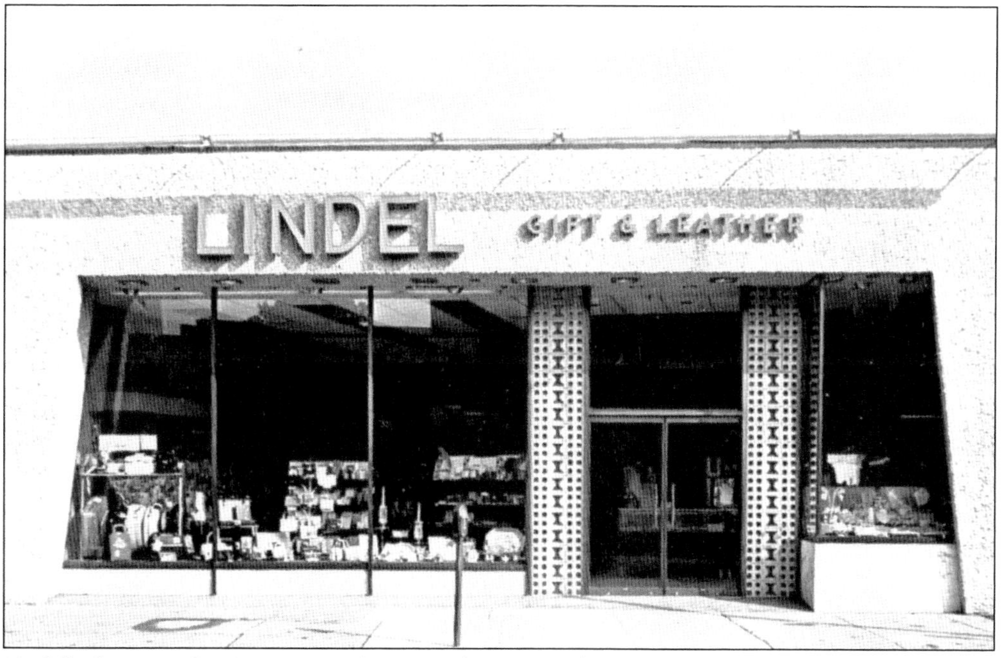

Lindel's shop stood at 26 Westwood Avenue from 1969 through 1991. The earliest records for this location show that it was occupied by Augenti Tailoring in 1913.

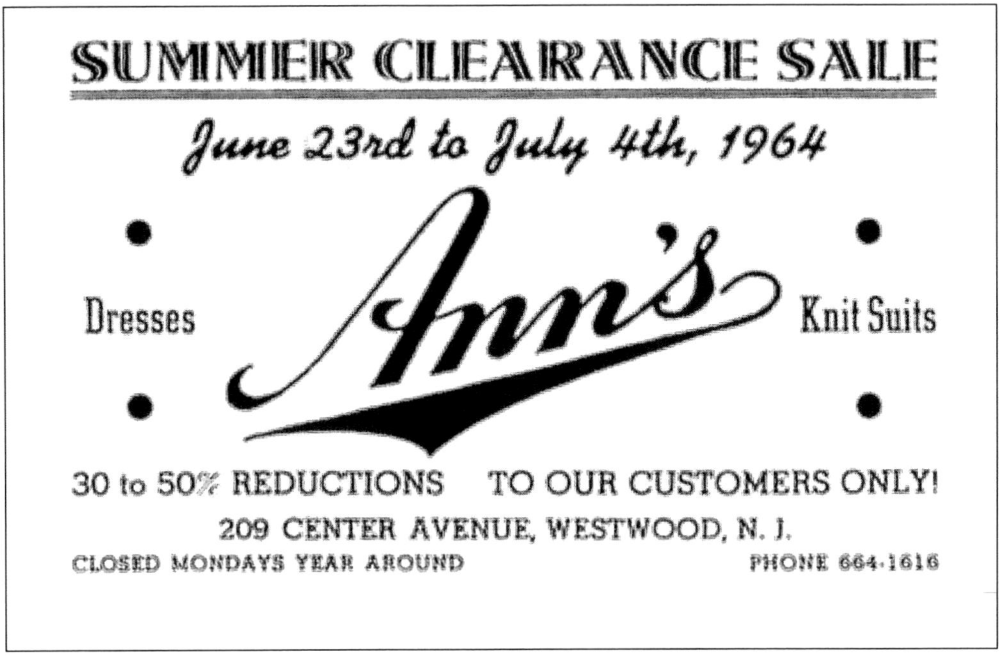

Ann's was a popular clothing store in the 1960s. Located at 209 Center Avenue, it is an example of how commerce spread up and down Westwood Avenue from the train station and then began to spread away from the avenue along Fairview and Center Avenues in the 1950s and 1960s.

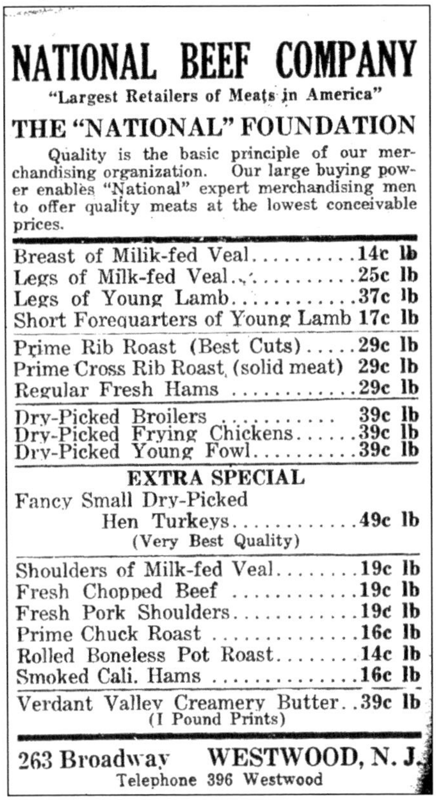

The National Beef Company was a meat distribution chain with locations across the country. This postcard advertises its Westwood shop, located at 263 Broadway, and lists veal for just 14¢ per pound.

Six

Early Places of Worship

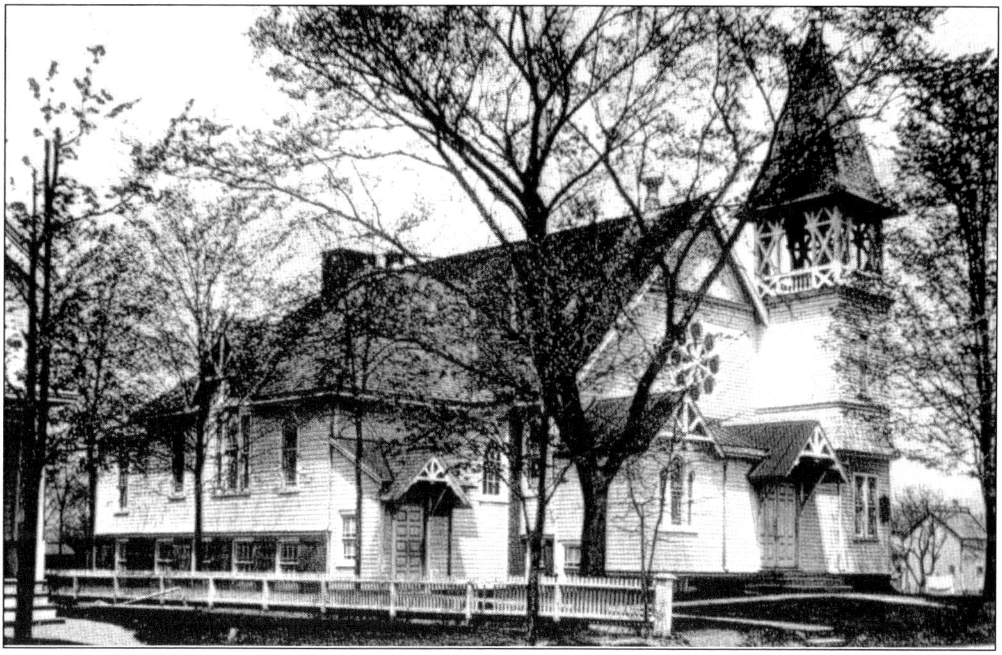

Westwood's first house of worship was a nondenominational chapel built at the west corner of Third and Park Avenues in 1872. Its members included names that are still familiar in Westwood today: Bogert, Brickell, Rumsey, Van Emburgh, and Westervelt. In 1885, a cyclone destroyed the structure. Just a year later, in 1886, the Reformed Church became Westwood's first denominational church. It was formed by the members of the destroyed chapel and was constructed at the same location. Completed in 1887, the new Reformed Church of Westwood seated 300 and cost just $5,800, including furnishings. The church building continued in use until a new building program was completed on December 24, 1961.

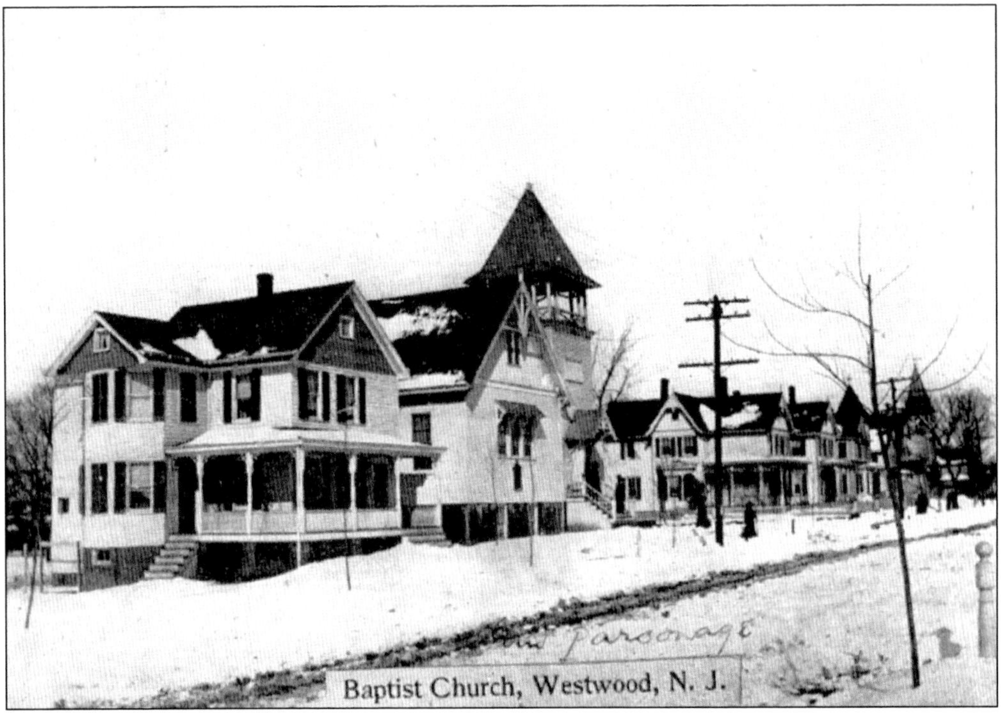

The Calvary Baptist Church was incorporated on June 21, 1902. Odd Fellows Hall was used for early meetings until land was purchased at the corner of Third Avenue and Elm Street.

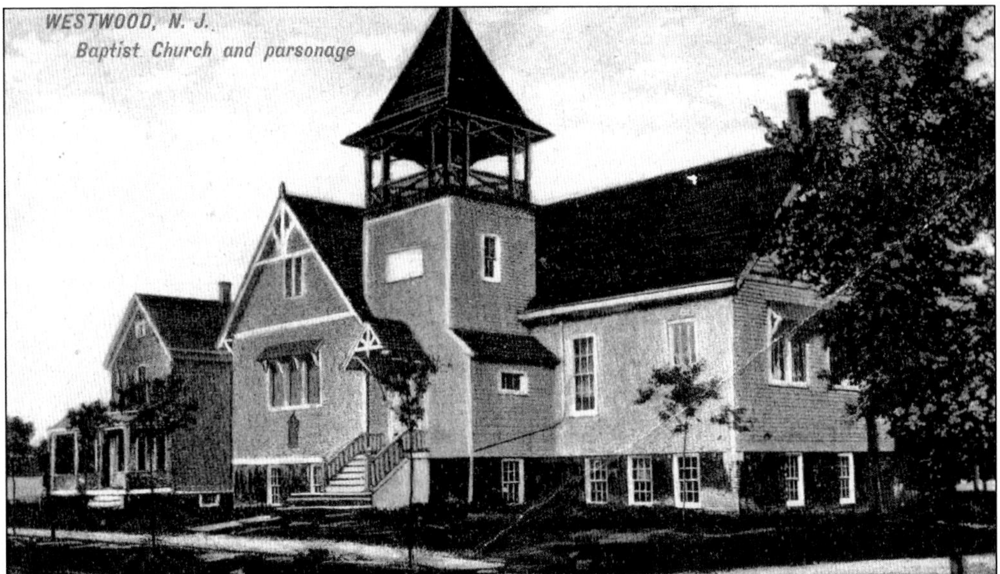

A former school building was moved from the corner of Fourth Avenue and Mill Street for transformation into a church house. The cornerstone was laid on October 17, 1902, and the first pastor was Rev. Thomas D. Wesley.

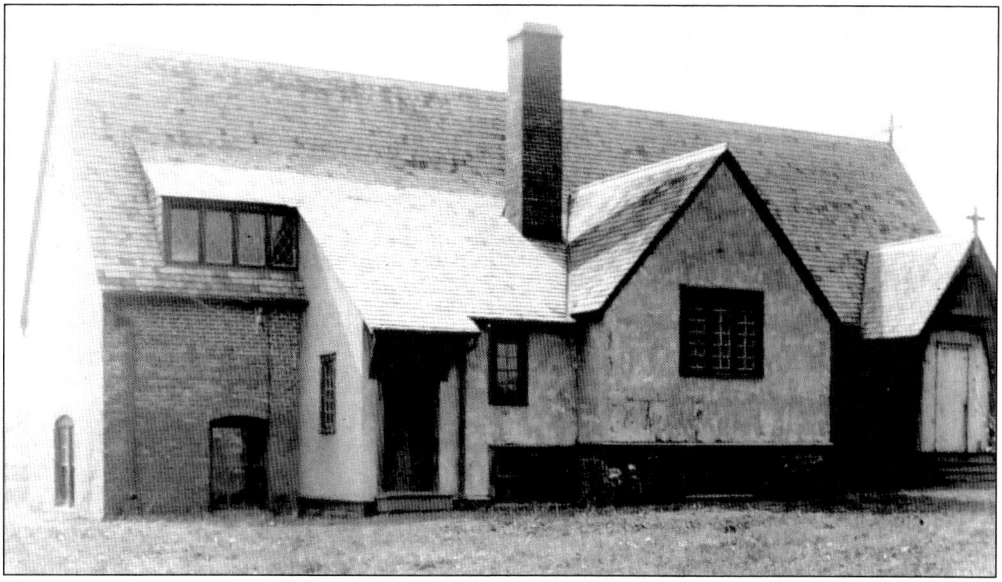

Grace Episcopal Church started as a mission station of the Diocese of Newark in 1905. Services were held at the Odd Fellows Hall until members acquired a portion of the Hopper's farmland near Five Corners in 1906 and built the church in 1909.

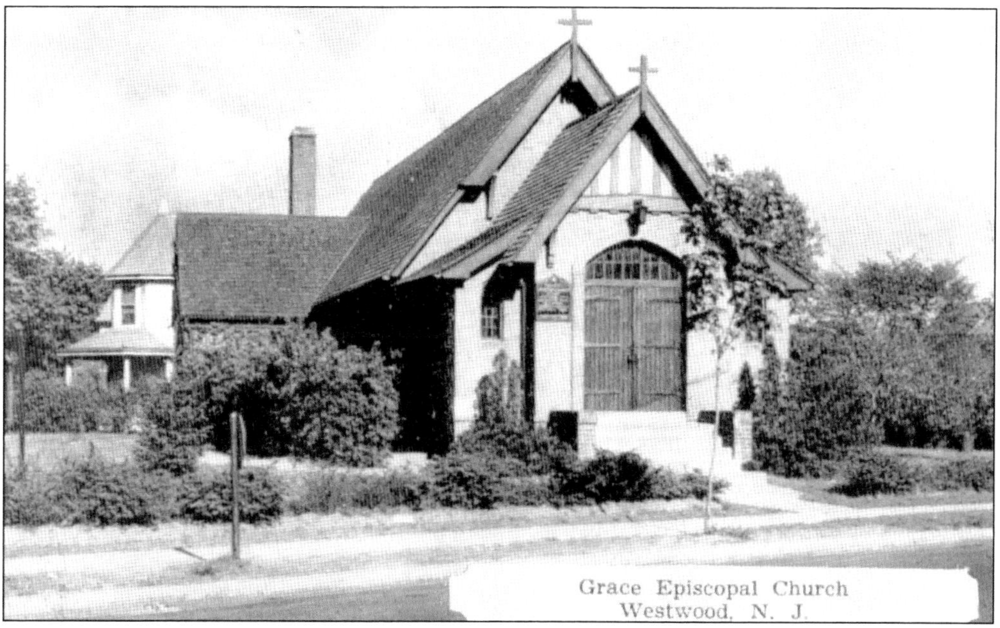

Although the church remains at this location, it has been rebuilt. The house in the background with the peaked roof is 15 Harrington Avenue.

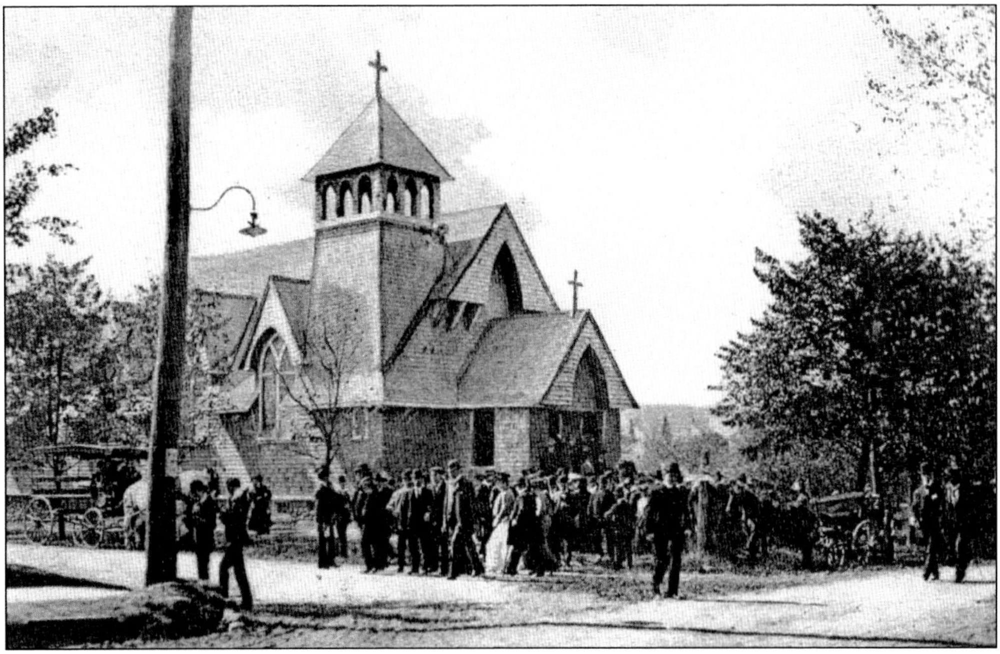

St. Andrew's Church was established in 1887, and its first location was where the American Legion Hall currently stands, on Washington Avenue. St. Andrew's continued to grow, and in 1905, a new larger church was dedicated at the corner of Fourth and Washington Avenues where the borough hall is now. Later, the church moved across Washington Avenue to its present location, and the old church building burned down in the late 1970s.

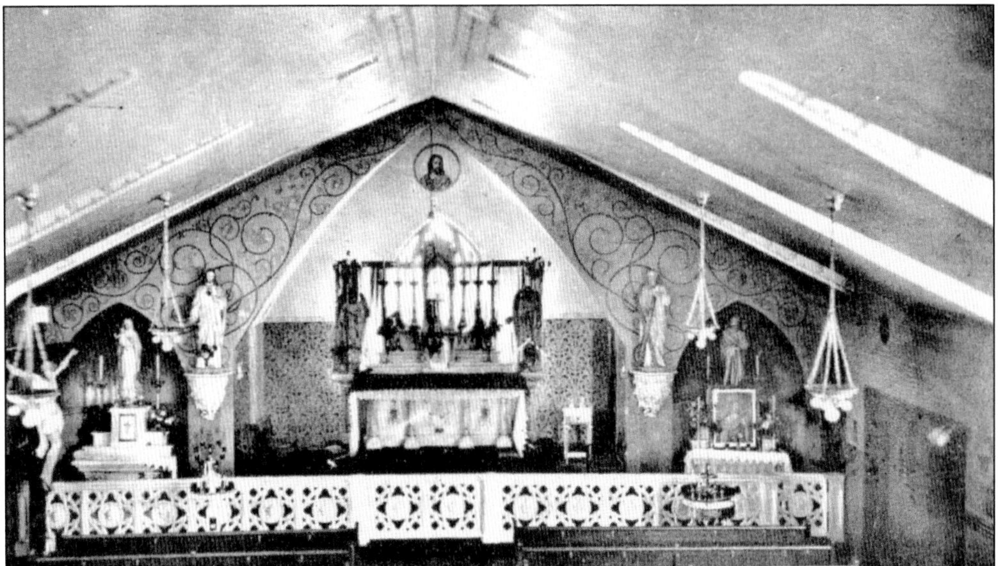

This card proudly displays the interior of St. Andrew's in the 1960s, when the church was located at the corner of Washington and Fourth Avenues.

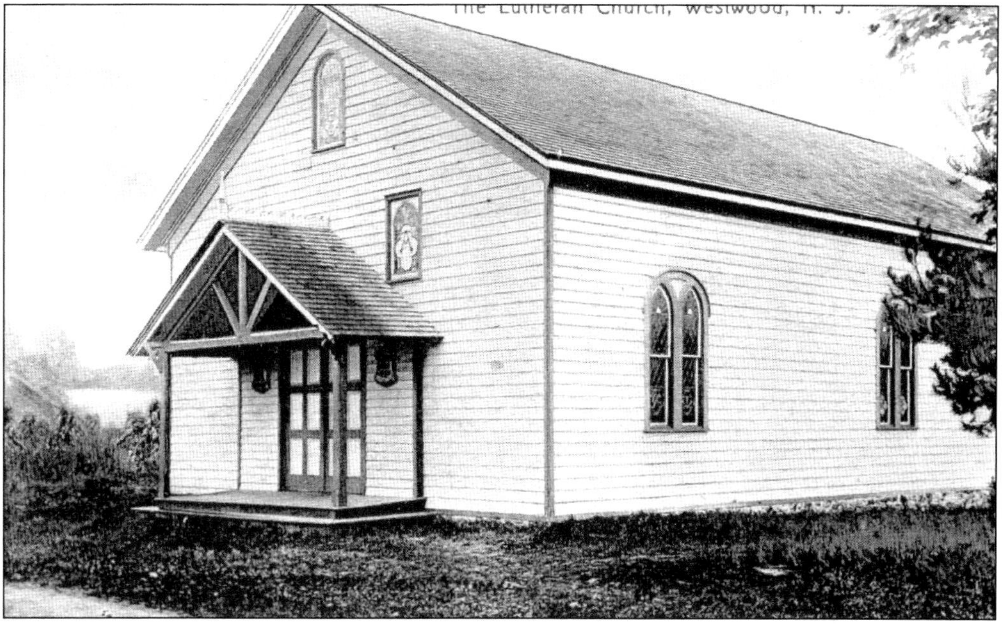

The Zion Lutheran Church of Westwood was formed in 1905 and was initially located in a frame building on Washington Avenue, which is now occupied by the American Legion. As with the other early churches in Westwood, Zion's initial meetings were held at Odd Fellows Hall (pictured on page 24). In addition to housing Zion Lutheran Church, this building on Washington Avenue served as a military drill house during the Civil War and housed several early churches and the Junior Order Hall.

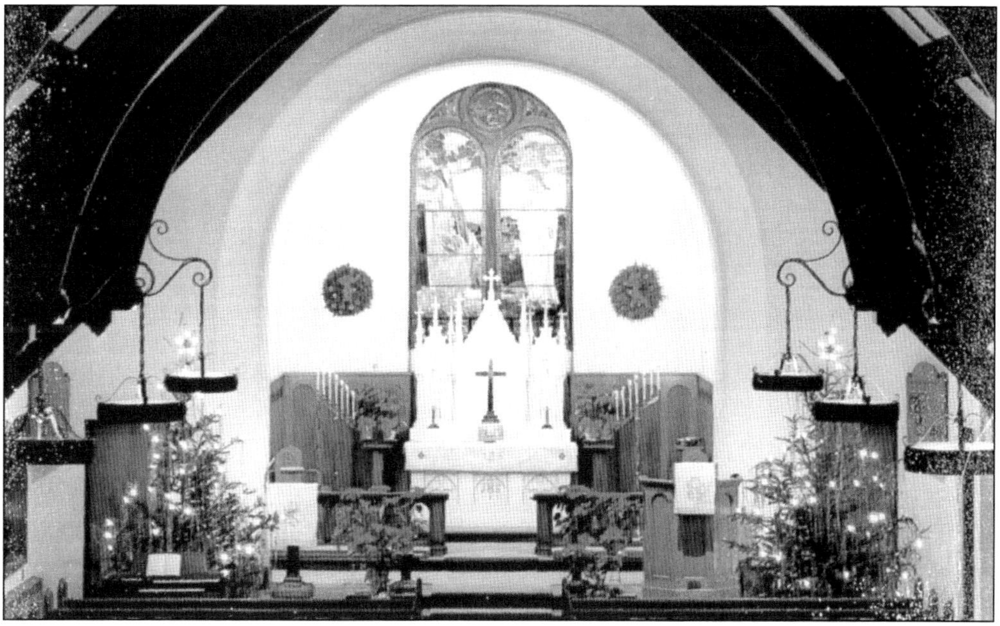

In 1926, Zion Lutheran Church moved to its current location on the corner of Second Avenue and Elm Street. This postcard depicts the interior of the present church.

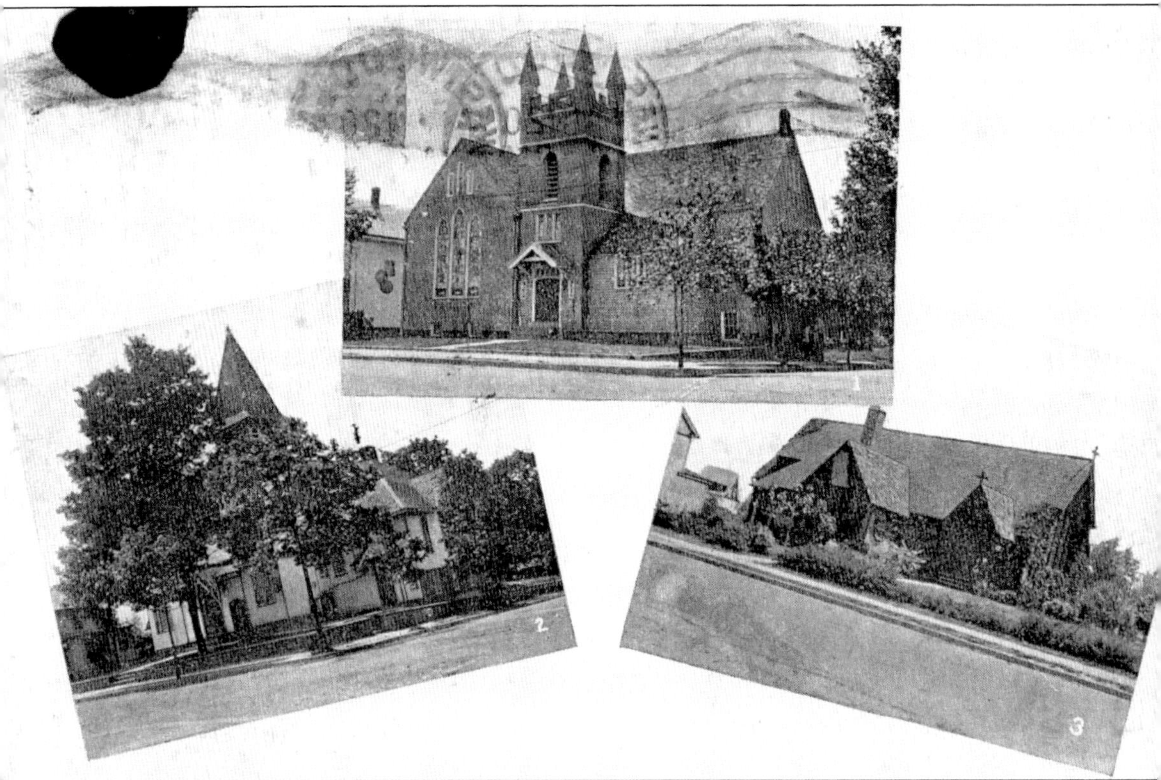

This card, mailed in 1922, appears to have been created for the multidenominational writer. It featured Westwood's Baptist church, Reformed church, and Episcopal church. Churches were commonly depicted in postcards because they were often the architectural and social centerpiece of a community. A church could also sell the cards to raise funds.

Seven

Recreation

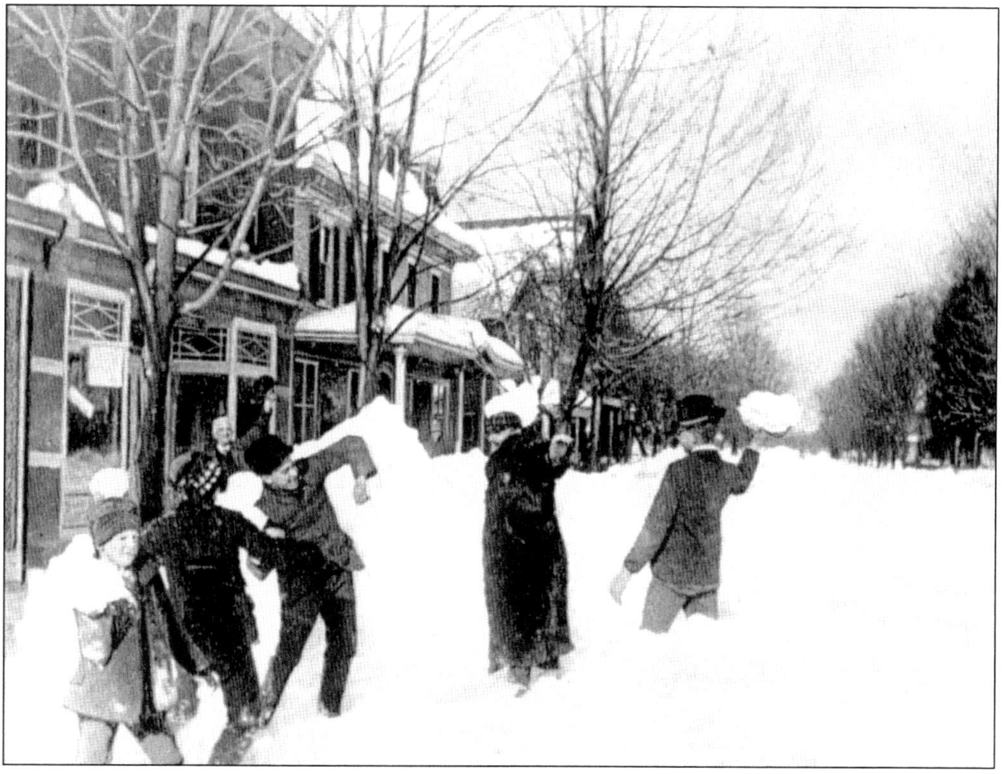

Until the mid-1900s, Westwood's development was limited to a one- or two-block radius around the train station and Westwood Avenue. People from larger cities like Hackensack, Paterson, Jersey City, and New York visited Westwood as a country getaway. Unspoiled streams, bridges, parks, and trails provided picturesque scenes for fishing, boating, or just passing the day. Mailed in 1909, this postcard captures a festive snowball fight in front of Westervelt's Ice Cream Emporium, which was located at 48 Westwood Avenue from 1884 to the 1920s.

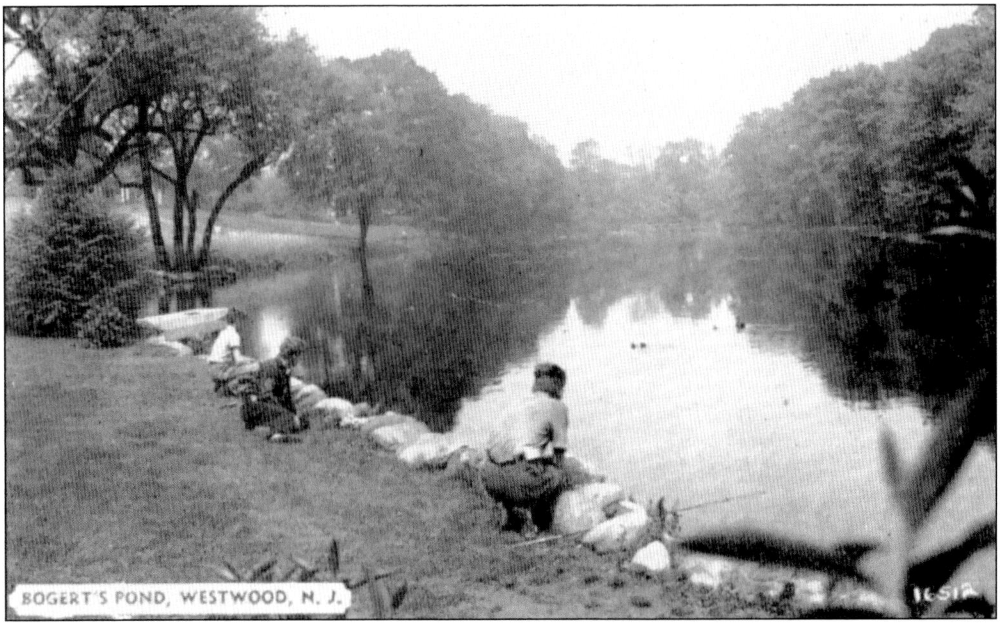

With the Pascack and Musquapsink Brooks winding their separate ways through Westwood, there is no part of town that is more than a few blocks from a body of water. Bogert's Pond, along the Musquapsink Brook, has been an appealing spot for fishing, skating, swimming, and boating for over 100 years.

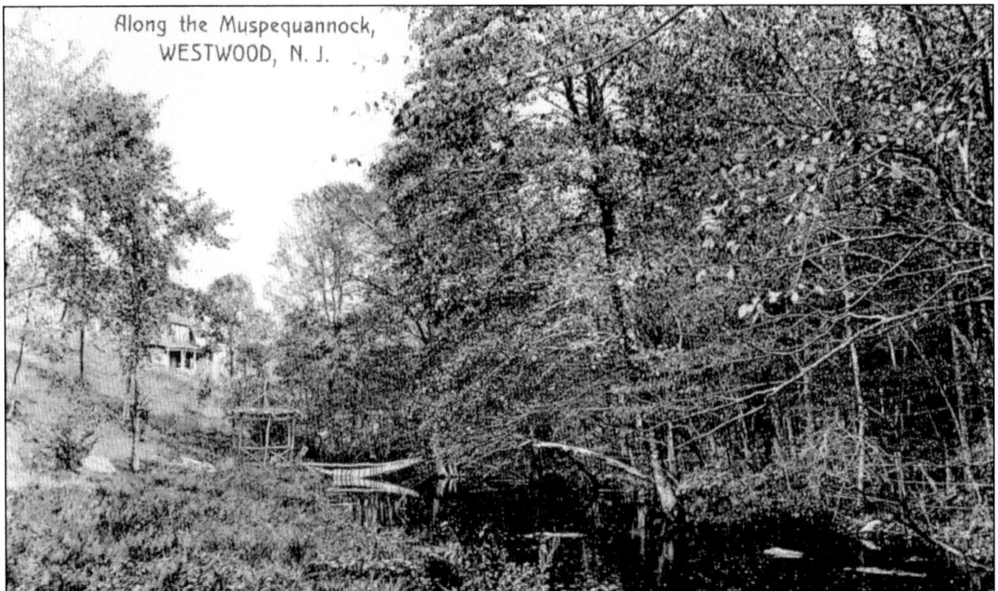

The Musquapsink Brook was named by the Lenni Lenape Indians, who inhabited the area of Westwood prior to 1850. Musquapsink means "water mingled with blood," which based on a legend similar to Romeo and Juliet, involving forbidden lovers from rival tribes.

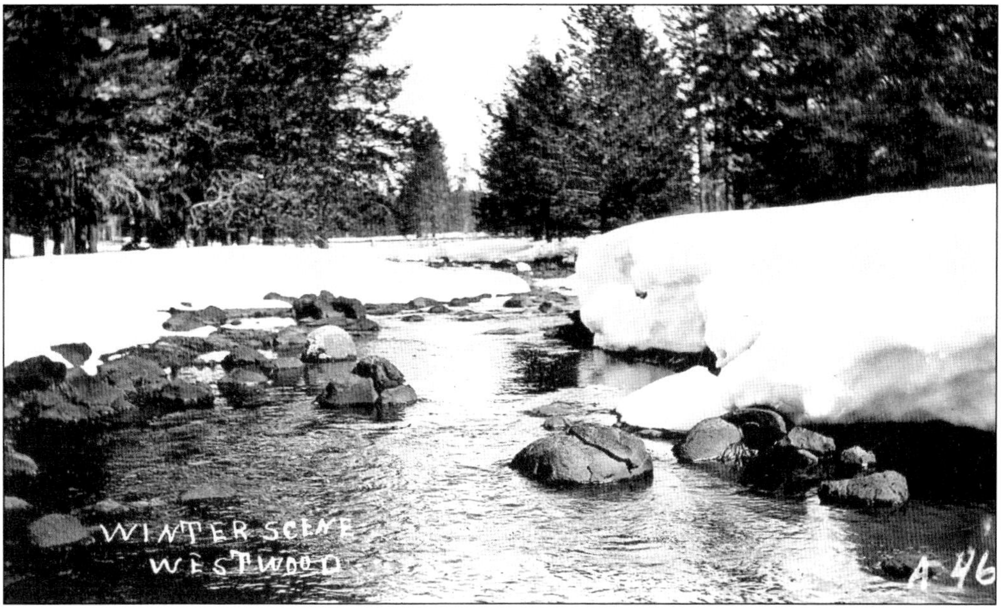

Neither of these scenes can be identified, but they are typical of many spots along the Musquapsink and Pascack Brooks, which thread their separate ways through Westwood.

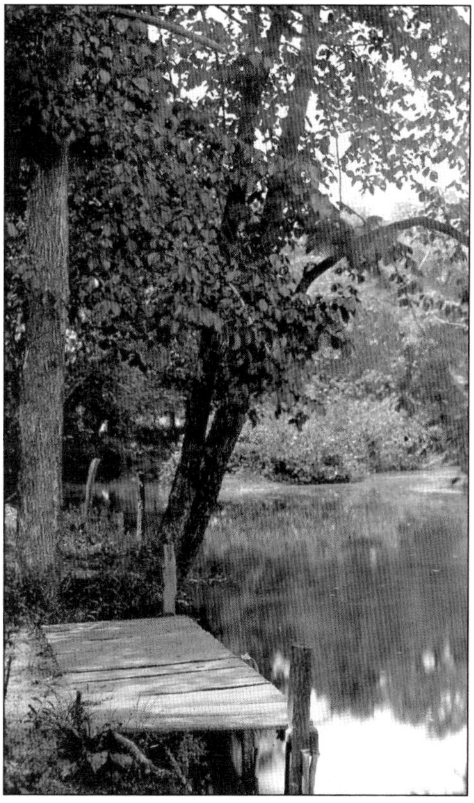

Both streams have historically provided Westwood residents with many opportunities for fishing, swimming, and boating.

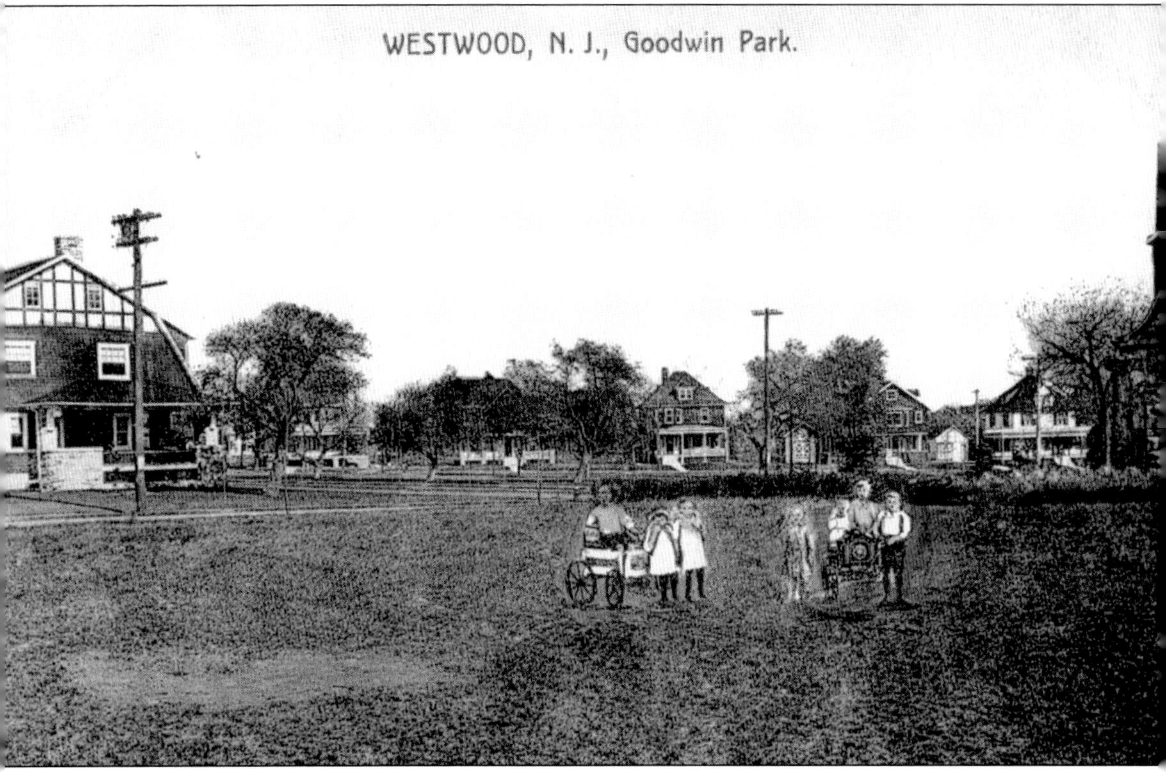

The Goodwin Park neighborhood, on the east side of Bogert's Pond, is named after Harry Goodwin, who was mayor in 1910 and owned much of the area. In 1921, a group of neighbors in the area pooled their money and purchased from Harry Goodwin the triangular lot surrounded by Carolyn Street, Prospect Avenue, and Bogert Street. The neighbors then deeded the property to the borough, with a perpetual restriction that the land could be used only "for the sole purpose of maintaining a park for general landscape purposes. . . . No paths . . . shall be allowed, no buildings of any kind . . . no benches . . . swings, and no construction for amusement purposes shall be allowed." Since the park had already been known as Goodwin's Park, the neighbors retained the name.

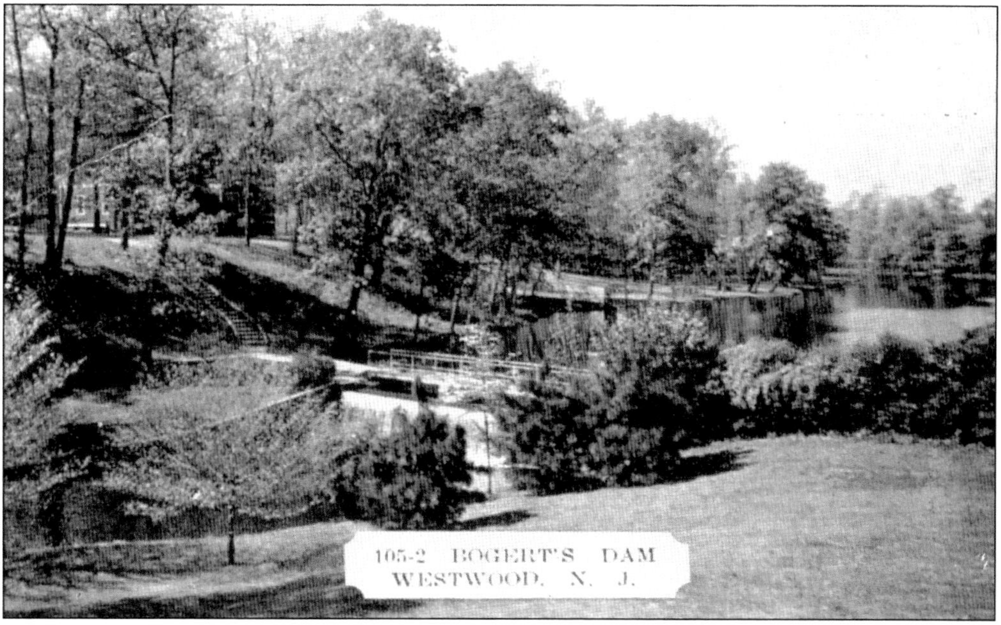

The old gristmills, although long gone, have left dams that create attractive ponds and wildlife habitats. This postcard of Bogert's Pond captures the beauty of the dam, pond, and bridge as they existed in the early 1900s.

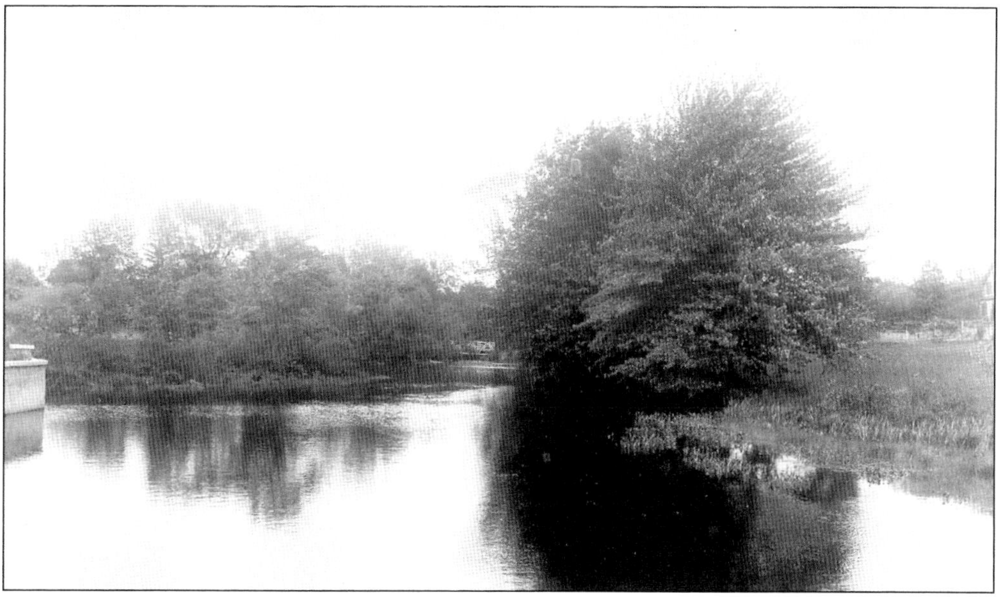

Located on the Hackensack River in what is now River Vale, Collignon's Mill also left a legacy of a scenic pond and landscape long after the mill was in ruins.

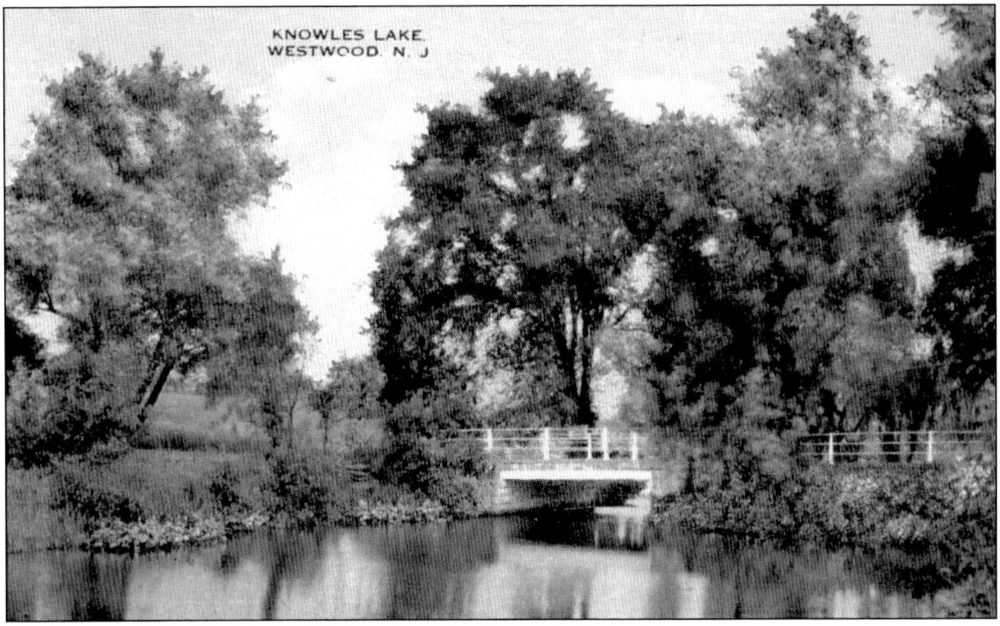

The pond created by Yates Mill was sometimes known as Knowles Lake.

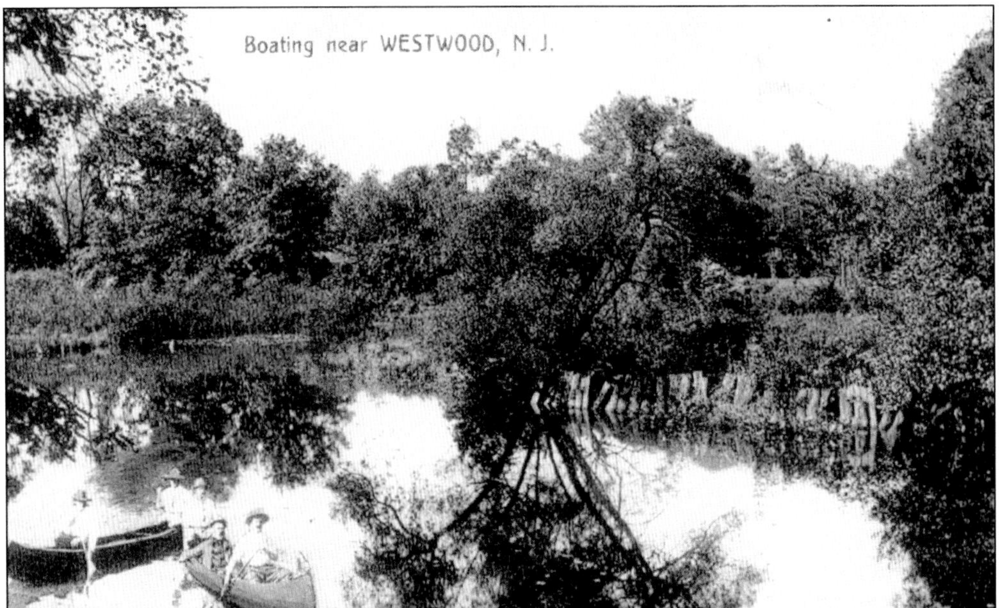

This location is unknown, but the three mills and winding brooks provided many scenic locations for boating and fishing in and around Westwood.

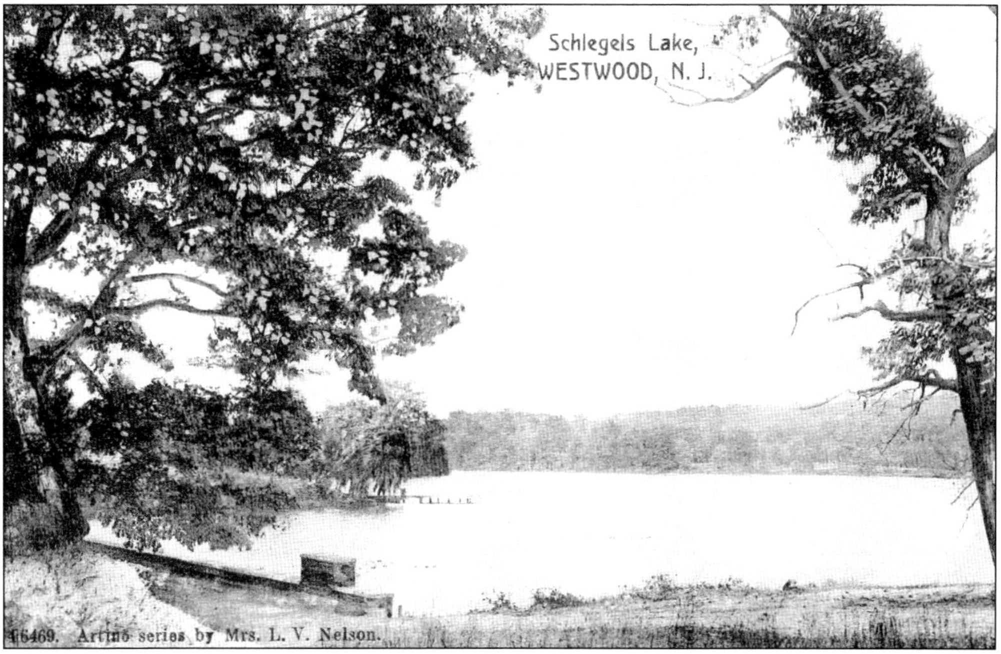

Back in 1910, when this postcard was mailed, the name Westwood was associated with a much larger area that included parts of River Vale and Washington Township. Schlegels Lake is now commonly known as Washington Lake. It is located in Washington Township near the Washington Township Library.

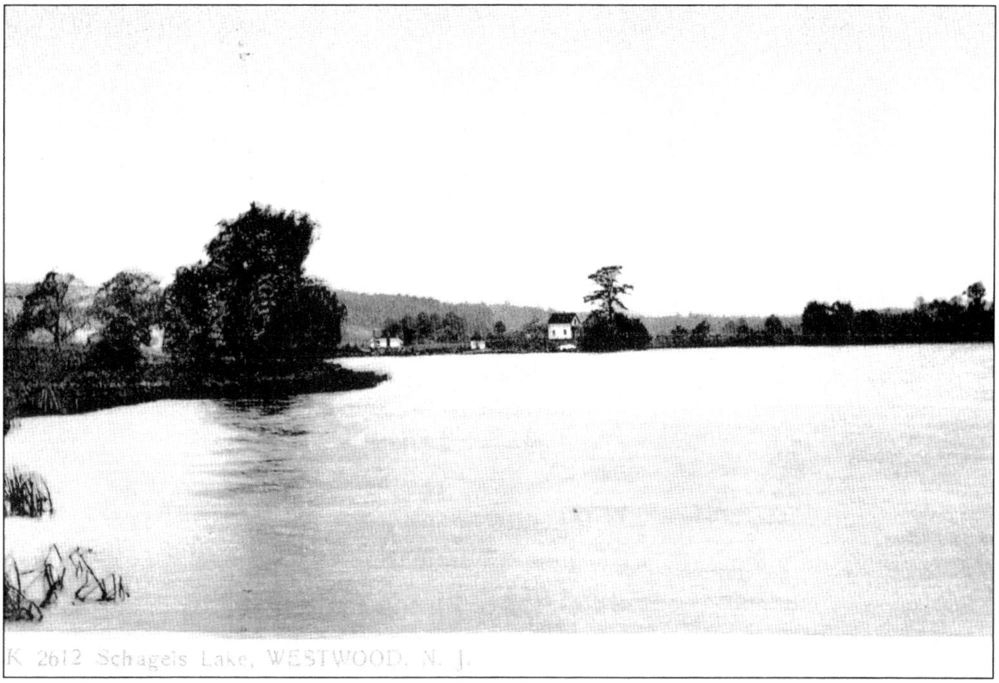

In the 1940s, Washington Lake Estates developed housing around Schlegels Lake. Houses were advertised for just $12,550. The surrounding neighborhood of 257 homeowners formed the Washington Lake Association in 1947 to manage and preserve the lake.

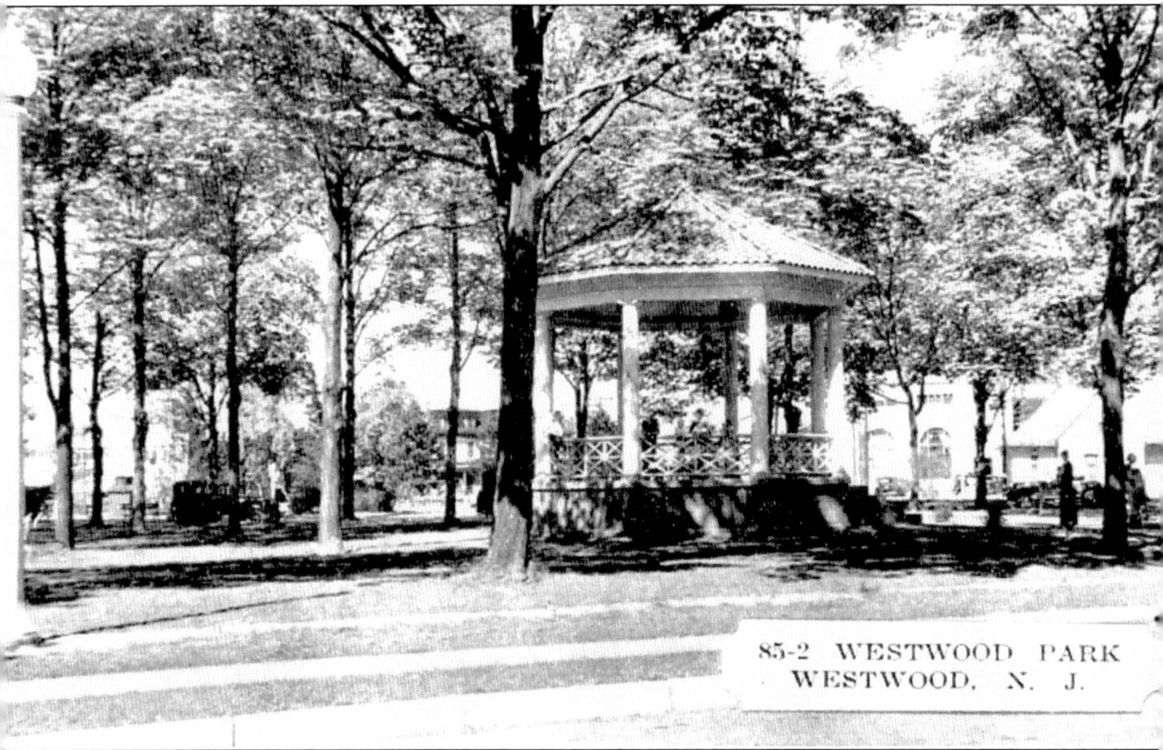

Veterans Memorial Park, located in the center of Westwood, just west of the train station, is the social heart of Westwood. Dedicated to war veterans, it has been preserved as open space used for community events. The most prominent structure in the park is the bandstand. It is located on the triangular section of the park that was donated by Isaac D. Bogert on July 18, 1894. Dedicated on August 2, 1922, the bandstand was built at the suggestion of Mayor Irving T. Brickell entirely by volunteers using donated funds and supplies. Over the years, it has been rebuilt and repaired by volunteers, and it is currently maintained by the Westwood Heritage Society. It is used for concerts, public presentations, parades, and other community activities.

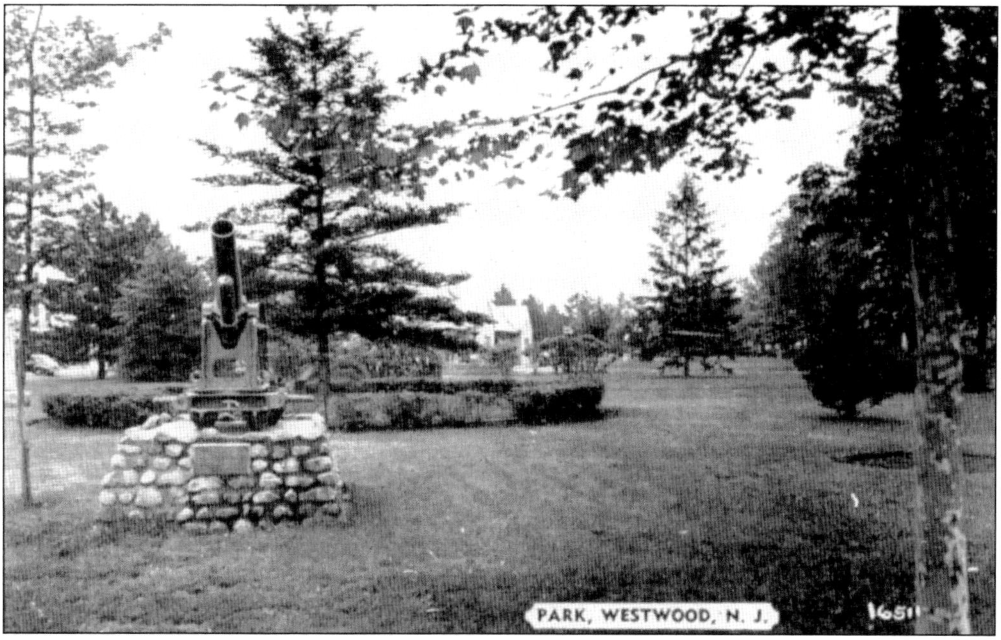

Veterans Park also contains this monument to Westwood's World War I veterans, which was dedicated on September 14, 1927. Located right across from the Iron Horse Restaurant, the monument includes a real trench mortar that was used to fire mortar shells in World War I.

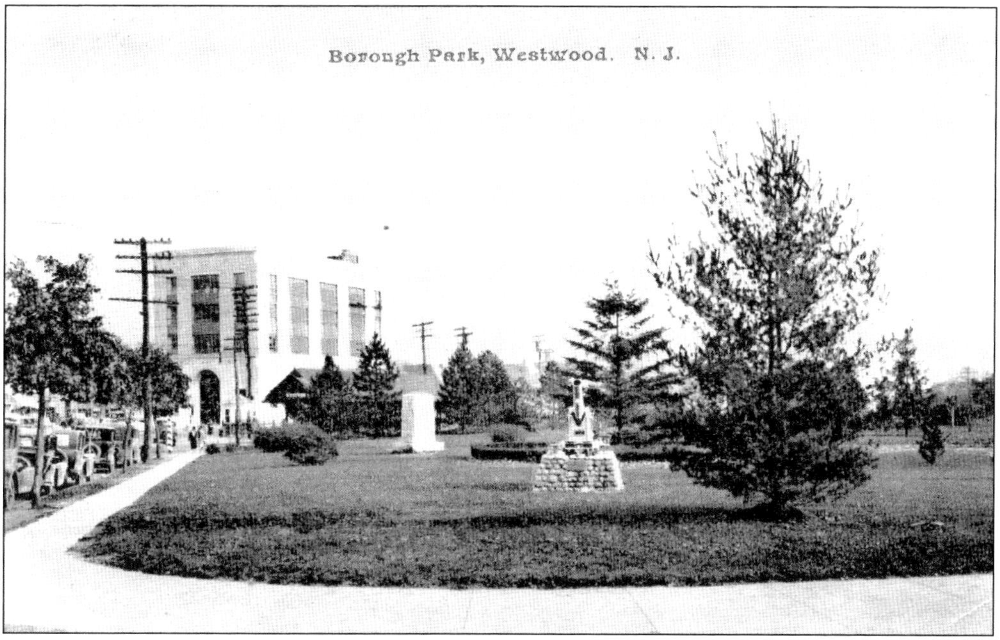

The mortar was presented to the borough on September 14, 1927, by the Ralph W. Lester Veterans of Foreign Wars Post No. 130, which is named after a Westwood resident who died in service during World War I. The old train station can be seen in the background.

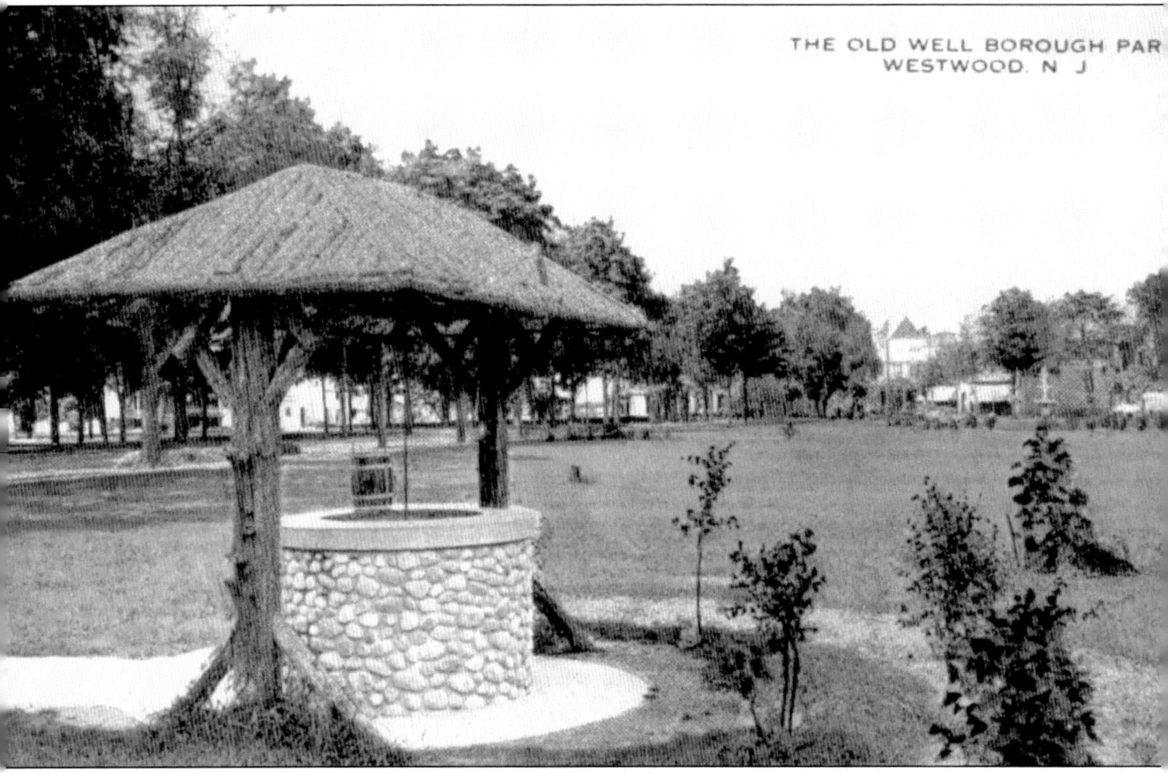

The old well remains in the southeast quarter of the park, but the roof structure is gone, and the well has been capped for safety reasons.

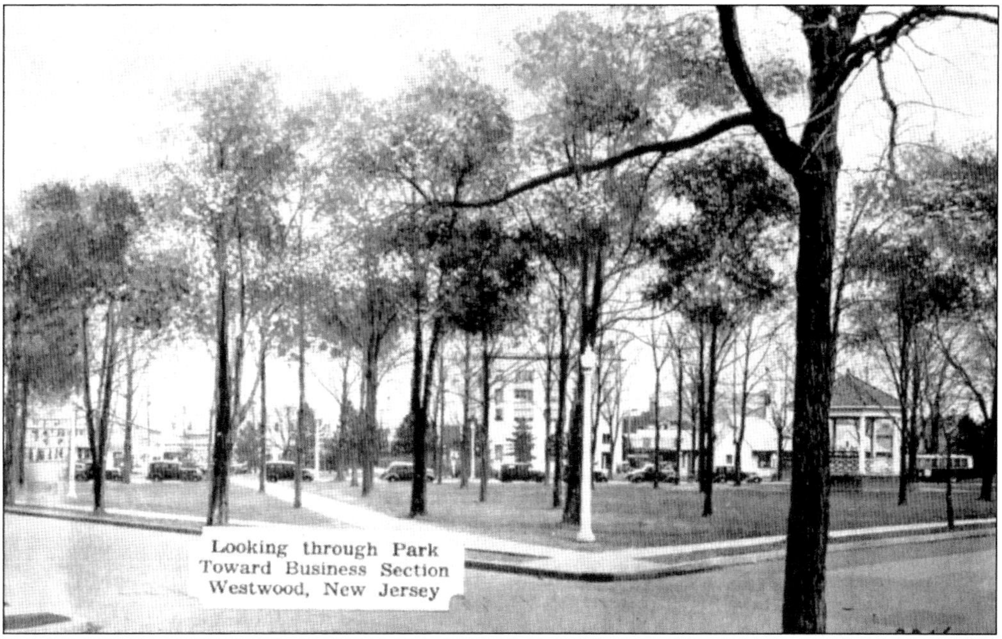

Scattered with tall trees, Veterans Memorial Park provides a restful, shady oasis in the center of town, just steps from the train station and shops. The park is used for antique shows, concerts, flea markets, and community gatherings of all types. In this 1939 view looking east through the park from the corner of Park and Third Avenues, the bandstand is visible and the bank building dominates the corner of Broadway and Westwood Avenue in the background.

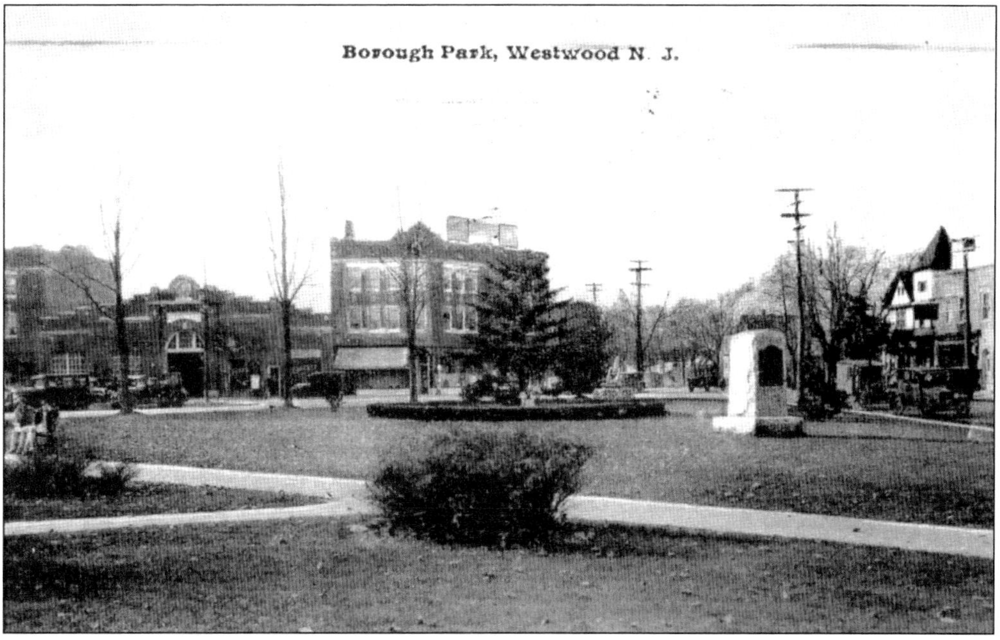

This view of the park, from a postcard mailed in 1932, features the bus terminal building in the background, at 318 Third Avenue, and the World War I Memorial on the right. The monument was dedicated on November 11, 1922, to American servicemen who lost their lives during World War I.

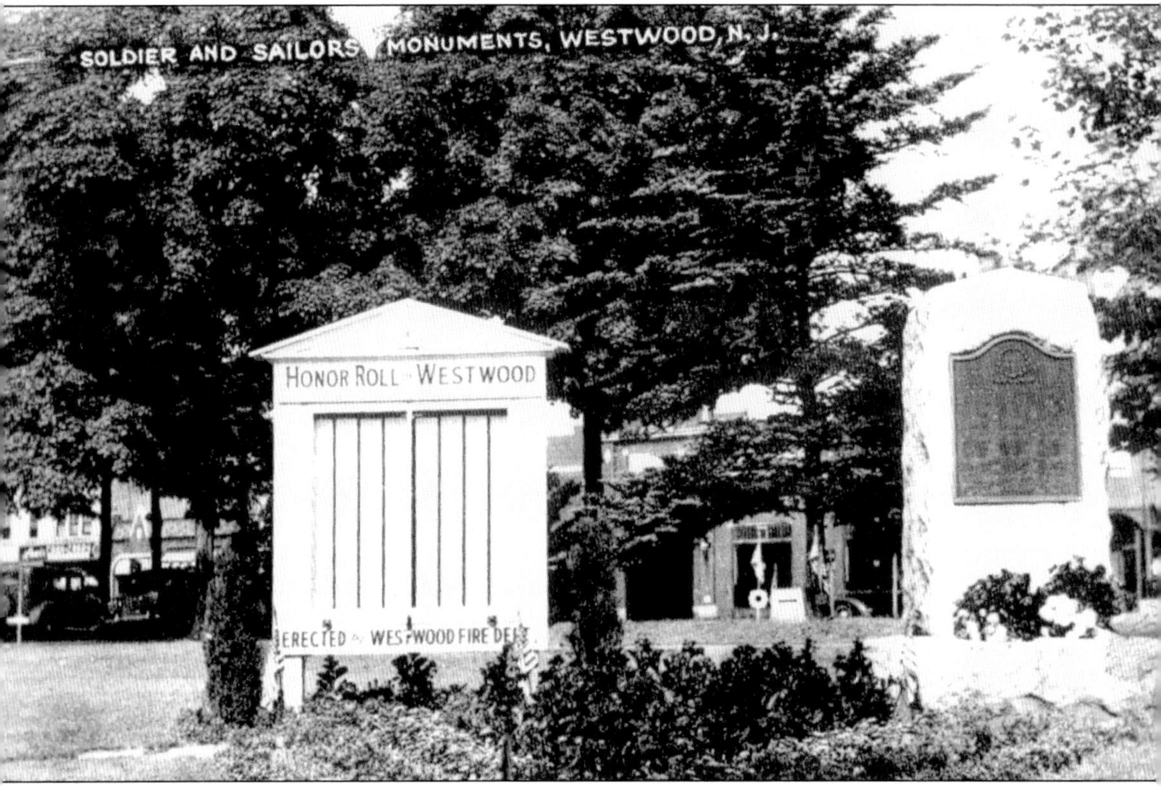

The original Honor Roll of Westwood, pictured on the left, was a simple wooden structure erected by the Westwood Fire Department to memorialize Westwood residents who sacrificed their lives in service to our country. The World War I Memorial is pictured on the right of this card, which was mailed *c.* the 1940s.

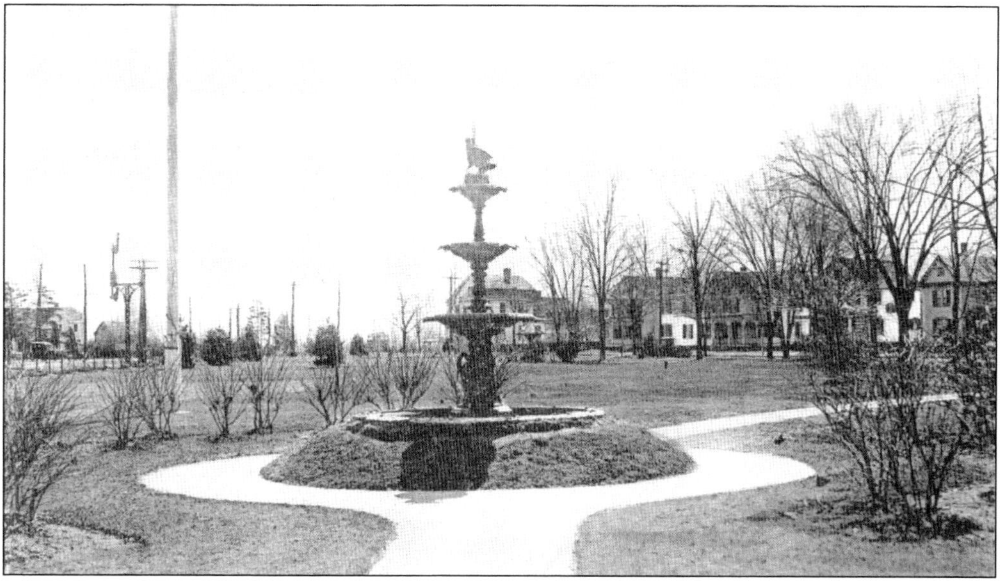

This large, ornate fountain was located in Veterans Memorial Park in the center of the circular path. The fountain was removed after a child climbed up it and was killed when the sections of it toppled over on him.

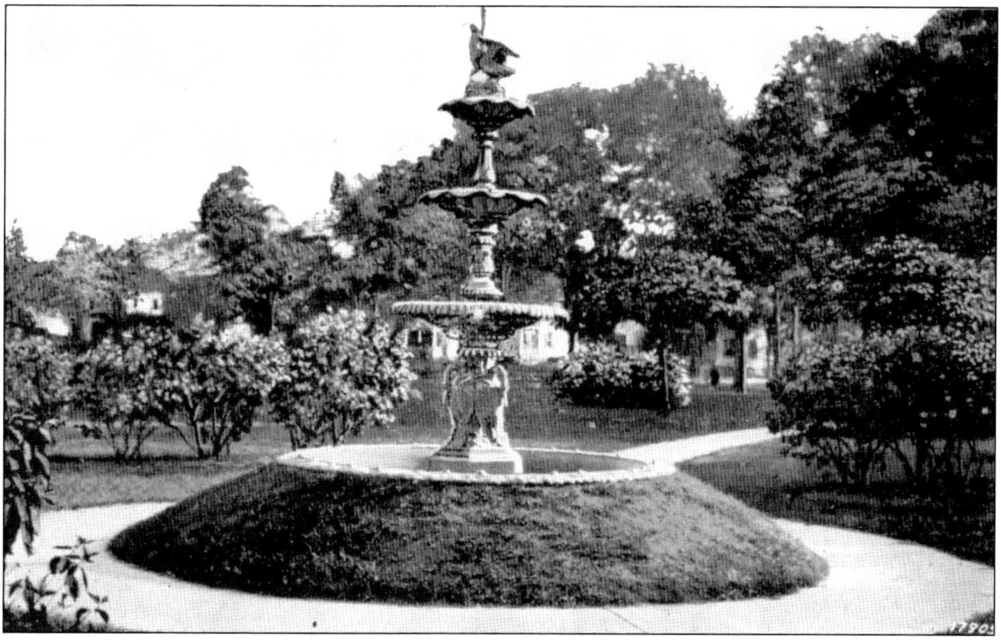

This circular path, where the fountain was located, is now the site of the World War I Memorial, which was relocated here from its original location in May 1949.

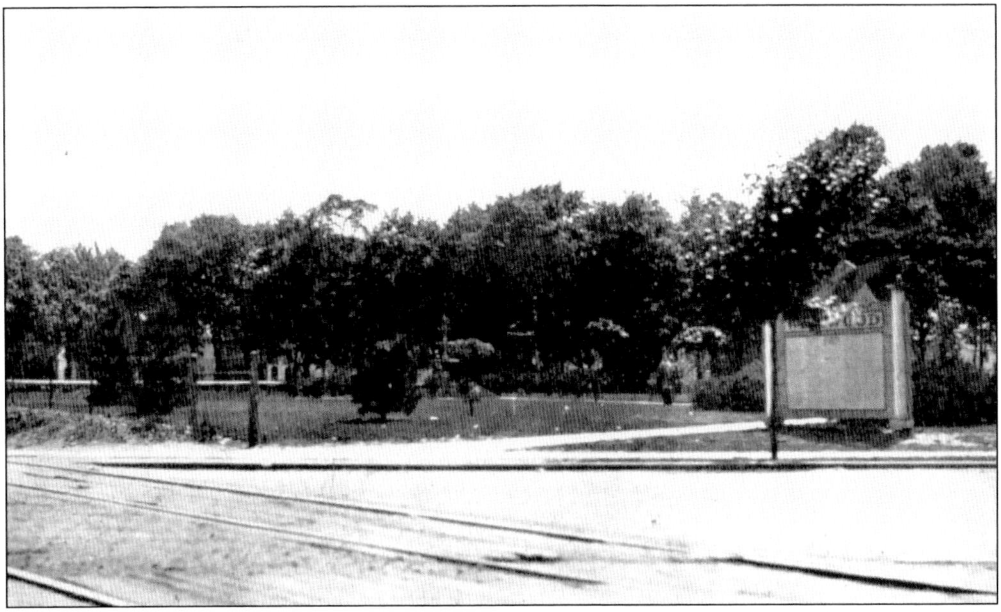

In the northeast corner of the park, just over the railroad tracks on Westwood Avenue, sits the Westwood Bulletin Board. All of the planned activities in the park and other local announcements appear on the official board.

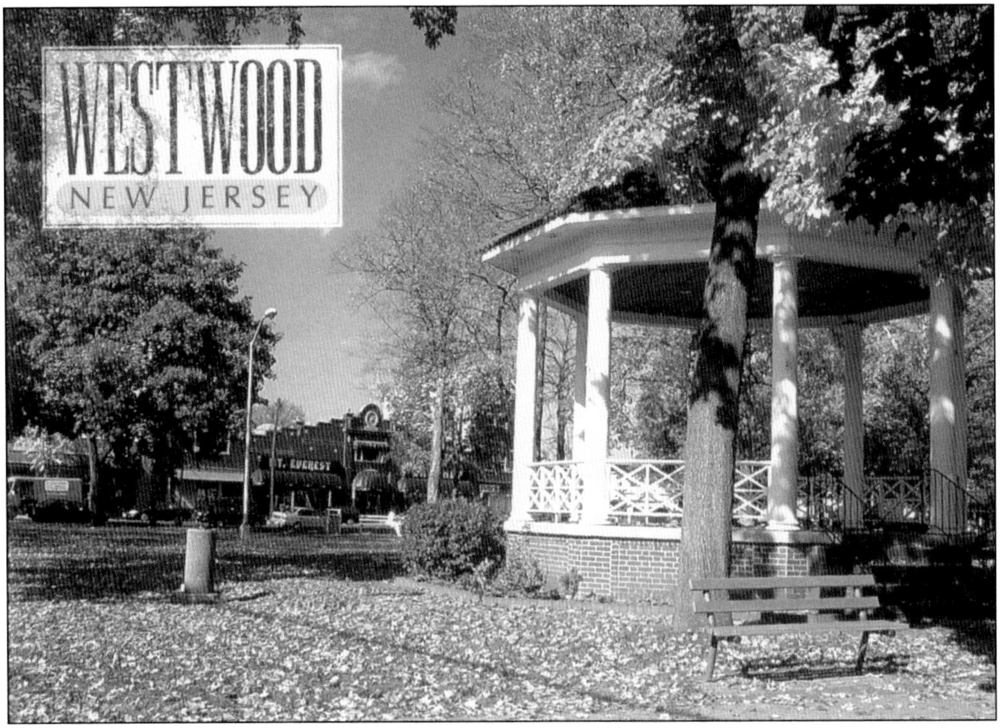

This modern postcard displaying Veterans Memorial Park and the bandstand shows that they remain strong symbols of Westwood.

Eight

The Train Station

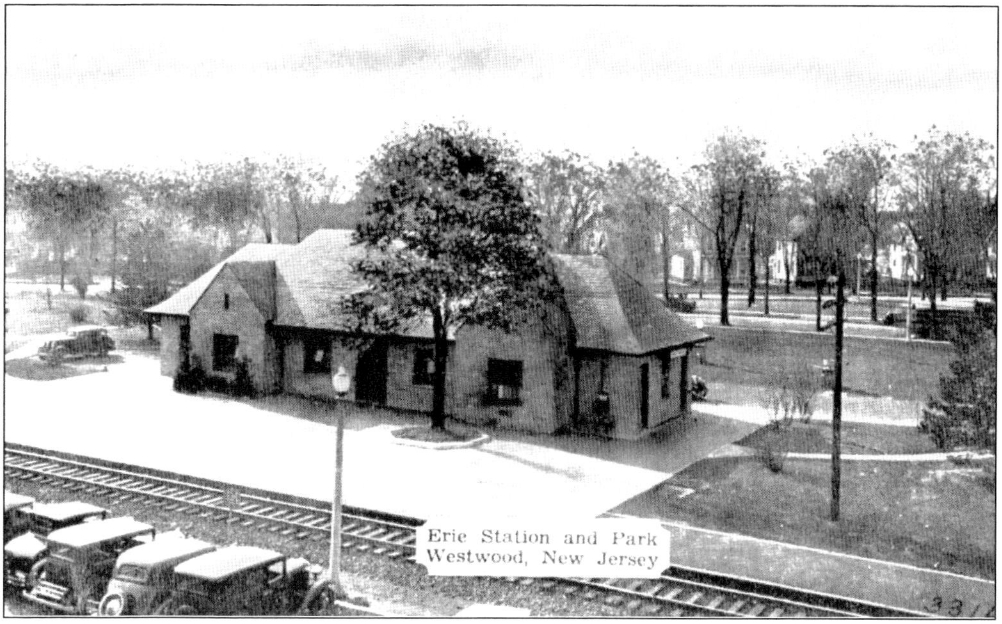

Prior to 1870, there was no train service to Westwood and stagecoach was the only means of public transportation. Before the Civil War, there was an early stagecoach route between Westwood and Hackensack, where travelers could take a second stage route to New York. By 1850, a daily stage route connected Westwood to Closter, where travelers could take a train to New York. This made it possible for commuters to make round trips to New York in a single day. In 1870, the railroad extended from Hackensack through Westwood to Hillsdale. This provided easy access to cities such as Paterson, Hackensack, and New York, and it ignited the growth and development of Westwood. This postcard depicts the train station in 1936.

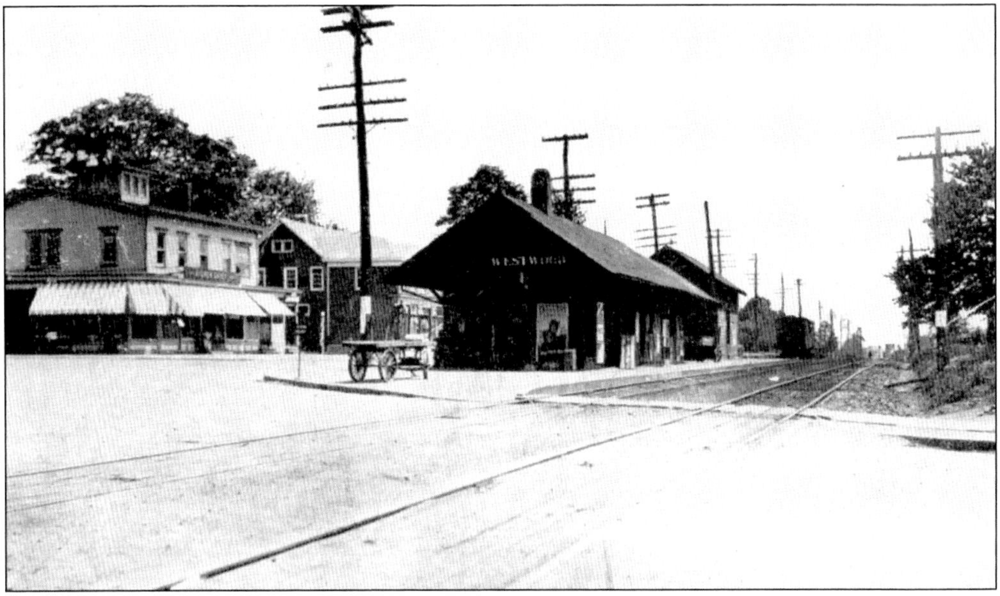

Because of the train station, pictured here in this postcard from 1923, Westwood rapidly grew into a desirable residential area for city commuters and became a country destination for city dwellers.

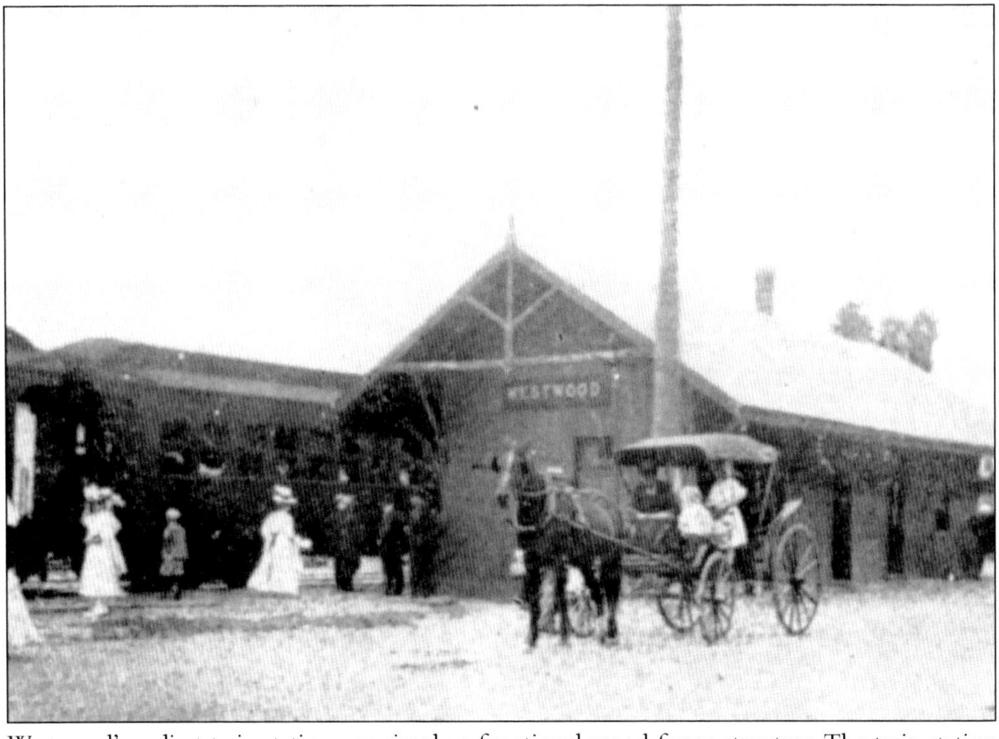

Westwood's earliest train station was simply a functional wood frame structure. The train station included a carriage house, through which horse buggies could enter and exit to unload baggage.

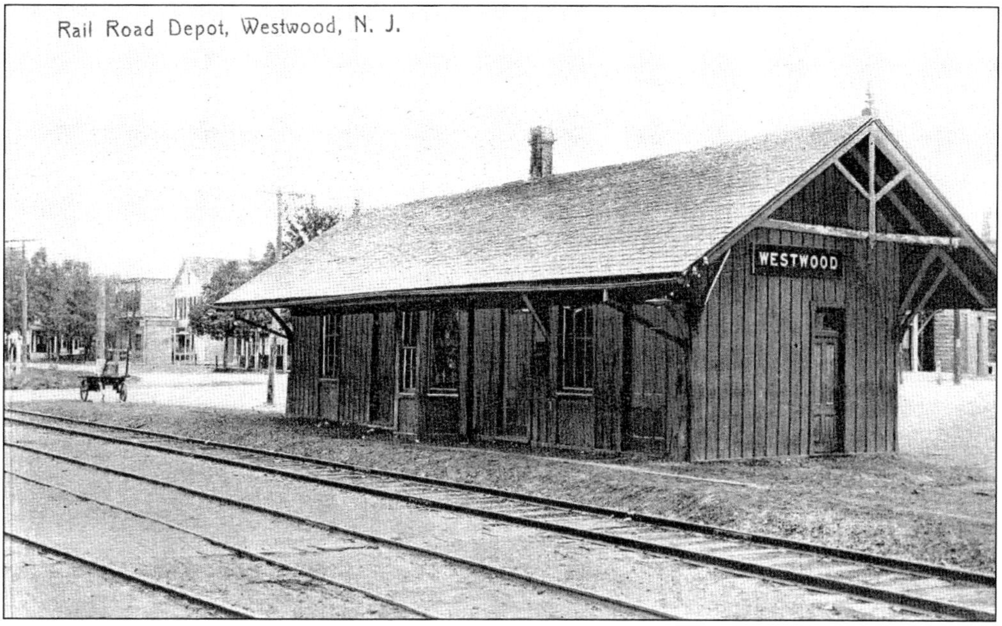

The original train station stood on the east side of the railroad tracks. There were a few houses on the west side of the tracks. Eventually, the houses were removed and the land became part of Station Plaza Park, which later was officially named Veterans Memorial Park (discussed in chapter 7).

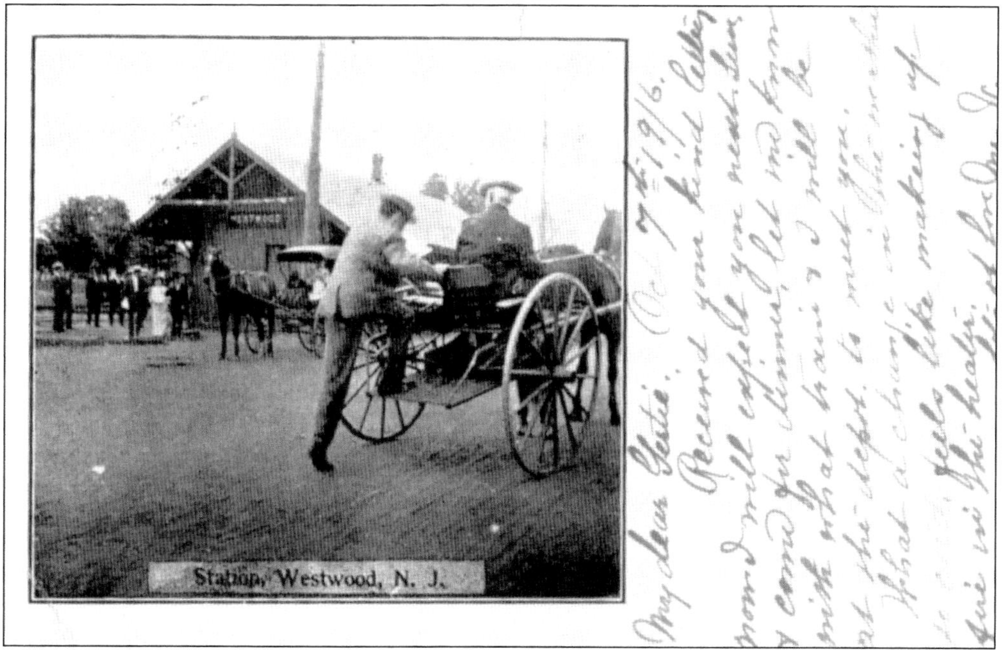

Just as they do today, residents from neighboring towns traveled to Westwood's train station and often stayed to shop, eat, or sleep in one of the hotels. Unlike today, however, back in 1906, when this card was mailed, travelers were picked up and dropped off by horse buggies and wagons.

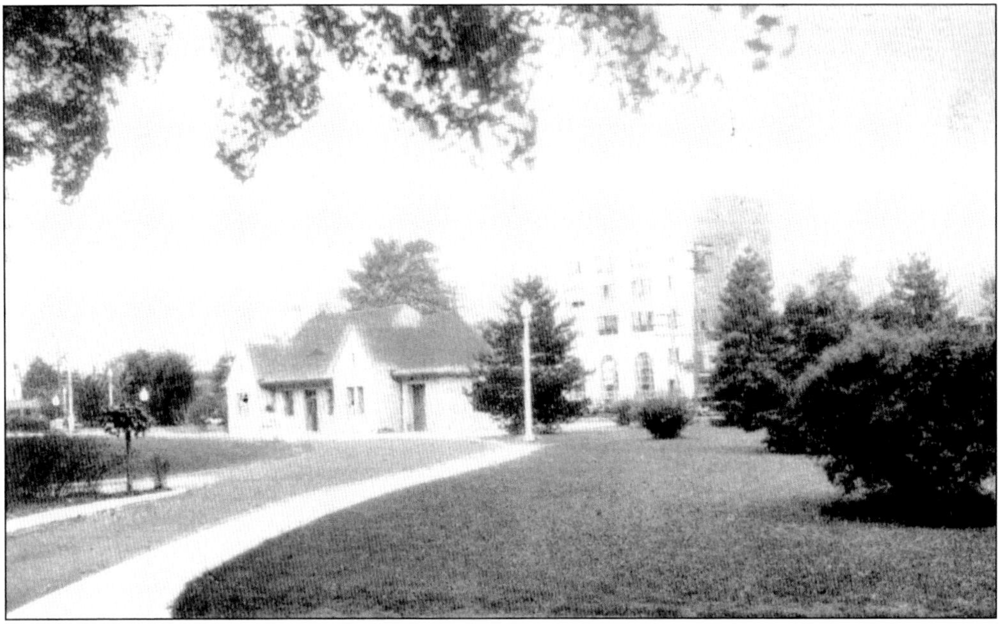

In 1932, the borough built a more aesthetic and permanent train station out of Briar Hill stone on the west side of the tracks in what had become Veterans Memorial Park. Built during the Great Depression, the new train station represented stability and promise for the future. At the dedication ceremony, Mayor Edward Ringrose referred to the event as "the happiest moment of our lives in Westwood." The four-story bank building can be seen in the background, standing at the corner of Broadway and Westwood Avenue. The train station has been rehabilitated but still stands today, essentially in its original design. It now also serves as the home of the Westwood Heritage Society's Museum, and is the home base for many events in Veterans Memorial Park.

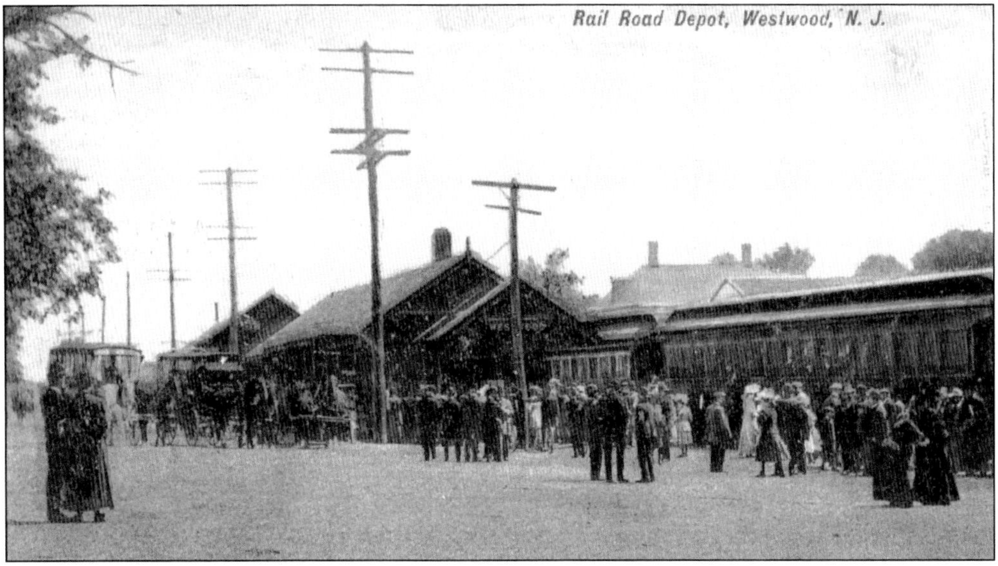

This postcard from the Artino series is purely an artistic creation, roughly based on the Westwood train station. The Westwood station never looked exactly like this structure, but this card provides a charming characterization of what the Westwood station would have looked like on a busy day in the early 1900s.

Nine

HOMES

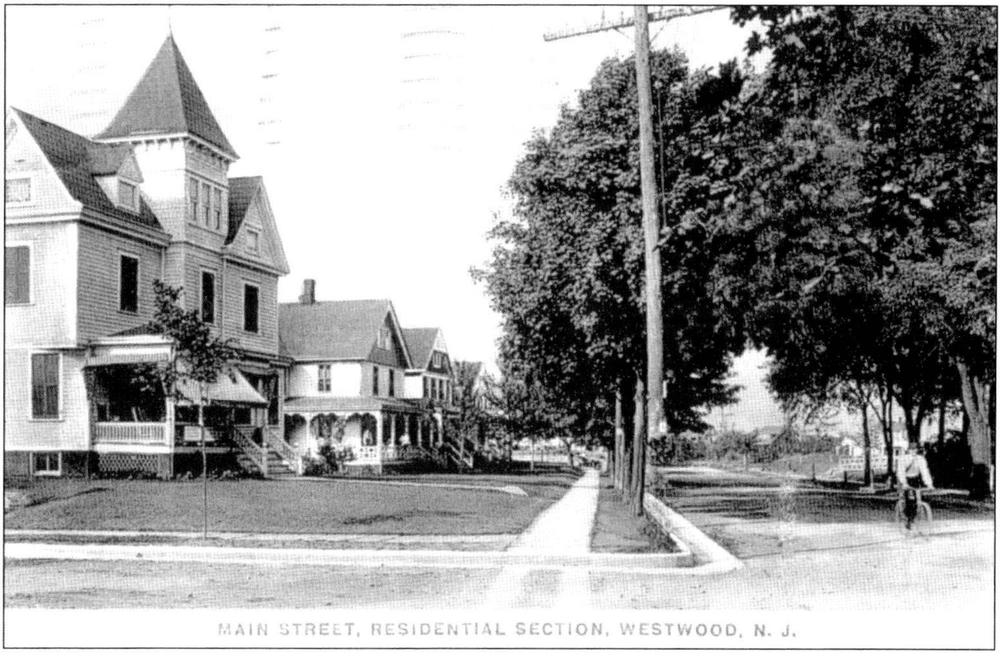

The earliest development in Westwood centered on and around Main Street and Railroad Avenue (now Westwood Avenue and Broadway). Until the late 1800s, the downtown area consisted of just a handful of shops. Small markets were mixed with beautiful Victorian and Colonial-style homes all along what is now known as Westwood Avenue. When the railroad extended to Westwood in 1870, the demand for both commercial space and housing shot up. Westwood became a popular stepping-off point for commuters who lived in surrounding towns, as well as an attractive place for commuters to live. The town grew from an estimated 25 homes in 1870 to a population of 828 in 1900. Eventually, more and more stores and commercial buildings squeezed the residences out of the downtown area. As the town became more developed, homes were torn down or literally moved off Westwood Avenue.

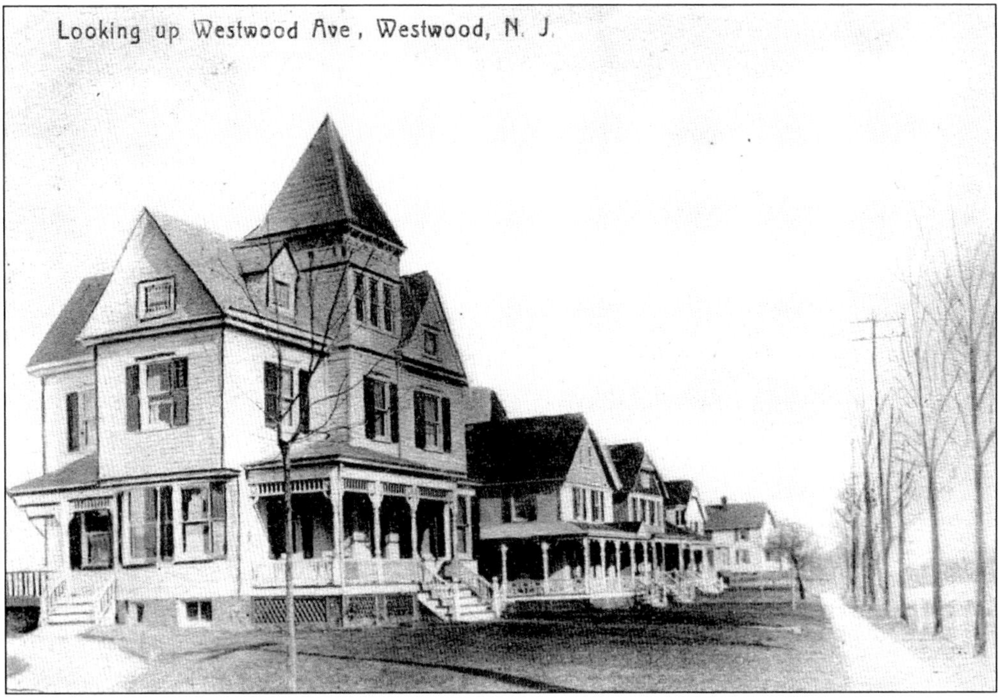

All of the houses on this card, mailed in 1907, are now gone. The house on the left was used as an early post office and was located on the site of the present post office, at the corner of Fairview and Westwood Avenues. The houses beyond it have been replaced with stores.

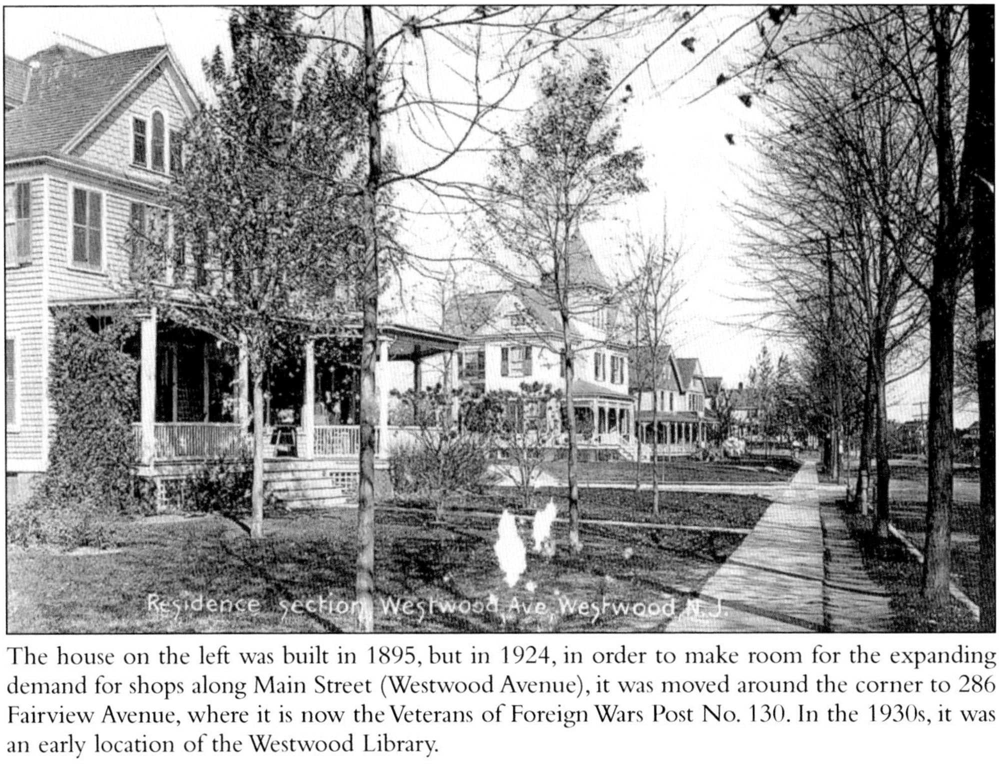

The house on the left was built in 1895, but in 1924, in order to make room for the expanding demand for shops along Main Street (Westwood Avenue), it was moved around the corner to 286 Fairview Avenue, where it is now the Veterans of Foreign Wars Post No. 130. In the 1930s, it was an early location of the Westwood Library.

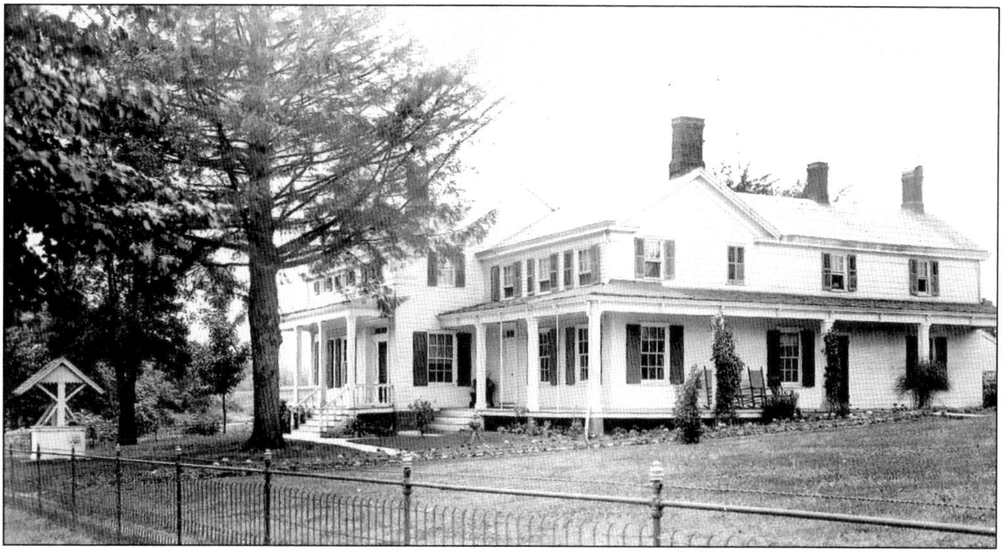

First Avenue became one of the premier residential areas in Westwood. Isaac Bogert was Westwood's first mayor, and his home can still be seen on the corner of First Avenue and Mill Street. A portion of the original house was separated and moved one lot west to 14 Mill Street *c.* 1950.

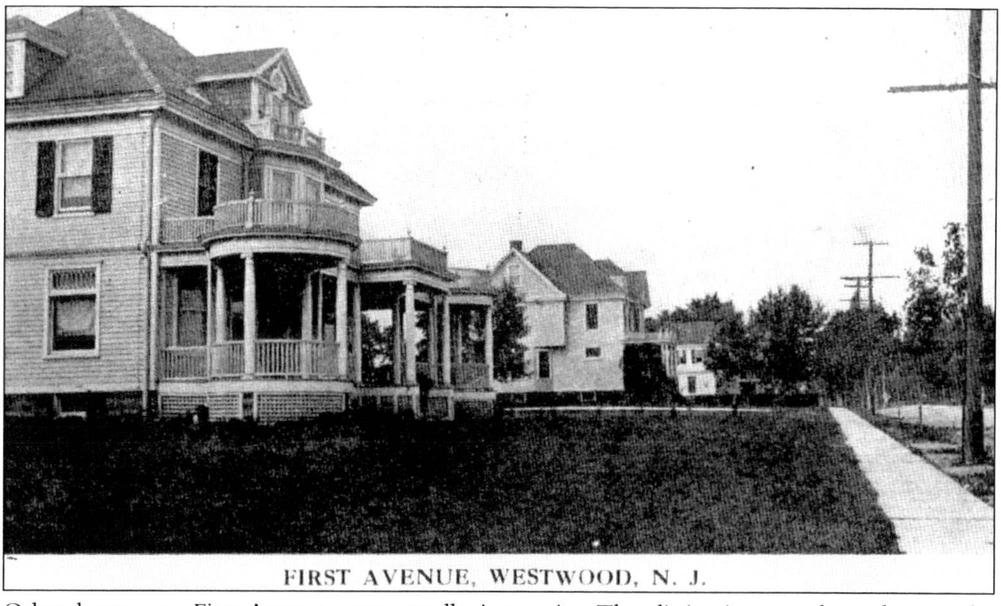

Other homes on First Avenue were equally impressive. The distinctive round porches on the house at 36 First Avenue are an example of the Victorian architecture that has been preserved in some of Westwood's older homes.

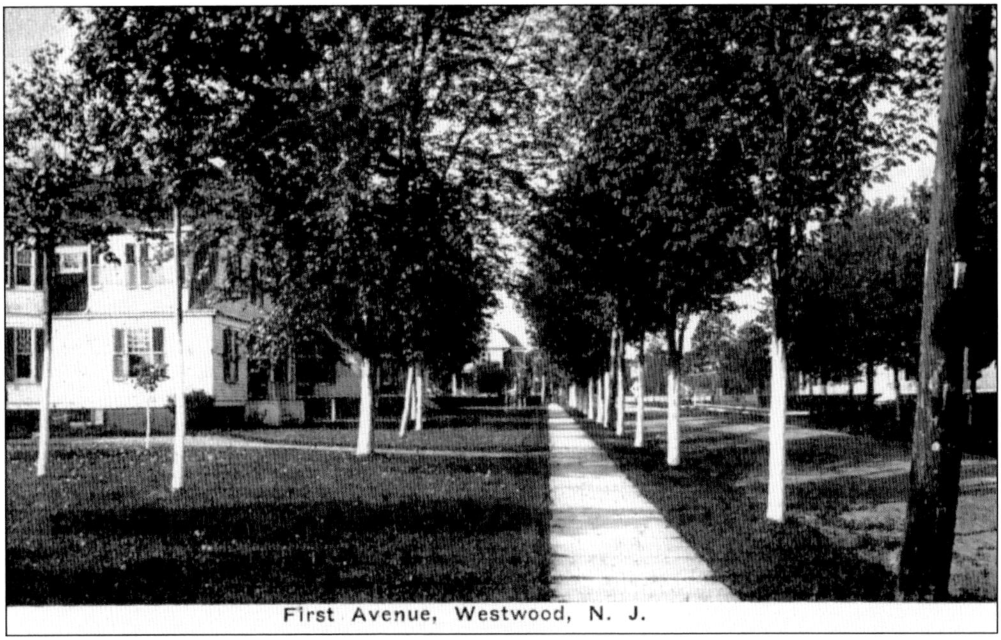

Facing the railroad tracks, this postcard view shows First Avenue including number 78. The vacant lot in the foreground is now the fenced-in field used by Zion Lutheran School at the corner of Elm Street and First Avenue.

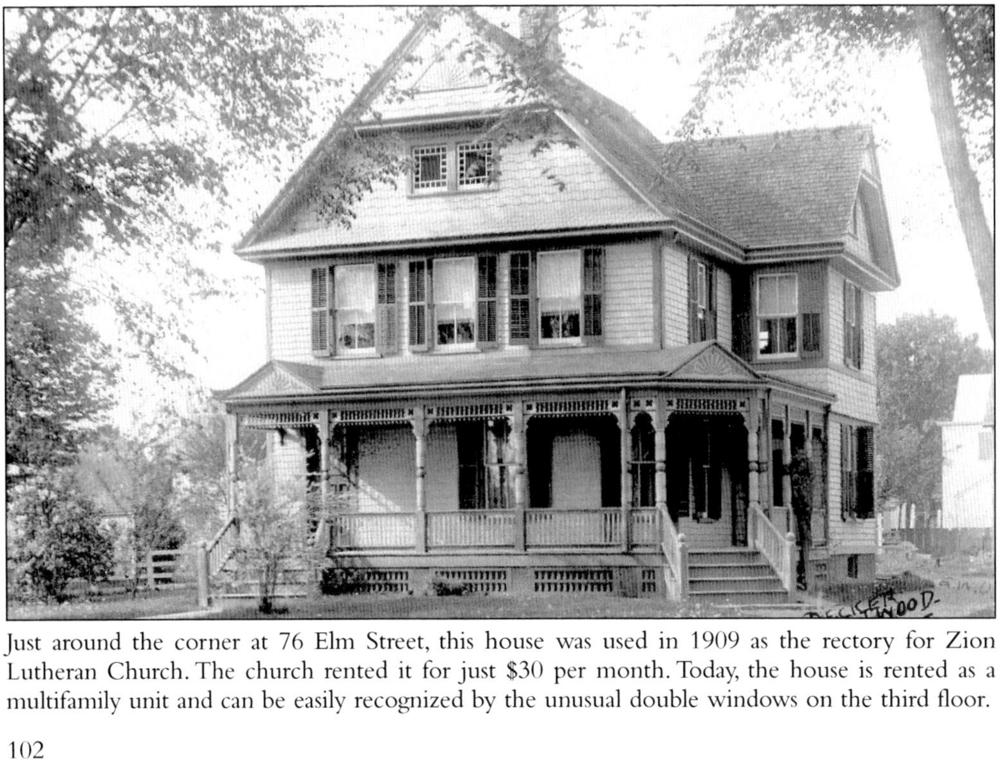

Just around the corner at 76 Elm Street, this house was used in 1909 as the rectory for Zion Lutheran Church. The church rented it for just $30 per month. Today, the house is rented as a multifamily unit and can be easily recognized by the unusual double windows on the third floor.

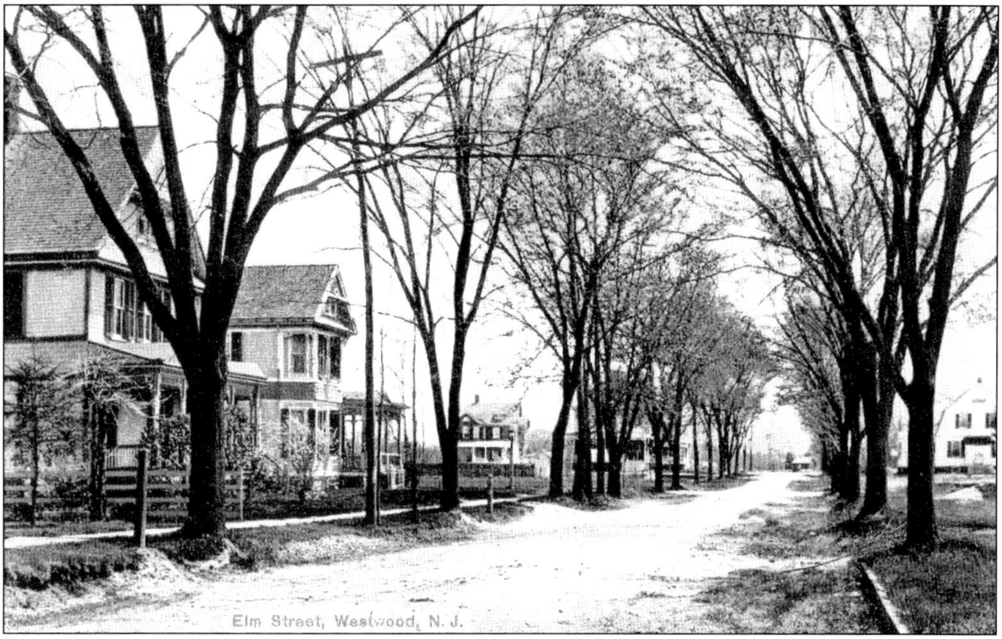

Mailed in 1912, this postcard features 76 and 72 Elm Street. Elm Street was also one of the earliest neighborhoods to be developed because of its proximity to the train station.

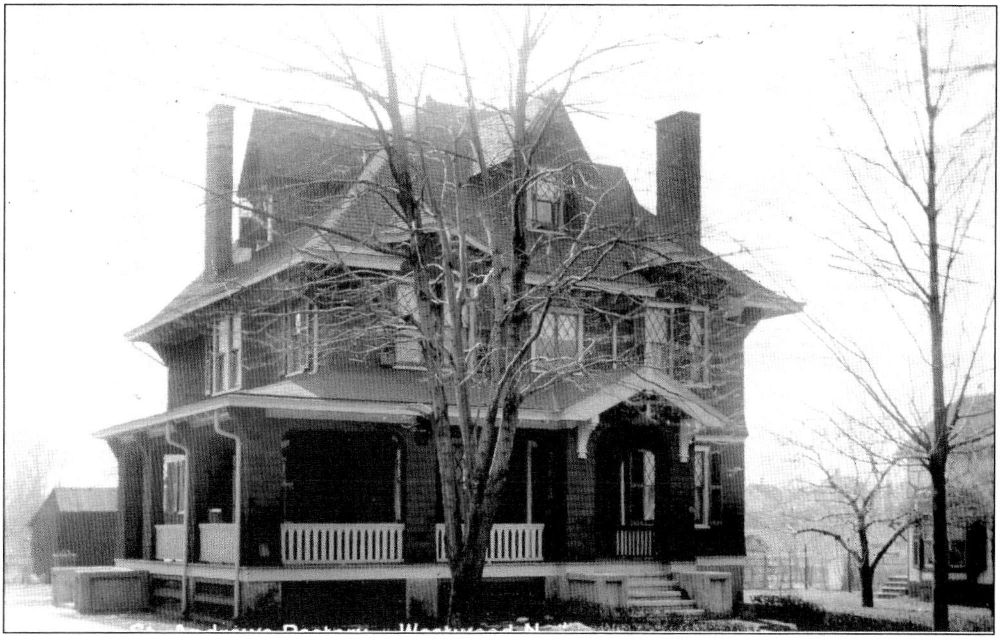

St. Andrew's Rectory was located next to the church at the corner of Washington and Fourth Avenues. The church burned down, and the rectory was demolished in 1982. This is currently the site of the Westwood Municipal Building parking lot.

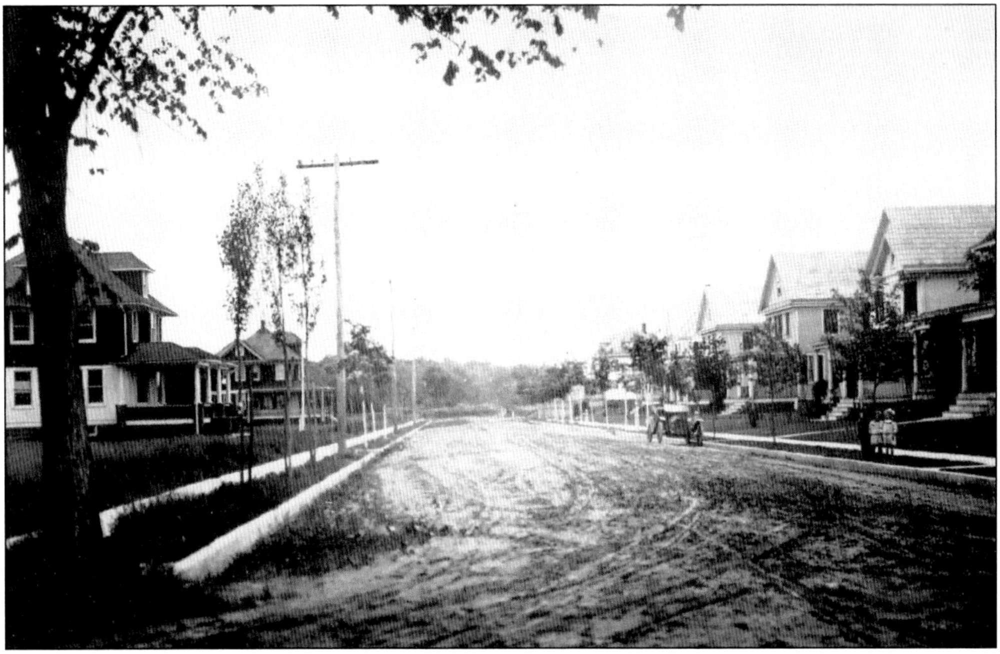

This view, facing south from near the corner of Elm Street, is Second Avenue as it appeared in the 1920s. The houses on the left are numbers 137 and 119, and the row houses on the right are recognizable as numbers 138 through 120.

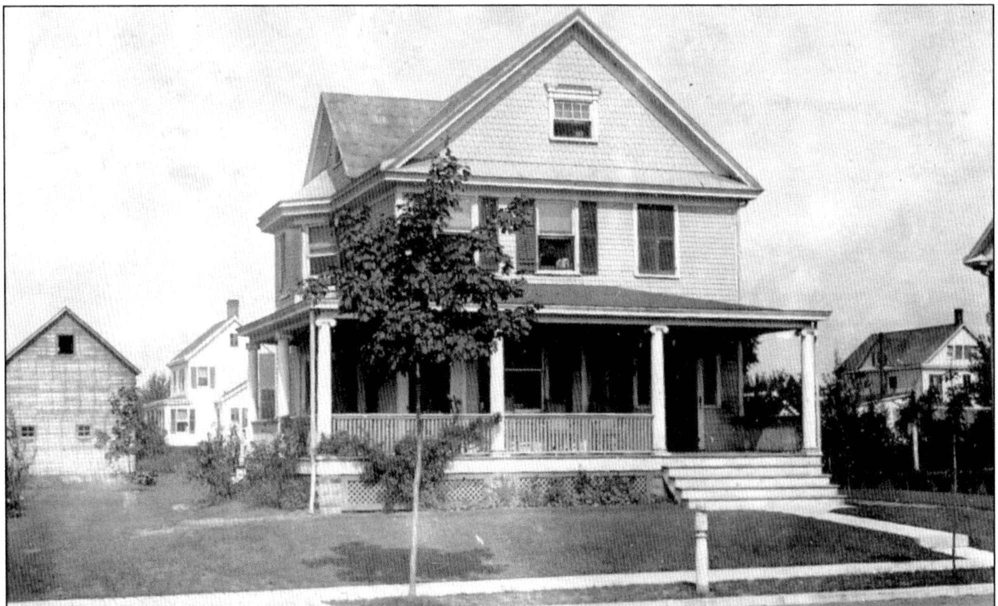

The house at 132 Second Avenue was built *c.* 1900. It is now occupied by the Volz family, who owned one of Westwood's earliest businesses, Volz Hardware.

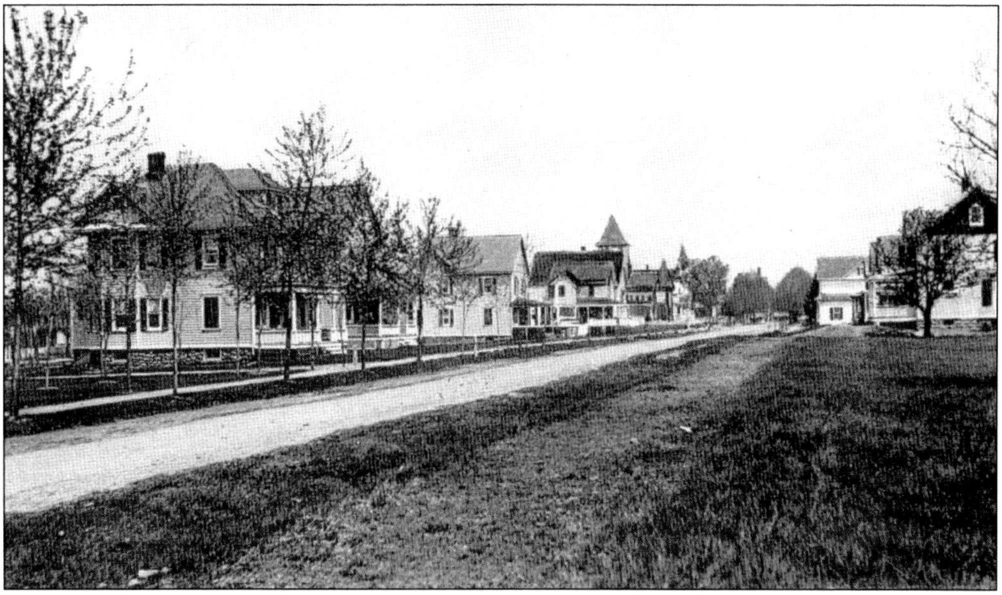

In 1908, the west side of Third Avenue included the Baptist church, which was on the corner of Elm Street. The peaked roof of the church stands out, and the smaller peaked roof far in the background was the C. S. DeBaun house, which was still located on Washington Avenue at the end of Third Avenue.

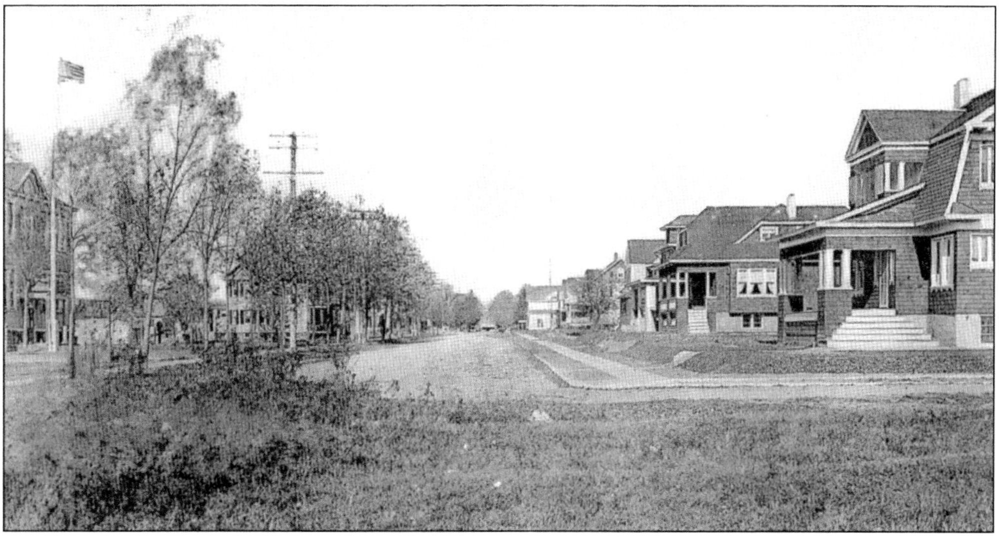

At the time this postcard was created, Third Avenue ended at Mill Street where the Lincoln School stood. Townhouses have taken the place of the school, and the front porch of 139 Third Avenue, on the right, has been closed in to make an office. The author wrote most of this book in this office.

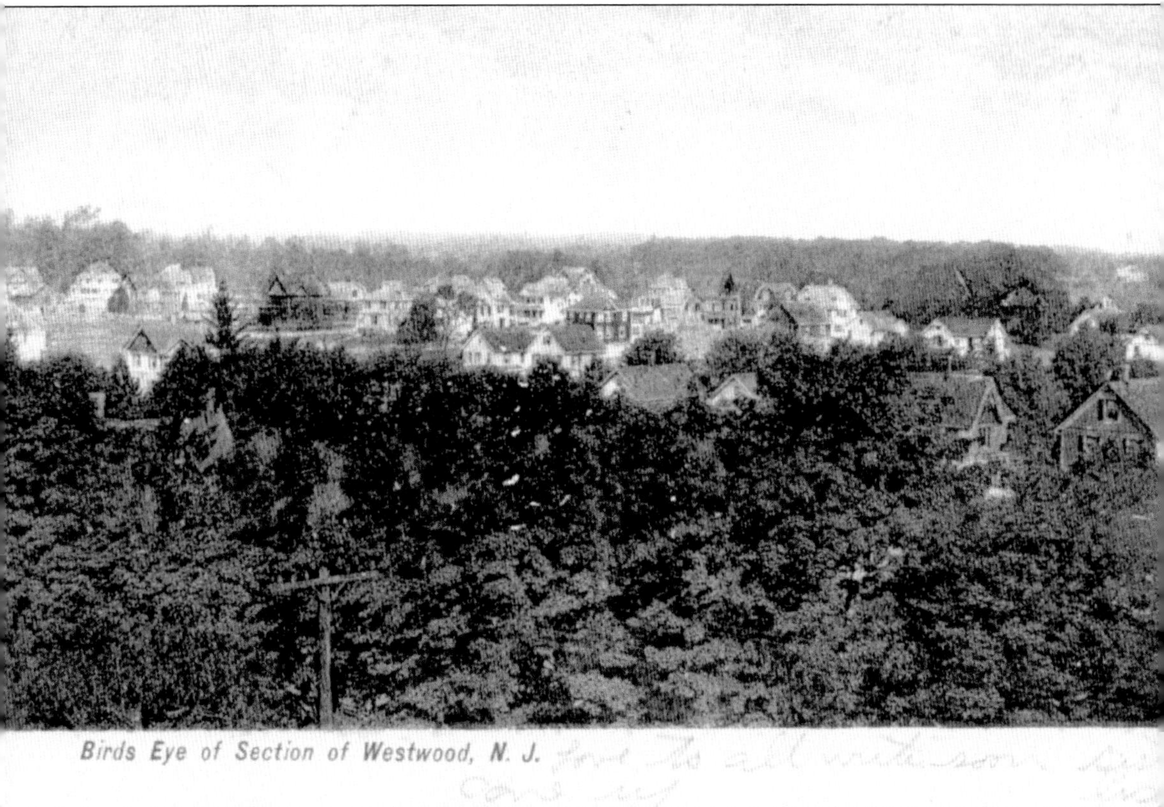

More and more homes and neighborhoods gradually spread away from the center of town throughout Westwood. Postmarked in 1908, this image appears to be an aerial view in a northeast direction toward Fairview and Center Avenues.

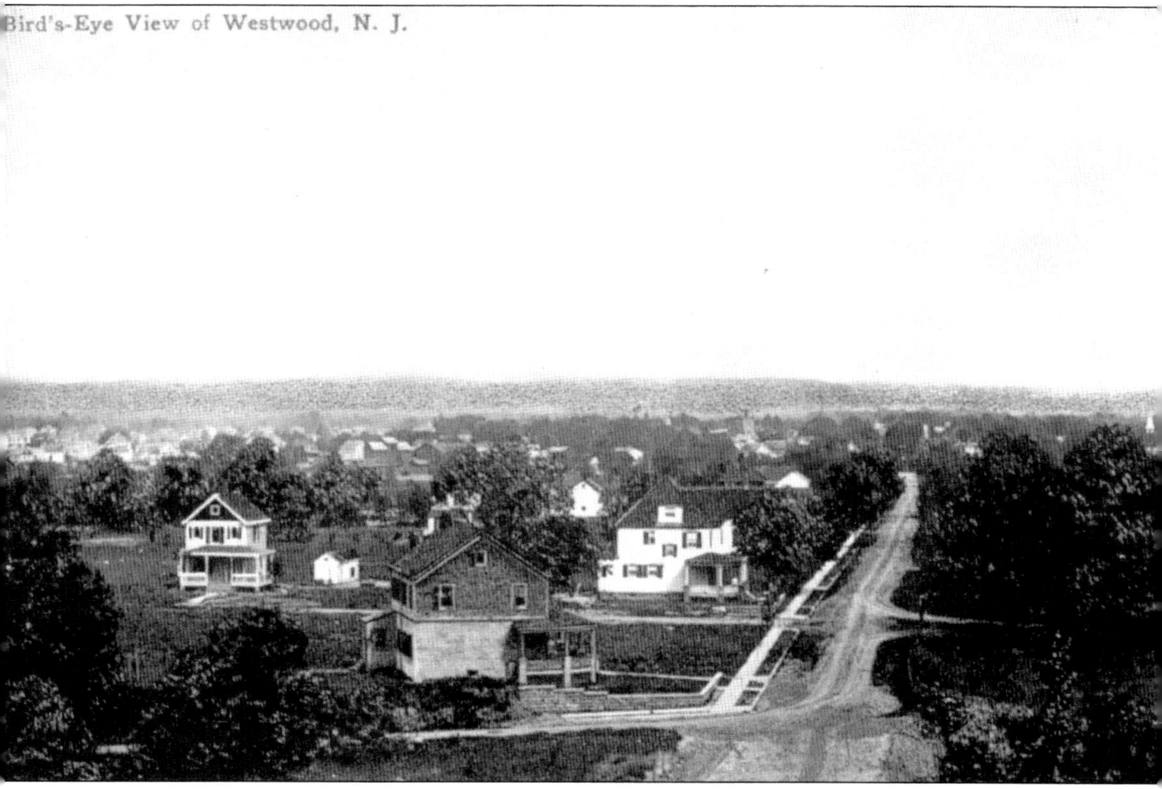

Although the neighborhood has filled in since 1909, these houses at 306 and 288 Washington Avenue still stand out today as drivers come down the hill from Washington Township. This hill provided a natural location for a brick-lined water reservoir used for Westwood's early pressurized water system, built by C. S. DeBaun. The house in the foreground was a stop on the Underground Railroad, used by escaping slaves during the Civil War.

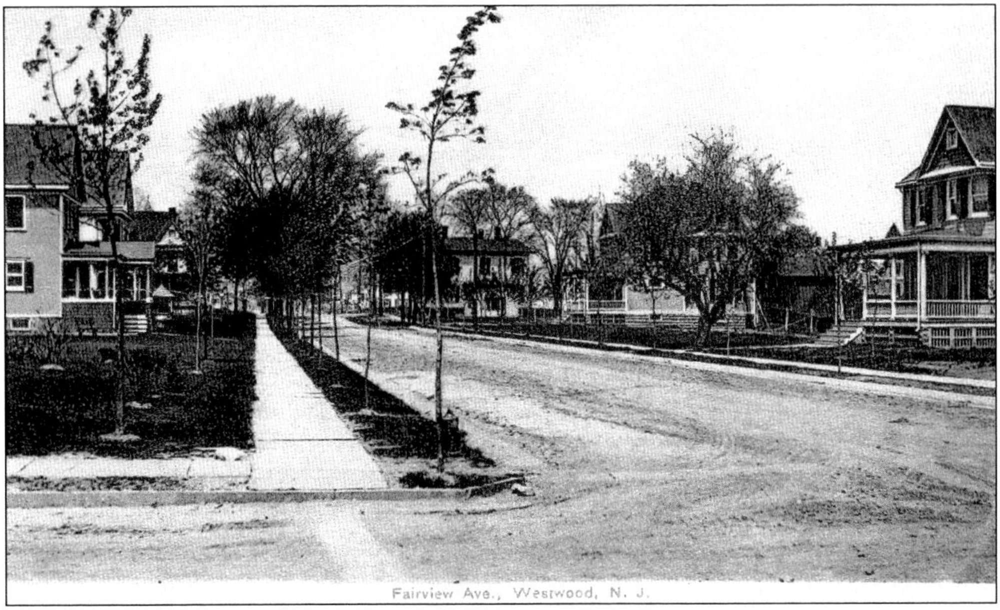

Fairview Avenue developed as the neighborhood grew out from Westwood Avenue. These homes appear to be at the corner of Fairview Avenue and Irvington Street.

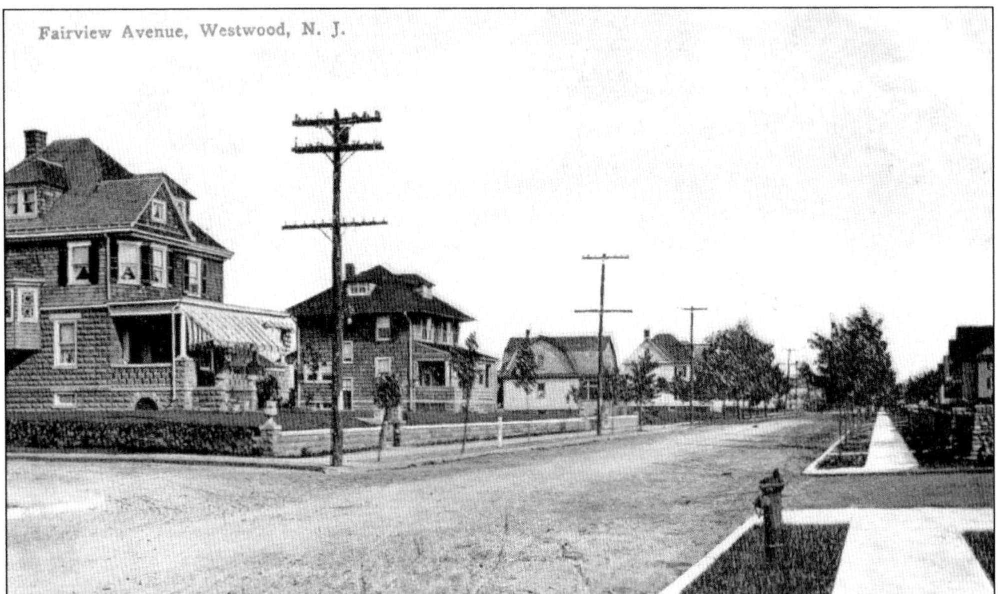

This postcard, mailed in 1912, provides a view of 479 Fairview Avenue at the corner of Lake Street, facing toward Westwood Avenue.

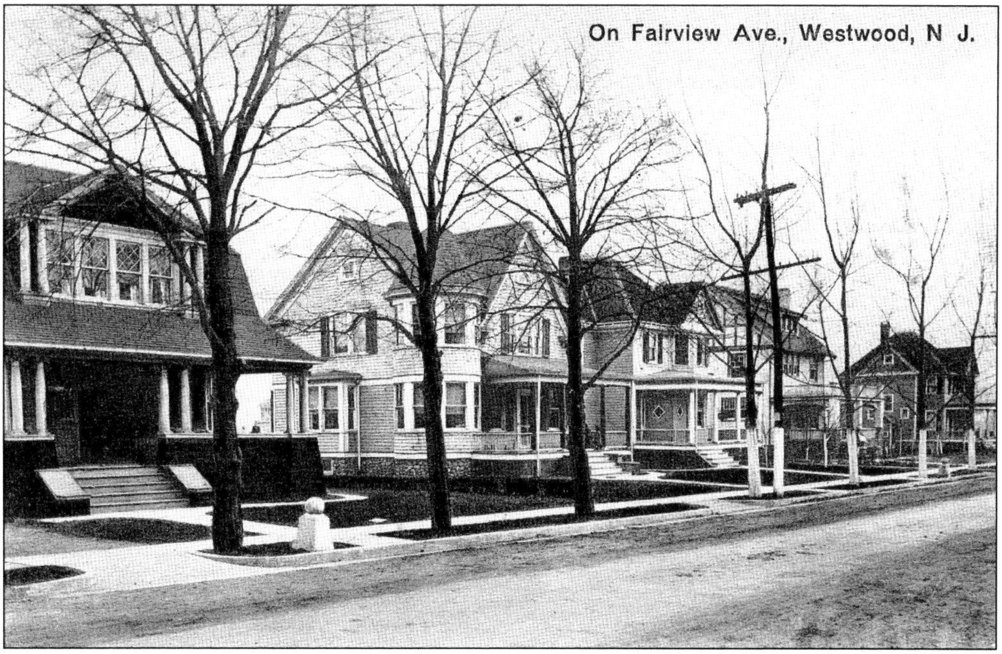

Both postcards on this page were mailed in 1918 and feature homes located at 219 and 205 Fairview Avenue. This block, just south of Westwood Avenue, has been almost entirely converted to commercial use.

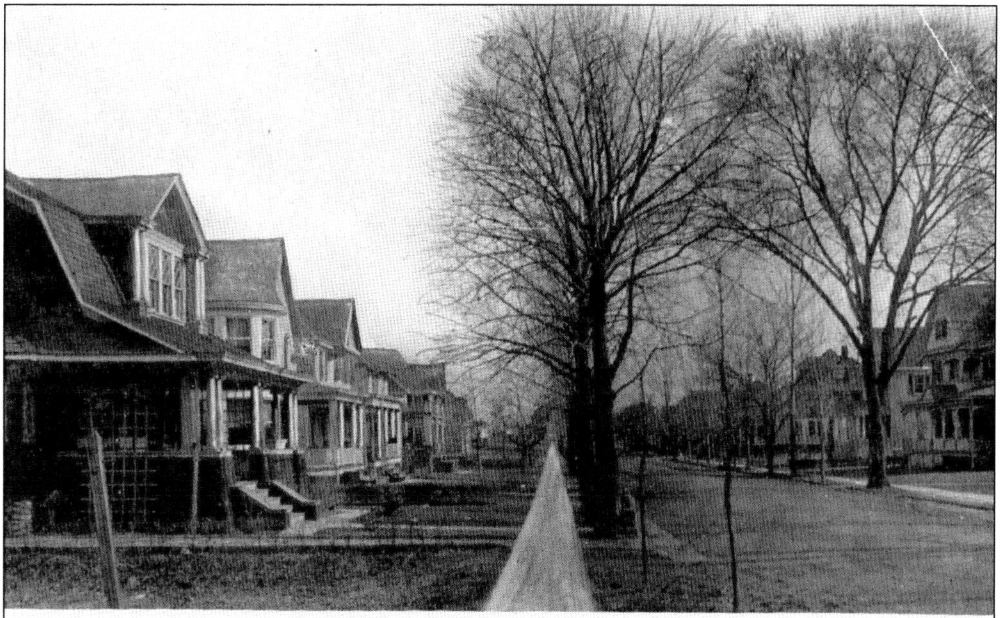

FAIRVIEW AVENUE, Westwood, N. J.

Although these houses are now used for retail stores, they remain easily recognizable due to their design. The house at 205 Fairview Avenue has a distinctive, rounded front corner that includes windows with rounded panes of glass.

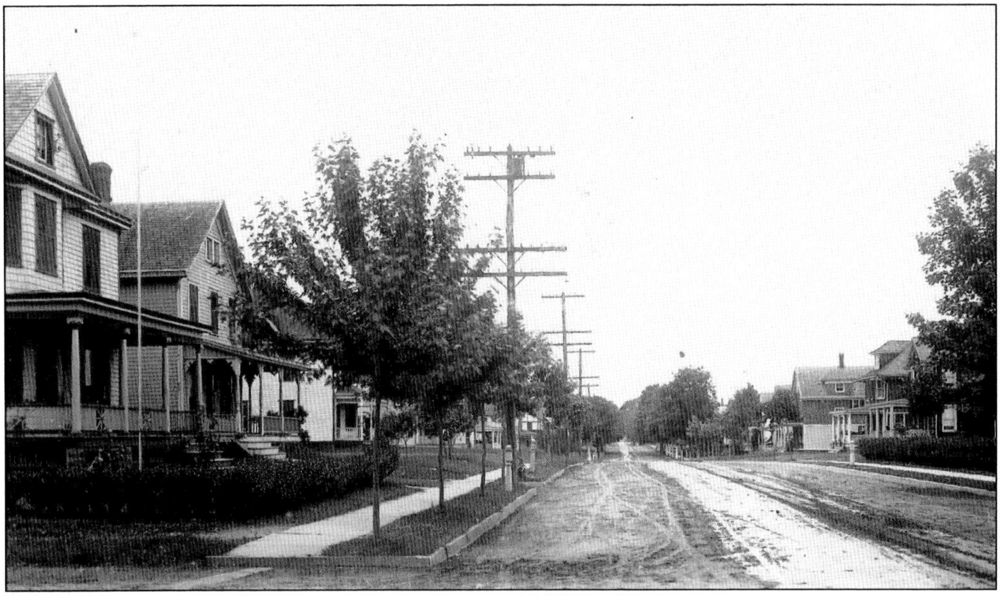

This card provides a view from the corner of Fairview Avenue and Grand Street, facing south toward Westwood Avenue. The houses on the left are numbers 437 and 433, and the house on the right side remains 418. The sidewalks, curbs, and trees shown in this card seem to be new, but the road appears to remain unpaved.

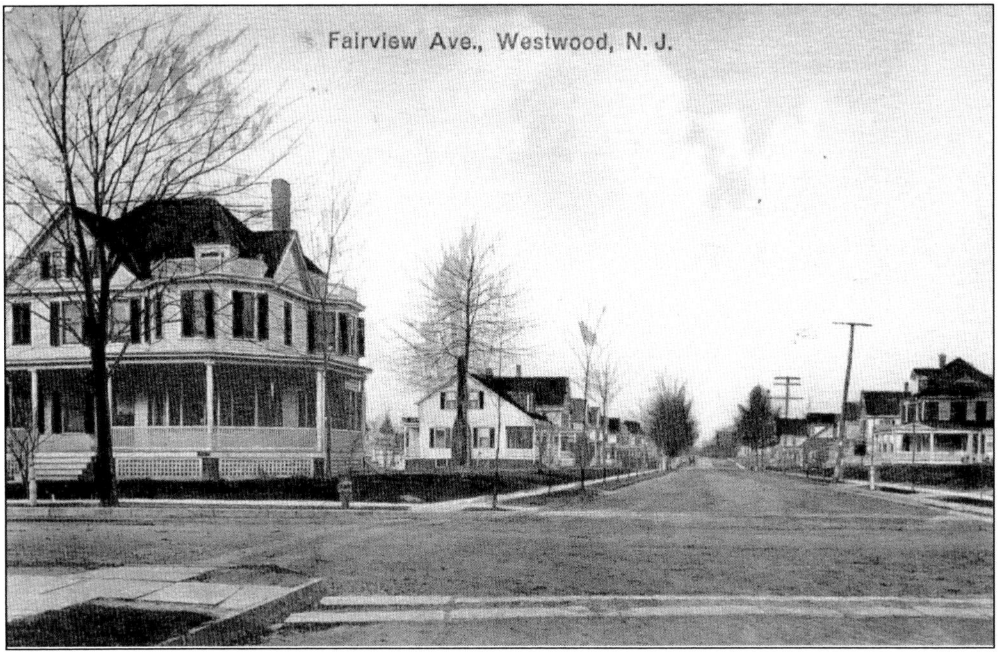

In 1910, the stately James Demarest House stood at the corner of Fairview Avenue and Main Street (now Westwood Avenue). The house was built in 1885 and was later moved around the corner to 286 Fairview Avenue, where it is now the headquarters of the Veterans of Foreign Wars Post.

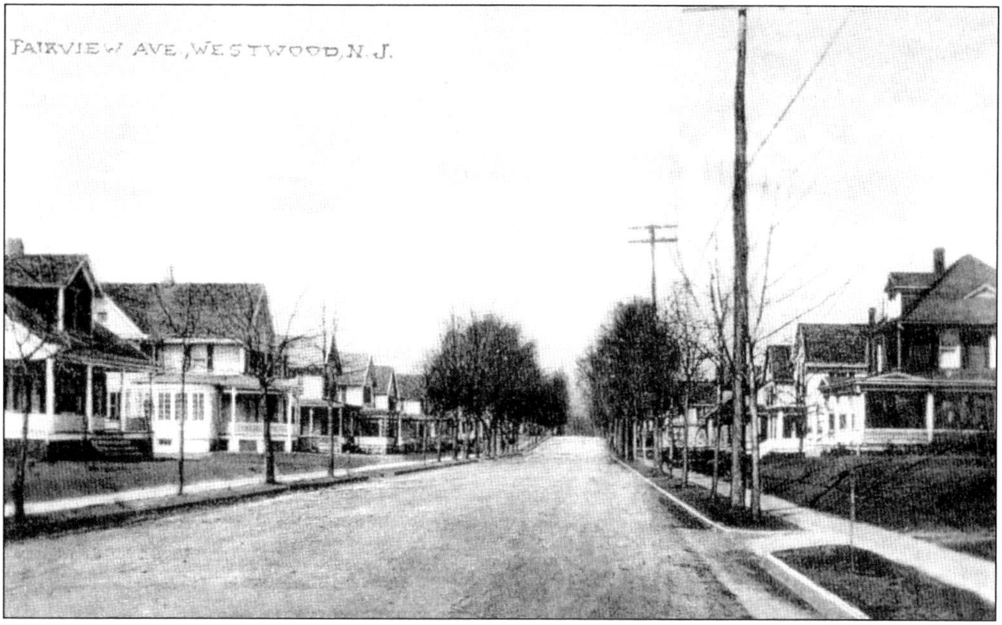

Although the house on the far right is no longer there, the two houses on the far left of this *c.* 1920 postcard are 344 and 350 Fairview Avenue.

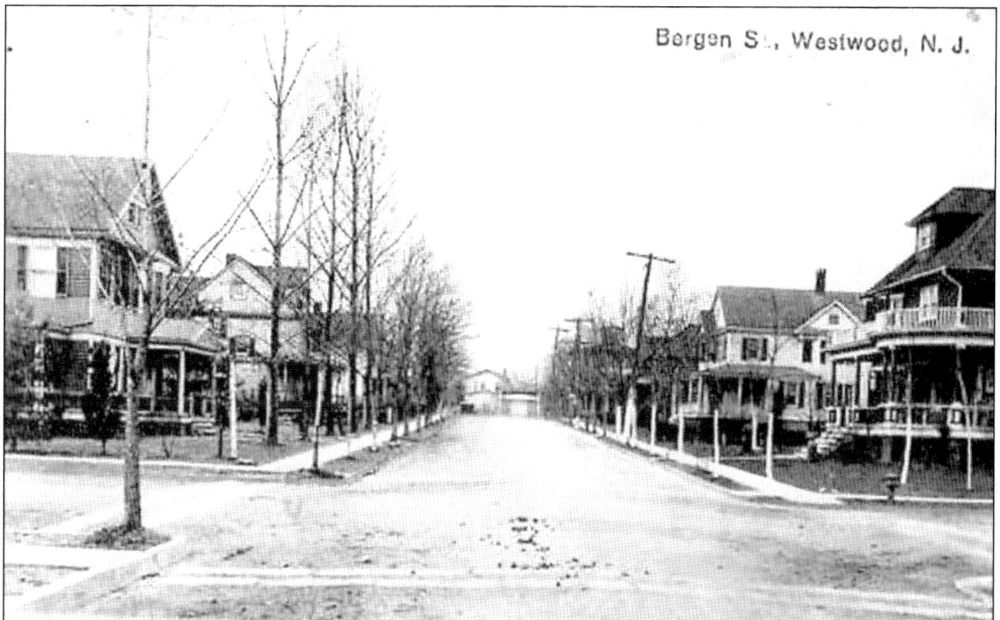

This card features the view looking west on Bergen Street from the corner of Fairview Avenue. The back of Volz Hardware can be seen in the center distance. The house on the left corner has been replaced with an apartment building, but the houses on the right side remain at 126 Fairview Avenue and 12 Bergen Street.

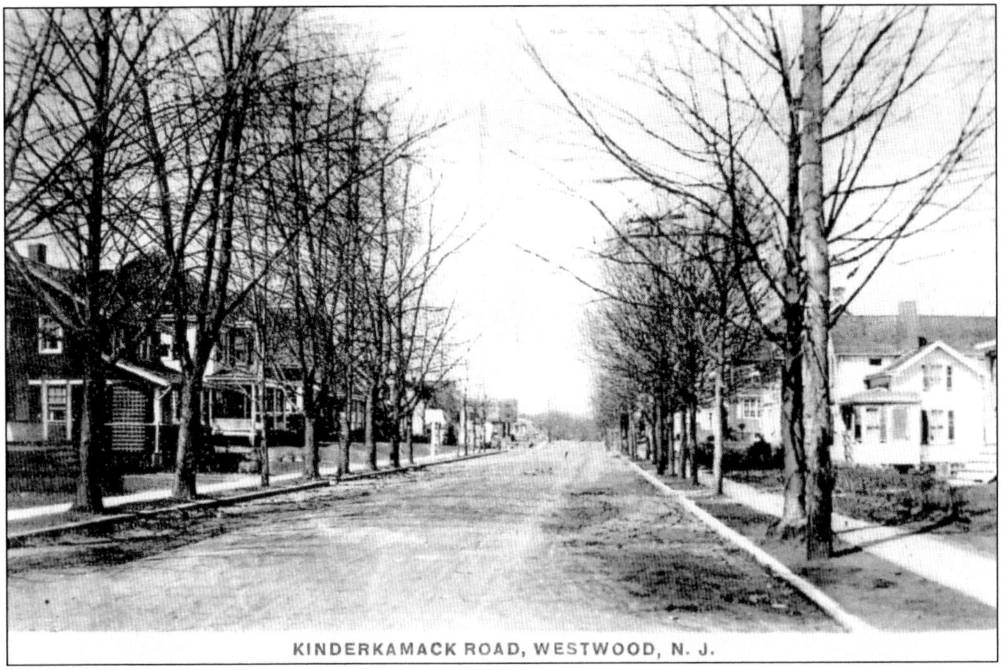

Kinderkamack Road is a busy county street today, but in the early 1900s, it was still an unpaved, narrow street in a quiet, residential neighborhood. The second house on the left was the last house in Westwood to be moved. It was moved to 416 Center Avenue (two doors north of Goldberg's Child Center). Moving houses was much more common in the early 1900s than it is today.

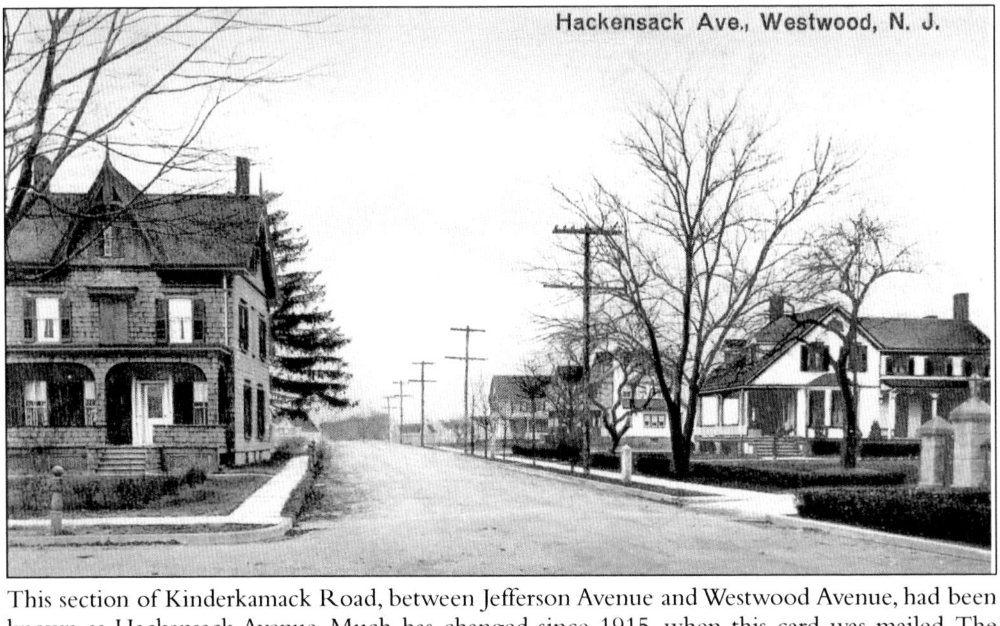

This section of Kinderkamack Road, between Jefferson Avenue and Westwood Avenue, had been known as Hackensack Avenue. Much has changed since 1915, when this card was mailed. The house on the left was replaced long ago by the Esso (Exxon) gas station, but number 231, on the right, is easily identified by the half-circle window at the peak of the roof. This house was later used as the Hitching Post Restaurant (page 63) and is now a dentist's office.

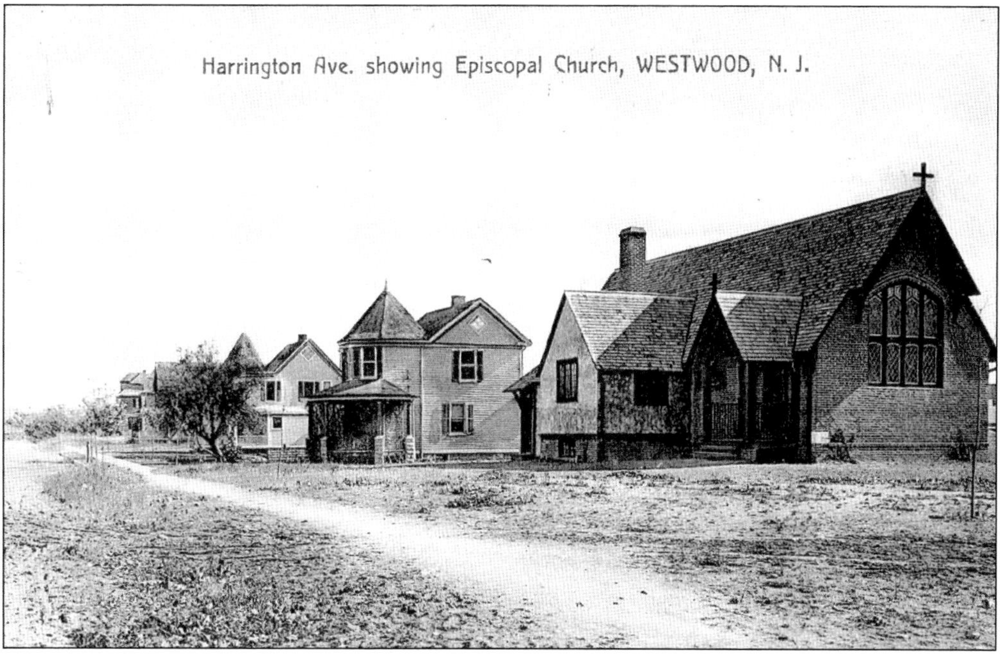

Although it has been rebuilt since this image was created *c.* 1910, the Episcopal church still sits at the corner of Kinderkamack Road and Harrington Avenue, as do its neighbors with the peaked roofs at 15 and 21 Harrington Avenue.

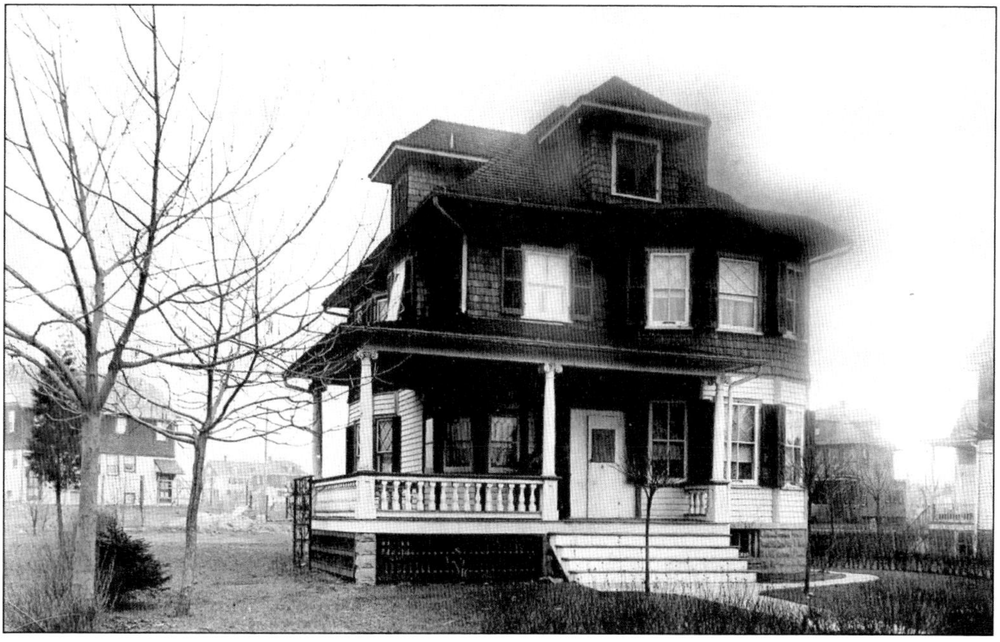

This card was mailed by the owner of 43 Harrington Avenue in 1913. The house has remained in the same family for three generations and is now occupied by the great-niece of the original owner.

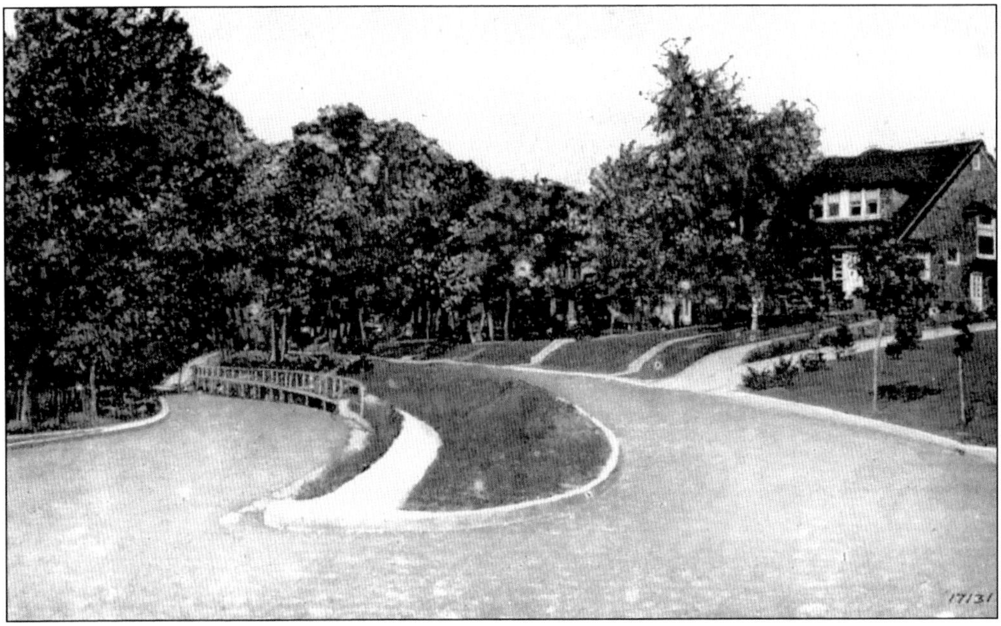

Terrace Drive has not changed very much since this postcard was created. The road to the left led over Yates Bridge into Hillsdale, and the homes on Terrace Drive had a great view of the pond created by Yates Mill and Dam, on the Pascack Brook.

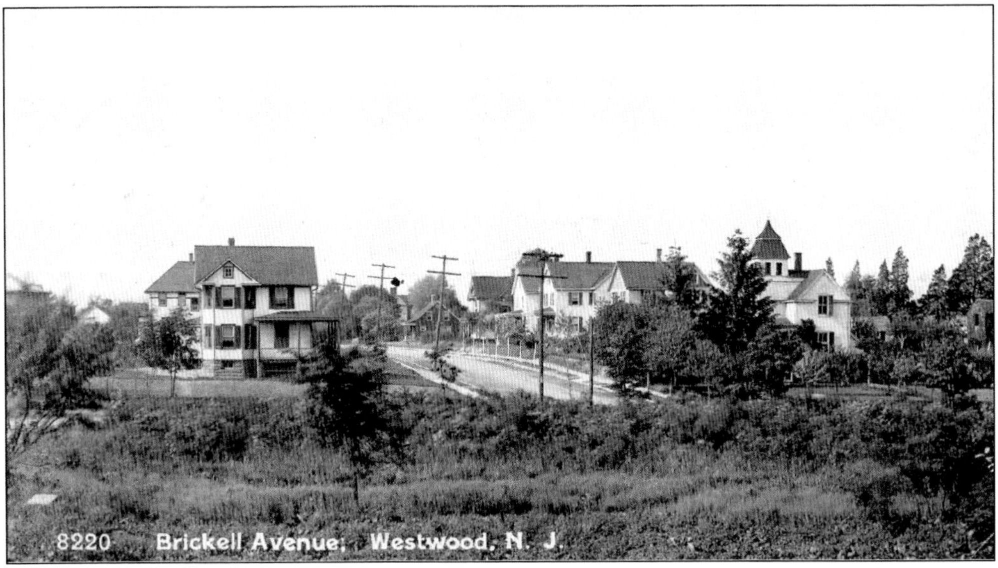

Back in 1912, Brickell Avenue ended with house number 12, pictured above. Today, these houses remain, but Brickell Avenue connects with Sixth Avenue, which continues to Mill Street. It is unclear whether Brickell Avenue was named after Thomas E., Thomas G., or George T. Brickell. George T. Brickell served as postmaster until 1862, ran the general store, and donated the land for the firehouse. His son, Thomas G. Brickell, served as mayor beginning in 1895. T. G. Brickell's nephew, Thomas E. Brickell, served as Westwood's postmaster from 1893 to 1897 and also served two terms as mayor, from 1903 to 1908 and 1914 to 1919. Each one of these early community leaders would have warranted the honor of having a street named after him.

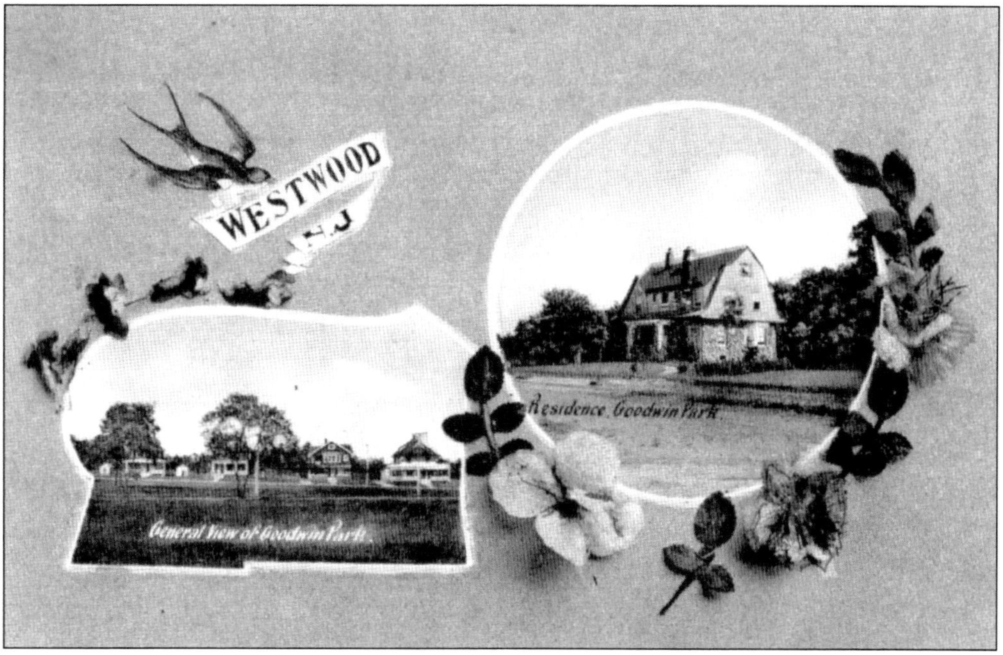

The Goodwin Park section of town has always been one of Westwood's more charming neighborhoods. The home pictured on the right side is located at 33 Bogert Avenue, and the homes at the left appear to be 131, 137, 145, and 151 Elm Street. Harry Goodwin, who was mayor from 1910 to 1911, bought the land to develop about 100 homes. He lived at 72 Goodwin Terrace.

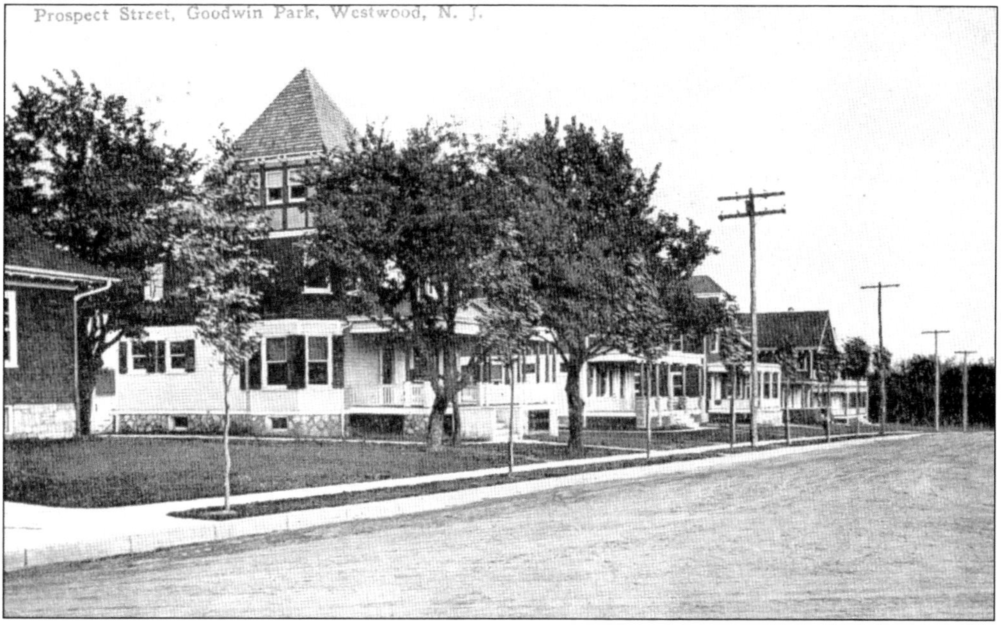

Many of the streets in the Goodwin Park area, such as James, Carolyn, Gladys, Vivian, and Hurlbut, are named after Harry Goodwin's children and other relatives. These houses on Prospect Avenue facing Goodwin Park date back to 1910. The peaked roof of 157 Prospect Avenue continues to add character to the neighborhood.

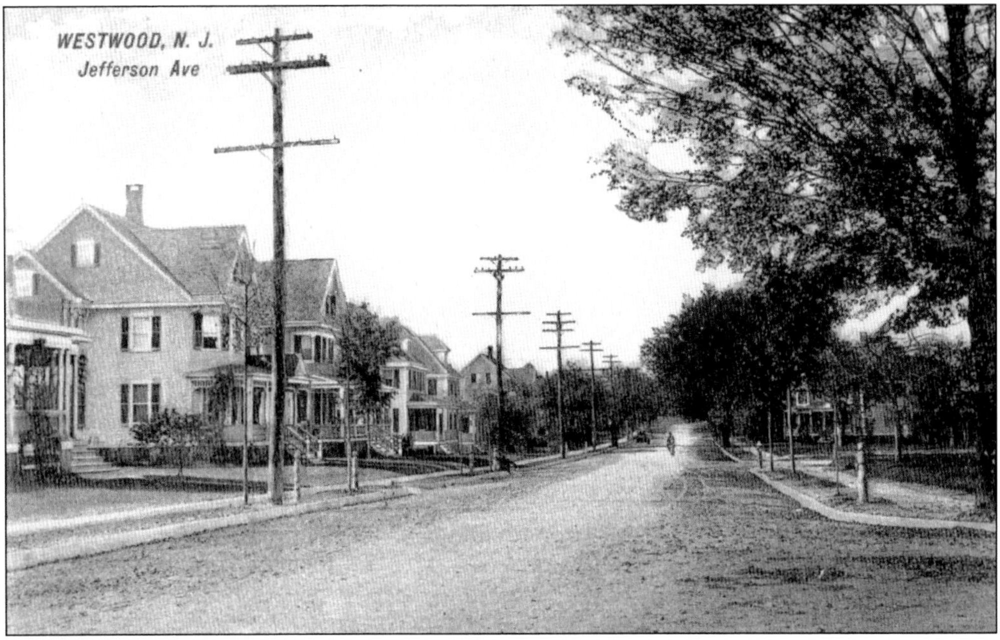

It is hard to imagine Jefferson Avenue unpaved, with no traffic or parked cars. This postcard was never mailed, so a date cannot be determined, but the scene is easily recognized as the view west on Jefferson Avenue. Although the street has changed from residential to commercial, many of the original homes remain as law offices and other small businesses.

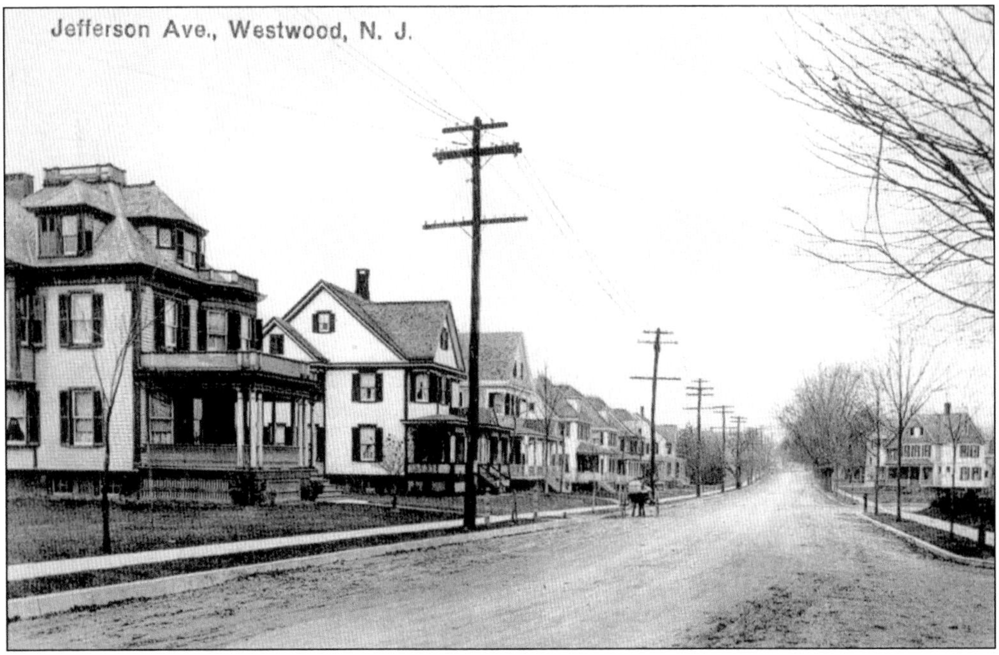

In 1906, Jefferson Avenue was entirely residential. Today, the house on the left has been replaced with the bank at the corner of Kinderkamack Road, but the two houses to the right remain at 77 and 73 Jefferson Avenue. They are used as charming offices.

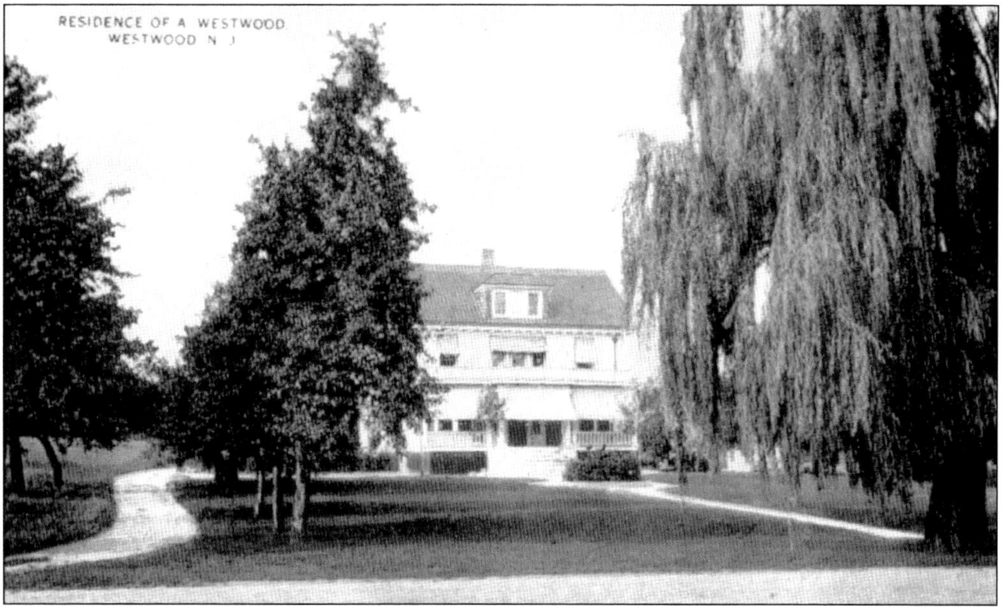

The Menschik residence, located at 124 Harrington Avenue, is across from the Berkeley School. The green roof and second-story balcony are quite distinctive. The house was originally owned by a wealthy family who lived in New York and used this as their country getaway.

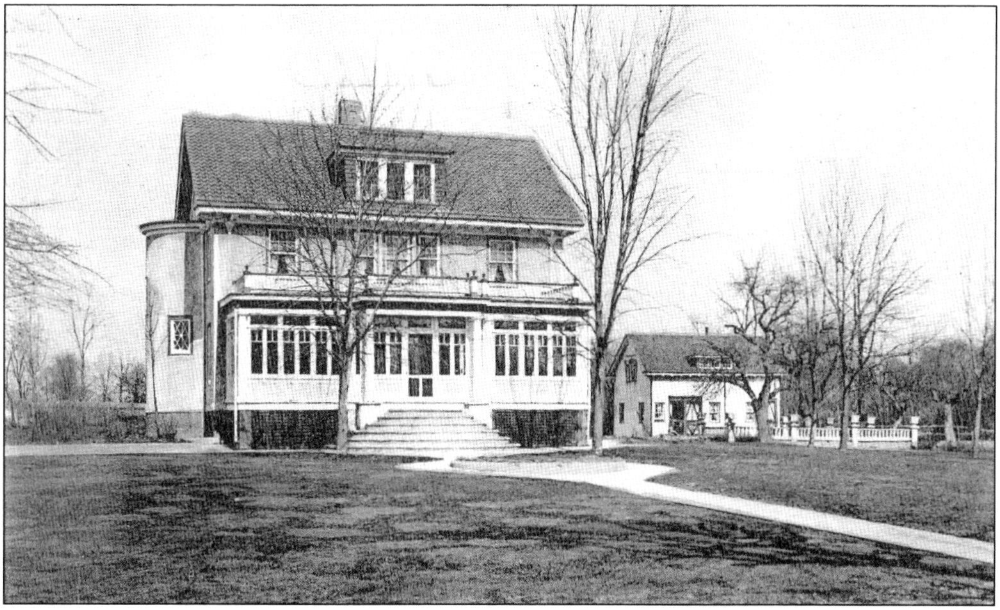

Neither of these postcards is dated, but the upper view appears to be older. This lower card depicts the house after the front porch was closed in.

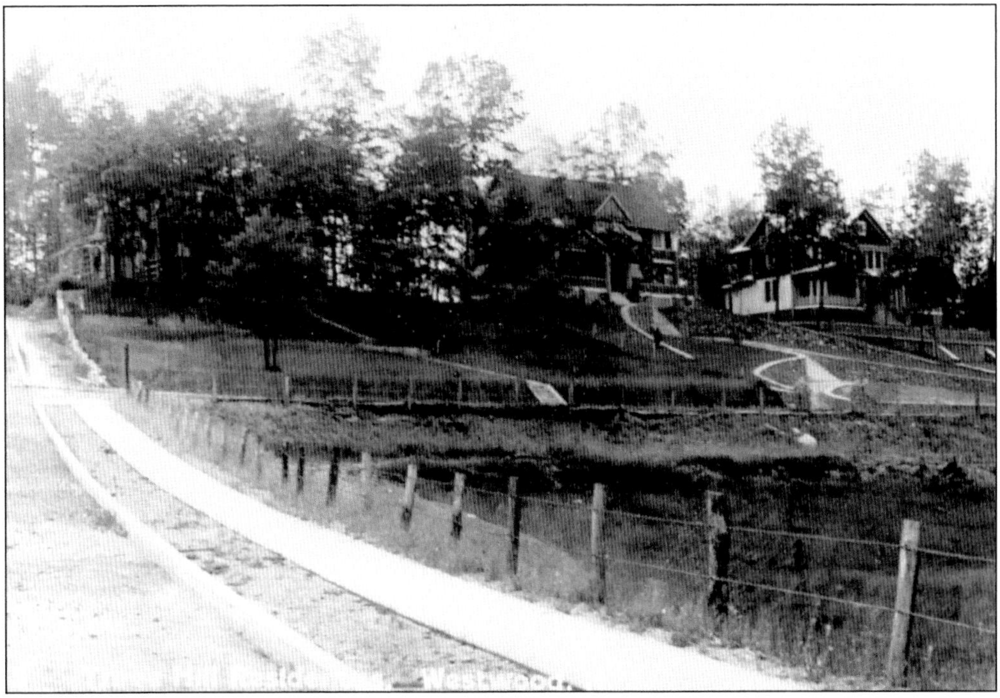

The three residences in this card, mailed in 1912, sit on top of the hill at the border with Washington Township. Their deep front yards originally reached down the hill to Mountain Avenue, but the properties were eventually subdivided, and today, there is another row of houses on Mountain Avenue, in front of the houses pictured. The entrances to these three houses are now on Koch Peak, on top of the hill that is named after the Koch family.

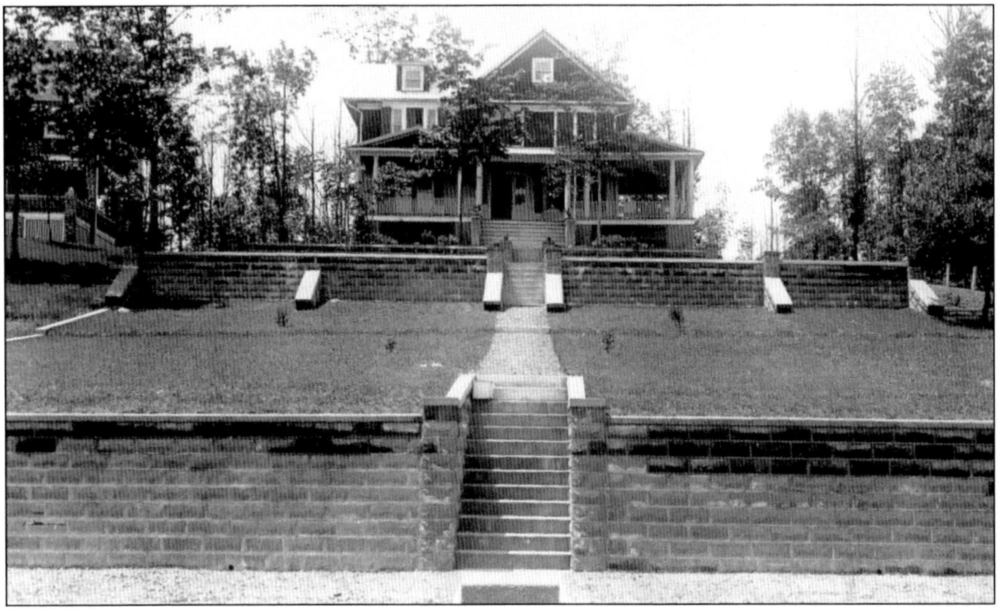

The third house in the row of residences was owned by F. H. Koch, for whom Koch Peak was named. This house is easily recognized as 657 Koch Peak. The large block retaining walls have been removed, and 22 Mountain Avenue is in their place.

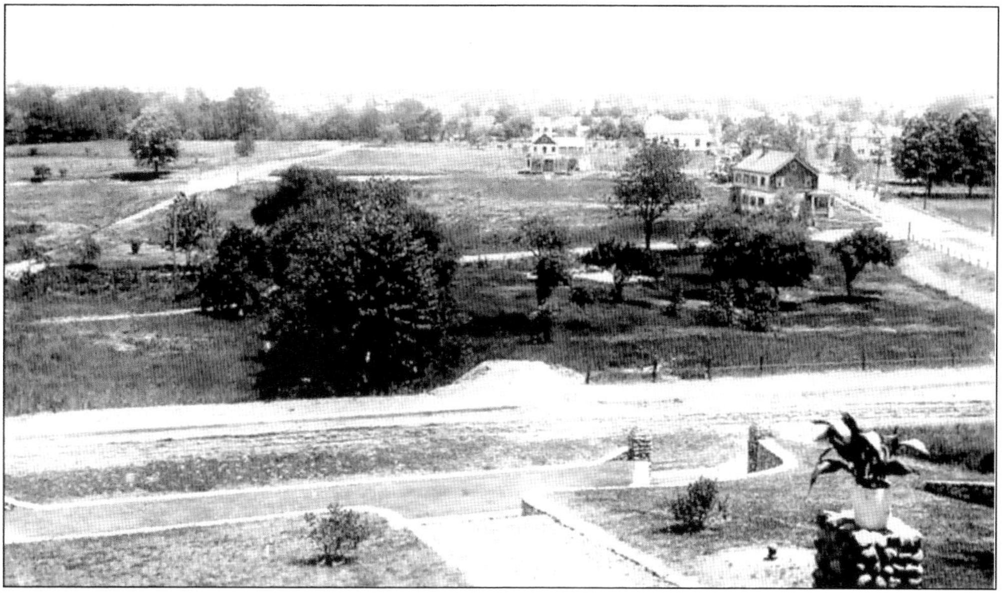

The house at the east corner of Washington and Mountain Avenues was not yet built at the time of this postcard. The image was taken from the present location of 490 Washington Avenue, near the border of Washington Township. The homes in the background also appear in the aerial photograph on page 107.

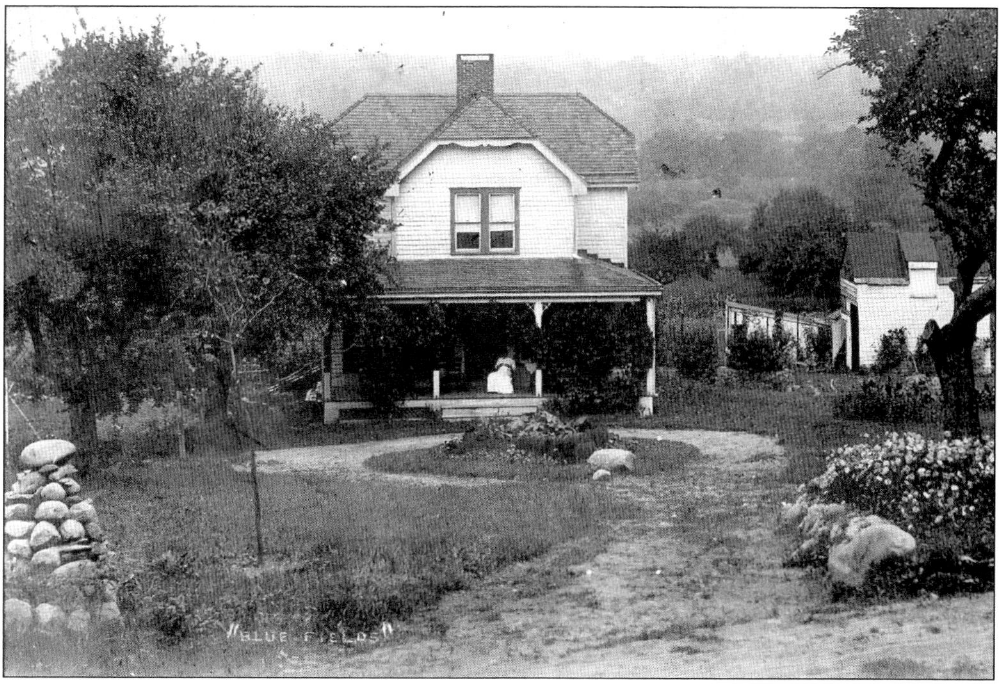

This house no longer stands in Westwood, and it is unknown where it stood in 1911, when this card was mailed. Based on the absence of other houses on the hills in the background, this house appears to have been on Berkeley Avenue or Sand Road, facing west.

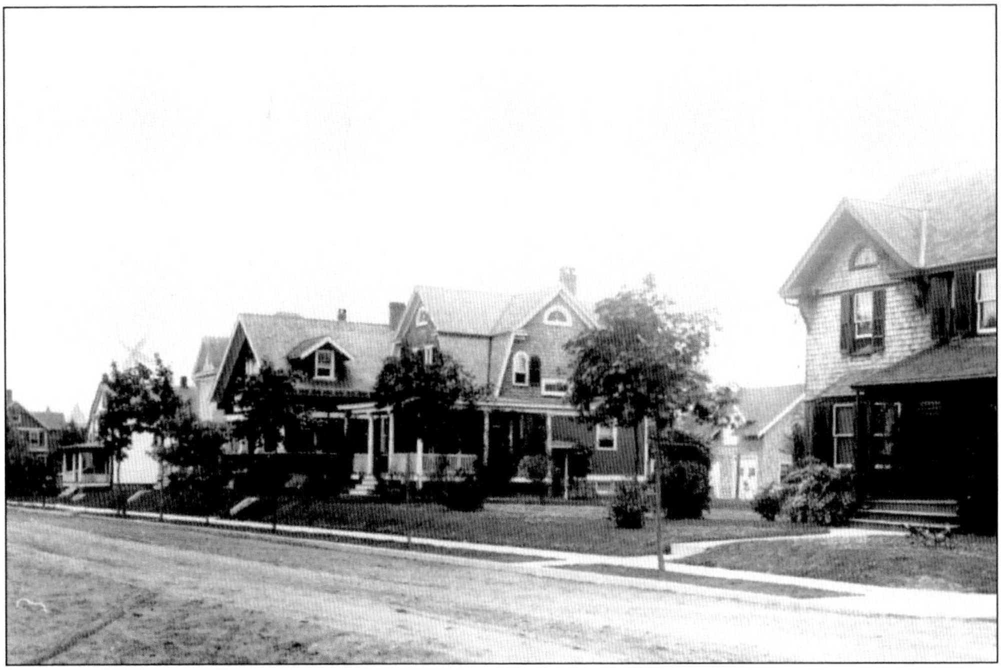

In the early 1900s, Hopper Avenue was a short segment of Kinderkamack Road between Westwood Avenue (at Five Corners) and Irvington Street. Today, the house on the far left has been replaced with a racquetball club, but the next three houses remain at 358, 362, and 366 Kinderkamack Road. The rounded windows and round columns of the house in the center of this image identify it as 366 Kinderkamack Road.

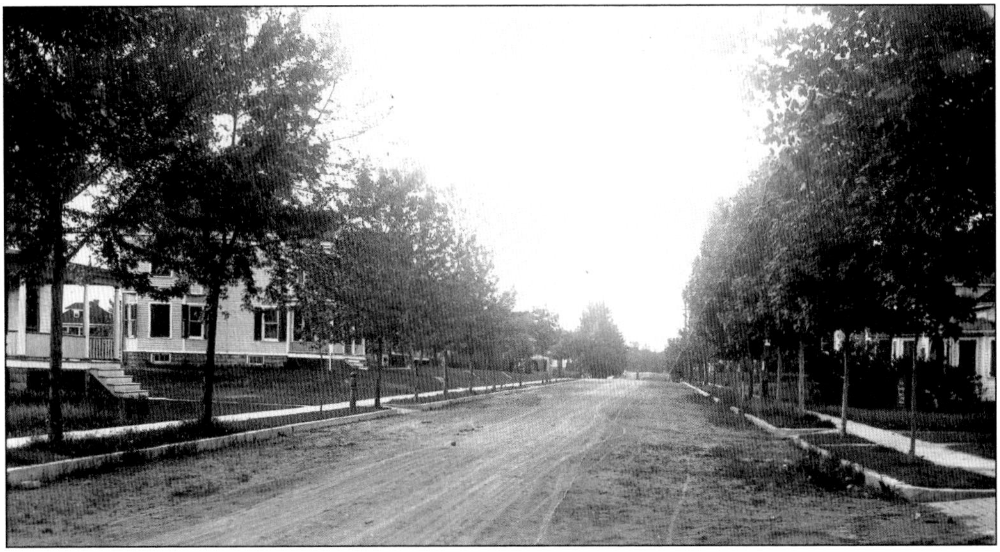

This card provides a view of Hopper Avenue facing north toward Hillsdale in 1912. On the far left, the house with the front porch is now known as 366 Kinderkamack Road. The Hopper family was one of the earliest families to settle in Westwood and was related through marriage to the Bogerts. The family owned a large tract of land in Westwood and ran a farm. Although this street is now part of Kinderkamack Road, another street near the border of Emerson was given the name Hopper.

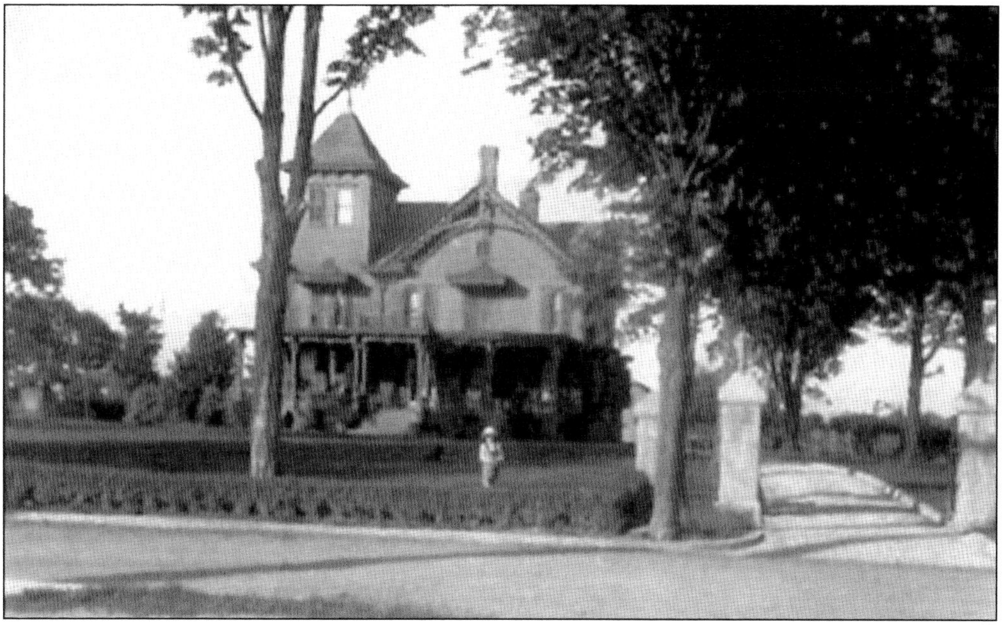

This beautiful estate was originally owned by the Hopper family, who operated a farm that stretched all the way to Five Corners, on the east side of Kinderkamack Road. The house was later used for Lyons Funeral Home and is now Becker's Funeral Home.

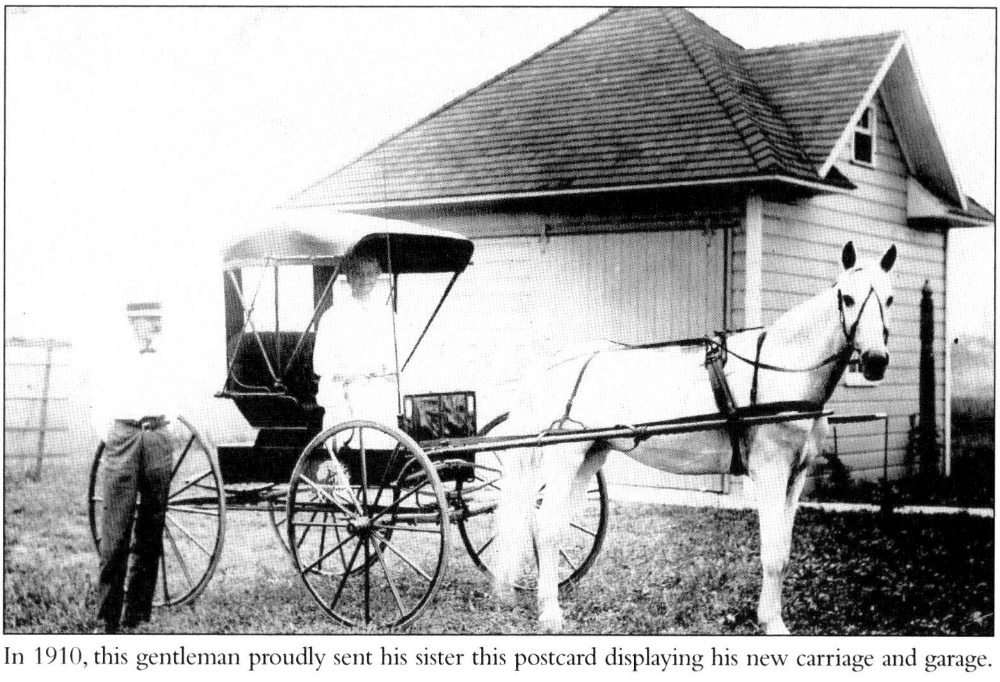

In 1910, this gentleman proudly sent his sister this postcard displaying his new carriage and garage.

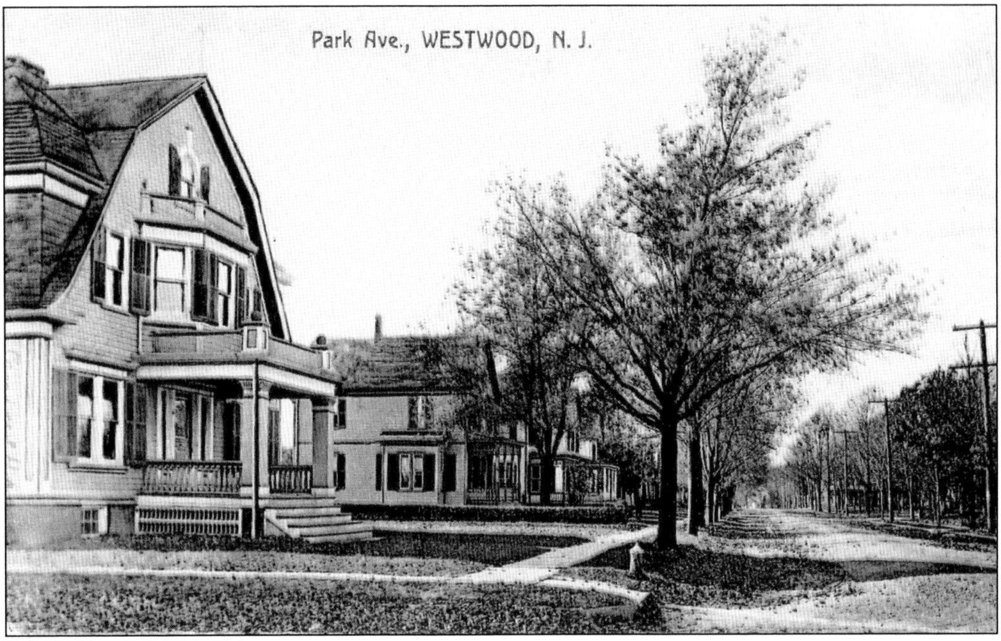

Park Avenue, just one block from the train station and the general store, was a very desirable neighborhood. The former De La Ree home, at the corner of Park and First Avenues, faces Veterans Memorial Park.

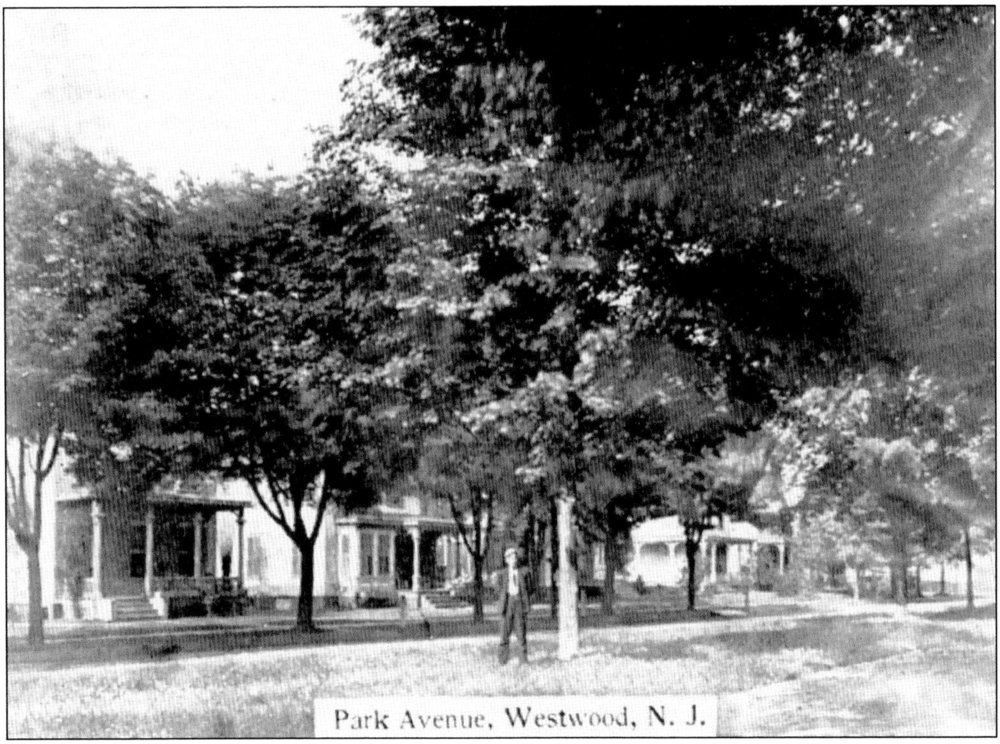

The two houses on the left side were removed *c.* 1938 for the construction of the Westwood Public Library, which opened at this location in 1939. The third house remains at 45 Park Avenue.

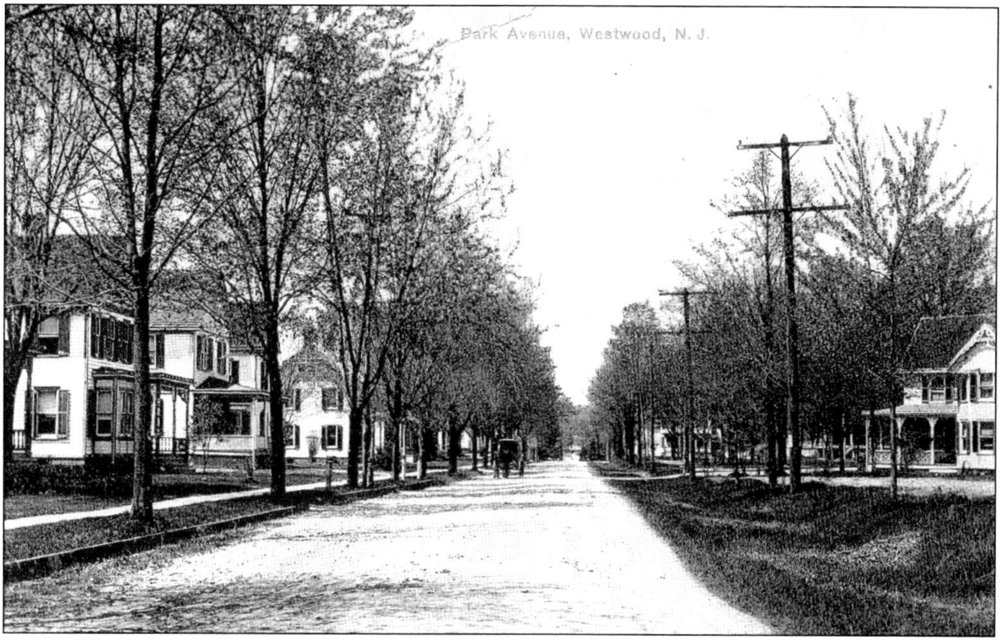

The houses on the right side of this postcard, mailed in 1912, were removed to clear the way for the expansion of Veterans Memorial Park. The houses on the left side still remain at 15, 21, 25, and 29 Park Avenue.

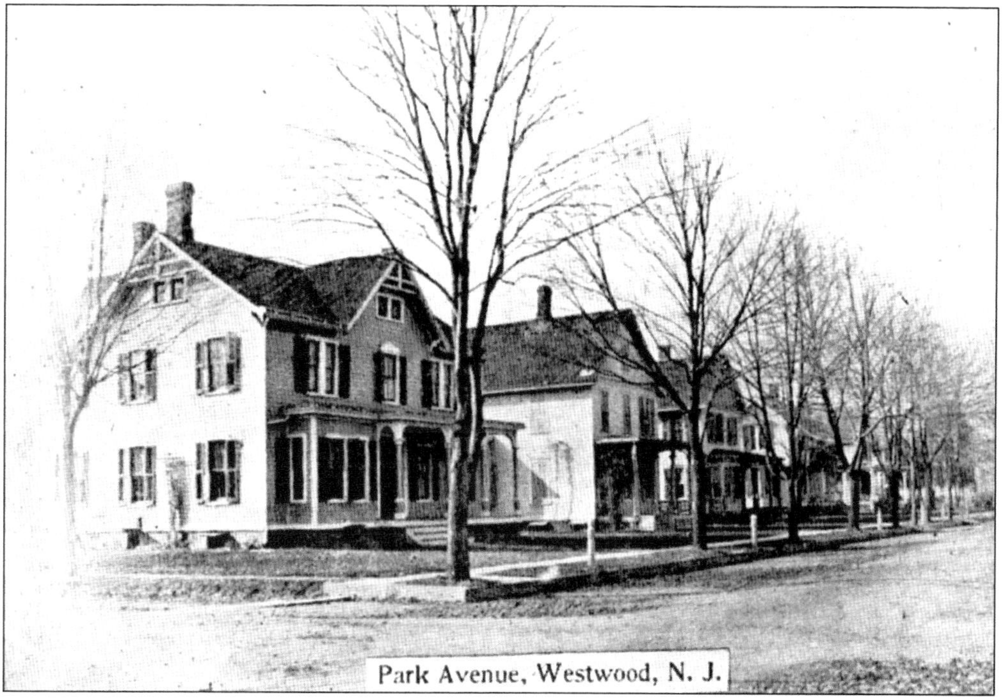

The distinctive windows in the peak of the home at the corner of Park and Second Avenues make it easy to recognize this house as 29 Park Avenue, although most of its surroundings have changed since 1907. The next two houses were removed for construction of the library.

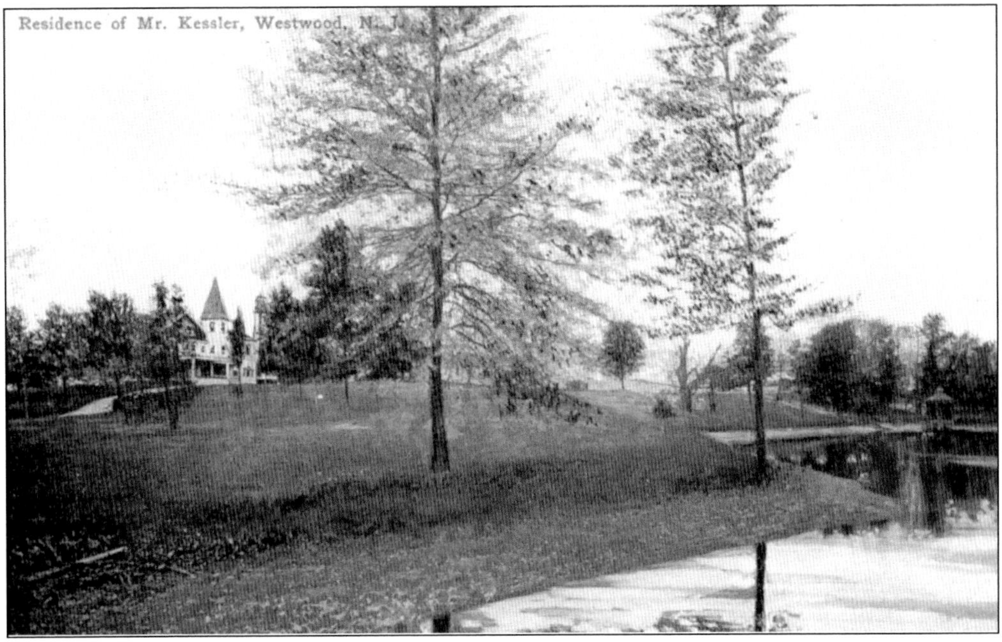

This postcard, mailed in 1911, shows the distinctive peaked roof of the Kessler residence, overlooking the pond formed by Yates Dam, on the border of Westwood and Hillsdale. The house later became part of the Overbrook Country Club. It no longer stands.

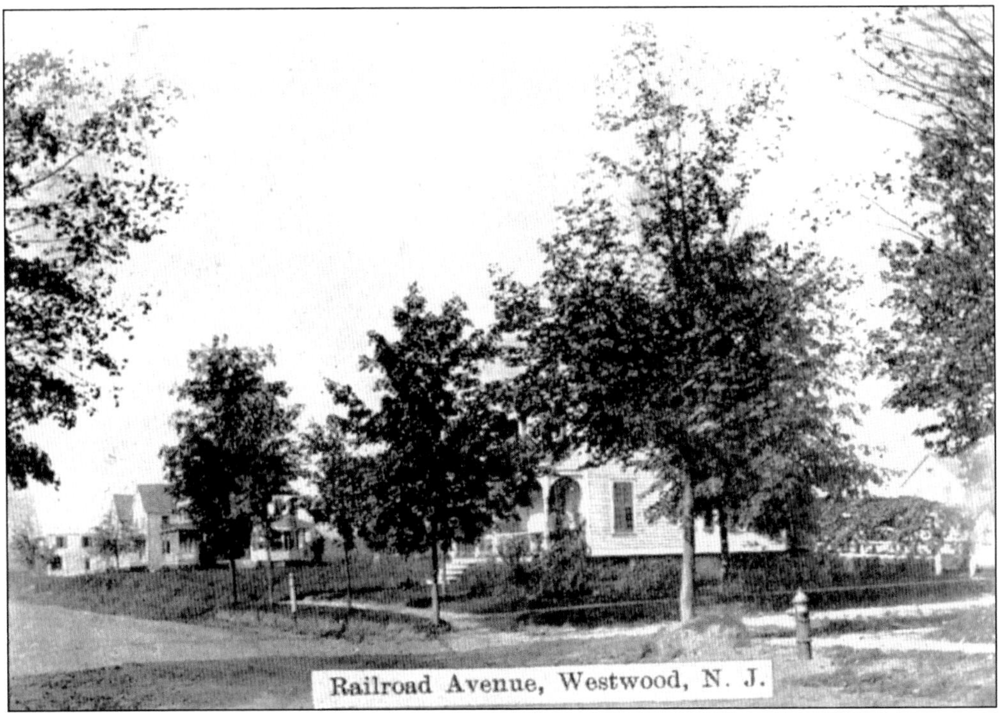

Railroad Avenue (now Broadway) was primarily a residential street in the very early 1900s. As Westwood grew, most of the buildings along Railroad Avenue converted to commercial use.

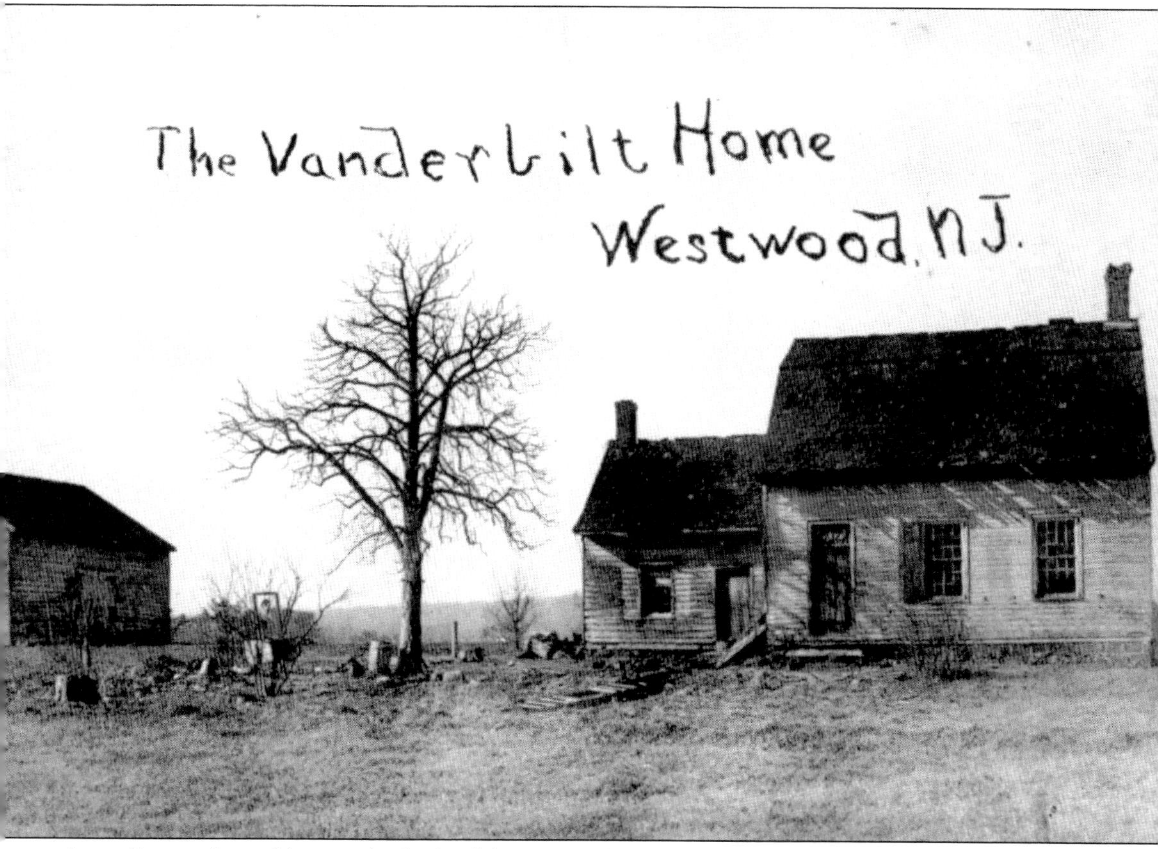

According to the writing on the back of this postcard, the Vanderbilt home was built in 1805 and lasted 101 years, until it was taken down by Martin West in 1906. Its location is unknown, but it looks like it was in a desolate area of town. This must have been the area of Westwood that a traveler named Guy Latourette visited when he referred to Westwood as "a dreary hamlet in a howling desert" in 1873. Thankfully, this was not a popular opinion of Westwood.

Westwood Firsts

As illustrated in the postcards printed throughout this book, Westwood residents have always been receptive to new ideas and have led the region in many ways.

In 1894, Westwood was the first town in the Pascack Valley to formally organize a firefighting company, the Continental Hook & Ladder Company No. 1.

Soon afterward, the first pressurized waterworks was built by C. S. DeBaun.

In 1907, the First National Bank of Westwood was organized as Pascack Valley's first bank, making Westwood *the* banking hub for the entire valley.

In 1919, the Westwood Public Library was the first in the Pascack Valley to be chartered by the state.

In 1924, Westwood planned the first modern sewerage system in Pascack Valley.

In 1929–1930, the first two cement streets were poured, at Fairview Avenue and Railroad Avenue (now Broadway).

Westwood developers and residents were also some of the first to experiment with houses built entirely of poured cement. Several of these cement homes were constructed, or poured, in the area of Seventh and Wheeler Avenues.

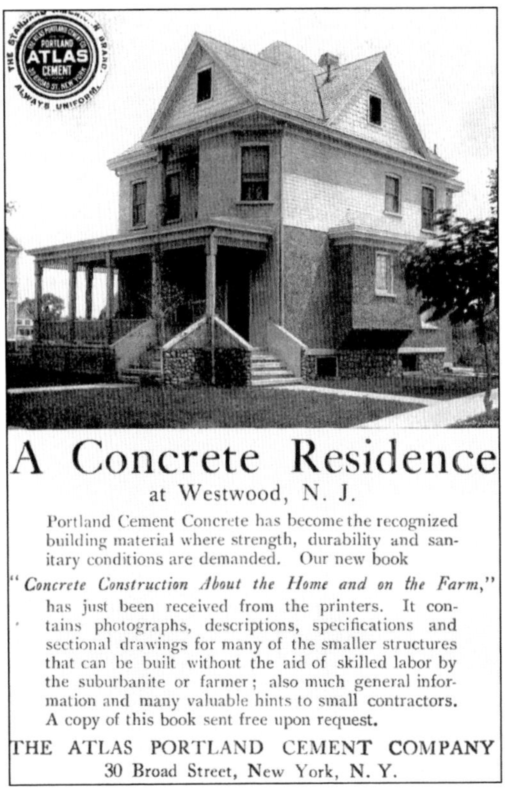

This postcard advertises the Atlas Portland Cement Company of New York City. The concrete house shown is in Westwood.

Index